DATE DUE

JУ 3 0 '98			
DE 16 '98			
MY 27 '99			
FE 9 '00			
JE 1 '00			

DEMCO 38-296

Stravinsky and
The Rite of Spring

Stravinsky and *The Rite of Spring*

THE BEGINNINGS OF A MUSICAL LANGUAGE

Pieter C. van den Toorn

University of California Press

BERKELEY · LOS ANGELES

The publication of this book was made possible in part
by a grant from the National Endowment for the
Humanities.

University of California Press
Berkeley and Los Angeles, California

Library of Congress Cataloging-in-Publication Data

Van den Toorn, Pieter C., 1938–
   Stravinsky and the Rite of spring.

   Bibliography: p.
   Includes index.
   1. Stravinsky, Igor, 1882–1971.   Vesna sviashchennaia.
I. Title.
ML410.S932V38   1987   785.3′2′0924   86-31778
ISBN 0-520-05958-1 (alk. paper)

Sources of the musical excerpts quoted in this volume are as
follows:

Examples 1–4, 9, 10c, 14–18, 27C, 28–31, 33b, 34–36, 38–44,
53–54, 61, 65, 69–72, and 74–91 from *Le Sacre du Printemps
(The Rite of Spring)* © Copyright 1921 by Edition Russe de
Musique. Copyright assigned 1947 to Boosey and Hawkes,
Inc.

Examples 2c, 3b, 4a–b, 5–8, 9a, 10a, 11a, 12a, 27a, 58, and 68
from *The Rite of Spring (Le Sacre du Printemps): Sketches, 1911–
1913* © Copyright 1969 Boosey and Hawkes Music Publishers
Ltd.

Examples 11c and 12d from *Le Sacre du Printemps: Danse Sacrale*
© Copyright 1945 by Associated Music Publishers, Inc.

Examples 20–24 from *Les Noces* © Copyright J&W Chester/
Edition Wilhelm Hansen London Ltd.

Example 26 from *Oedipus Rex* © Copyright 1927 by Edition
Russe de Musique. Renewed 1944. Copyright and renewal
assigned to Boosey and Hawkes, Inc. English translation
Copyright 1949 by Boosey and Hawkes, Inc.

Example 37 from *Agon* © Copyright 1957 by Boosey and
Hawkes, Inc.

Examples 51 and 52 from *Scherzo fantastique* © Copyright B.
Schott's Sohne, Mainz, 1931

to Cattarina

Contents

Acknowledgments

The idea for this book came to me shortly after I completed *The Music of Igor Stravinsky* (1983). I had wanted to develop and in certain instances reshape a number of ideas in that earlier volume in terms of a single work, *The Rite of Spring*. The choice of *The Rite* was at least partially determined by the surfacing of a wealth of source material in recent decades. My idea was, quite simply, to expand on earlier formulations within the context of *The Rite*'s conception as a ballet, the sketches, the emergence of a critical tradition, and the numerous revisions that followed its celebrated premiere on May 29, 1913.

In the fulfillment of this task I am indebted above all to Andrew Imbrie for his careful reading of the text and his many helpful suggestions. Imbrie's ideas on the nature of meter and rhythm were instrumental in sorting out a number of thorny issues.

I am grateful as well to Joseph Kerman, whose editing helped clarify many important points. Simon Karlinsky graciously offered his assistance in tracking down valuable sources and in translating crucial Russian texts.

I would also like to thank the Music Library at the University of California at Berkeley. The final version of the manuscript was prepared with care and skill by Mrs. Dottie Milani of the Novato Secretarial Service.

Finally I extend my thanks to Anna-Marie, Linnea, and Cattarina.

1
Point of Order

Here we are in a little difficulty, because the upholders of the "Sacre" tell us that it is to be judged on its musical merits exclusively, and on the other hand that it is conditioned by the story of the ballet for which it was originally written. This form of mental gymnastics seems a little difficult to the uninitiated, especially as some of the brutalities of the music, and the strong, relentless reiterated rhythms, seem to have no reason apart from the story in question.

Alfred Kalisch, "London Concerts," *The Musical Times,* July 1, 1921

The latest catchword of the partisans is that the "Sacre" is abstract music. We do not take that too seriously, however. We know how dependent Stravinsky's music has hitherto been upon the action it was designed to accompany.

Ernest Newman, "The End of a Chapter," *The Sunday Times,* July 3, 1921

For the greater part of this century our knowledge and appreciation of *The Rite of Spring* have come from the concert hall and from recordings. The facts surrounding its conception as a ballet have of course always been known. Commissioned, following the extraordinary success of *The Firebird* (1910) and *Petrushka* (1911), by Sergei Diaghilev for the Ballets Russes, *The Rite's* premiere in Paris on May 29, 1913, precipitated a celebrated riot. (Stravinsky later claimed to have been taken unawares, the rehearsals having been without intimation of a disturbance.[1] To

---

[1] Igor Stravinsky and Robert Craft, *Expositions and Developments* (Berkeley: University of California Press, 1981), p. 142. [First published by Doubleday, 1962.]

what extent members of the audience might actually have been predisposed toward riotous behavior would be a question difficult to assess. We do not hereby minimize the novel or "revolutionary" character of the music or the choreography.) Other credits have routinely been acknowledged: Nicolas Roerich collaborated on the scenario and was responsible for the decor, Vaslav Nijinsky composed the choreography, and Pierre Monteux conducted the rehearsals and the premiere.

But the scenario itself, the choreography, and, above all, the close "interdisciplinary" conditions of coordination under which the music is now known to have been composed—these are matters which, after the 1913 premiere, quickly passed from consciousness. Like pieces of a scaffolding, they were abandoned in favor of the edifice itself and relegated to the "extra-musical." They became history, as opposed to living art. Even the title, with its clear suggestion of pagan rites or "primitivism," lost its specific ties to the subject matter and became almost exclusively a musically descriptive label: *The Rite of Spring* is a translation from the French, *Le Sacre du printemps,* under which heading the work largely became known; the French in turn is a translation from the 1911 Russian title *Vesna sviashchennaia,* "Holy Spring"; this was preceded by the still earlier (1910) conception whose title, *Velikaia zhertva,* the "Great Sacrifice," became Part II in the final version; and this latter was itself inspired by a dream or "vision" that occurred to the composer in the spring of 1910. Similarly, the titles of the individual dances, preserved in Russian and in French translation in the first 1921 edition of the score and in most subsequent editions, became increasingly obscure and pretentious: *L'Adoration de la terre* or "Adoration of the Earth," *Cercles mystérieux des adolescentes* or "Mystic Circles of the Young Girls," *Glorification de l'élue* or "Glorification of the Chosen One." In what capacity could this verbiage serve a musical substance that, in logic and continuity, had become so utterly self-sufficient? (The early French translations, as Stravinsky later remarked, were by someone "with a special taste in titles."[2] English titles were added to the 1967 edition, which retained the French translations but deleted the Russian originals. The phony, "shamanistic" origin of the original Russian titles has been noted by a number of scholars familiar with Russian cultural trends at the time of *The Rite*.)[3]

Whether *The Rite* should be heard and understood as ballet rather than as concert music is not an appropriate question. We can doubtless have it both ways, even if there is little tradition behind the work as dance music, while its hold as a relatively autonomous piece of music has been virtually indestructible. Nijinsky's original choreography was quickly forgotten after the 1913 performances; it was ignored by the Diaghilev revival of 1920 and by nearly all subsequent productions. The music has, in contrast, remained a permanent fixture, even given the extensive revisions in instrumentation and barring. This is not to question the aesthetic incli-

---

[2]Robert Craft, "*The Rite of Spring*: Genesis of a Masterpiece," *Perspectives of New Music* 5, 1 (1966), p. 28. This article was reprinted as an introduction to Igor Stravinsky, *The Rite of Spring: Sketches 1911–1913* (London: Boosey and Hawkes, 1969).

[3]See Simon Karlinsky, "The Composer's Workshop," *The Nation,* June 15, 1970, p. 732.

nations of those for whom some contact with the ballet, in whatever form, remains an indispensable part of their appreciation, but only to point out that, in the absence of a tradition with accompanying terms of reference, it is not easy to assess the conditions or, indeed, the nature of these inclinations.

The really curious element in this story is that it was Stravinsky himself who initiated and then encouraged the music's dissociation from its scenic and choreographic ties. The first signs of a move in this direction were apparent directly after the premiere, and their roots can be traced back to the inception itself. Unlike *The Firebird* and, especially, *Petrushka,* whose illustrious "chord" so spectacularly complements, like an *idée fixe* in the second, third, and fourth tableaux, the quirky antics of the maligned puppet—*The Rite* never accompanied an actual plot. The scenario was conceived as a loosely aligned succession of imagined prehistoric rites, to which the music was in turn composed as a succession of dance movements. The idea had been presentational and had sought, in episodic fashion, to *depict* a series of primitive ceremonies, not to describe such rites in the form of narration or story.

Similar intentions obviously lie at the heart of many of Stravinsky's subsequent works for the theater, from *Les Noces* (1914–23) to *Agon* (1953–57). His observations on *Les Noces* are applicable more broadly:

> As my conception developed, I began to see that it did not indicate the dramatization of a wedding or the accompaniment of a staged wedding spectacle with descriptive music. My wish was, instead, to present actual wedding material through direct quotations of popular—i.e., non-literary—verse. . . .
>
> As a collection of clichés and quotations of typical wedding sayings, [*Les Noces*] might be compared to one of those scenes in *Ulysses* in which the reader seems to be overhearing scraps of conversation without the connecting thread of discourse. But *Les Noces* might also be compared to *Ulysses* in the larger sense that both works are trying to *present* rather than to *describe*.[4]

And later he recalled his impatience with the naive story element in *The Firebird,* those portions of the scenario that had corresponded with the more strictly narrative, pantomime sections of the dance. After the 1919 concert suite he preferred this abridged version to the original ballet.[5]

All of which is not to deny, in the case of *The Rite* or, indeed, any of the ballets, the intimacy of Stravinsky's contact with the scenario and its stage action, both before and during actual composition. In a letter to Roerich dated September 26, 1911, apparently written just after he had begun to compose, Stravinsky writes about a passage from the "Augurs of Spring": "The music is coming out very fresh and new. The picture of the old woman in a squirrel fur sticks in my mind. She is constantly before my eyes as I compose the 'Divination with Twigs': I see her run-

[4]Stravinsky and Craft, *Expositions and Developments,* pp. 114–15.
[5]Ibid., pp. 128, 132.

ning in front of the group, stopping sometimes and interrupting the rhythmic flow."[6] There are cues for "the old woman" at rehearsal nos. 15, 19, and 21 in the composer's four-hand piano score with choreographic notation,[7] and the syncopated, offbeat figure signaling the women's arrival at no. 15 is the first entry in the sketchbook of *The Rite* dating from 1911 to 1913.[8] (This initial sketch is shown in Example 58, Chapter 6.) But these sources are equally explicit about the ban on pantomime. In the same letter to Roerich, Stravinsky wrote: "I am convinced that the action must be danced and not pantomimed." And following the completion of the score, a synopsis of the scenario, sent to N. F. Findeizen, editor of the *Russian Musical Gazette,* is framed by the admonition that "the whole thing must be danced from beginning to end; I give not a single bar for pantomime."[9]

Still, the real change of heart began with what has been described by Robert Craft as "the *Montjoie!* affair."[10] Just prior to the premiere, Stravinsky granted an interview to Ricciotto Canudo, an author and founder of the Parisian arts journal *Montjoie!* Publication of this interview followed on the morning of the premiere, under the now infamous title "Ce que j'ai voulu exprimer dans *Le Sacre du Printemps*."[11] For reasons that are still not altogether clear, the essay sparked an angry reply from Stravinsky, who claimed that his ideas had been misrepresented. Yet the article contains many passages that now seem typical of the composer. Apropos of the Introduction or Prelude to Part I, Stravinsky is quoted as remarking that the principal melodic line was given "not to the strings, which are too symbolic and representative of the human voice," but to the wind instruments, "which have a drier tone, and which are more precise and less endowed with facile expression."[12] And the description of the scenario is relatively straightforward, consistent not only with the synopsis sent to Findeizen (and with other apparently authorized accounts at this time), but also with what we now know, from letters, documents, and sketches, of the initial collaborative effort. Compare the following excerpts from the interview with the description Stravinsky prepared for Sergei Koussevitsky's concert performances of *The Rite* in Moscow in February, 1914. (The latter is given in full in Chapter 2, pp. 26–27.) Note the initial references here to the

---

[6]"Letters to Nicholas Roerich and N. F. Findeizen," Appendix II in the accompanying booklet to Stravinsky, *The Rite of Spring: Sketches 1911–1913*, p. 30.

[7]See "The Stravinsky-Nijinsky Choreography," Appendix III in the accompanying booklet to Stravinsky, *The Rite of Spring: Sketches 1911–1913*, p. 36.

[8]Stravinsky, *The Rite of Spring: Sketches 1911–1913*, p. 3. This assumes a standard left-to-right and top-to-bottom chronological ordering of the entries on page 3 (the first page of musical illustrations), a matter to which we shall be turning in Chapter 6.

[9]Stravinsky, "Letters to Nicholas Roerich and N. F. Findeizen," p. 33.

[10]Vera Stravinsky and Robert Craft, *Stravinsky in Pictures and Documents* (New York: Simon and Schuster, 1978), p. 522.

[11]*Montjoie!,* May 29, 1913. Reprinted in François Lesure, ed., *Le Sacre du Printemps: Dossier de presse* (Geneva: Editions Minkoff, 1980), p. 13. An English translation by Edward B. Hill appeared in the *Boston Evening Transcript*, February 12, 1916, and is reprinted in V. Stravinsky and Craft, *Stravinsky in Pictures and Documents*, pp. 524–26.

[12]Vera Stravinsky, *Stravinsky in Pictures and Documents*, p. 525.

"old woman," an image which, as already mentioned, accompanied some of the composer's earliest sketches for the "Augurs of Spring."

> In the first scene [Part I], some adolescent boys appear with a very old woman, whose age and even whose century is unknown, who knows the secrets of nature, and teaches her sons Prediction ["Divination with Twigs"]. She runs, bent over the earth, half-woman, half-beast. The adolescents at her side are Augurs of Spring, who mark in their steps the rhythm of Spring. . . . During this time the adolescent girls come from the river. They form a circle which mingles with the boys' circle. . . . The groups separate and compete, messengers come from one side to the other and they quarrel.
>
> It is the defining of forces through struggle, that is to say through games ["Ritual of the Rival Tribes"]. But a procession arrives ["Procession of the Sage"]. It is the Saint, the Sage, the Pontifex, the oldest of the clan. All are seized with terror. The Sage gives a benediction to the Earth, stretched flat, his arms and legs stretched out, becoming one with the soil. His benediction ["The Sage"] is as a signal for an eruption of rhythm ["Dance of the Earth"]. Each, covering his head, runs in spirals, pouring forth in numbers, like the new energies of nature.[13]

On the other hand, the interview's opening paragraphs may now seem extravagant in tone and imagery. "In the *Prelude,* before the curtain rises, I have confided to my orchestra the great fear which weighs on every sensitive soul confronted with the potentialities, the "being in one's self," which may increase and develop infinitely."[14]

The Moscow journal *Muzyka* published a Russian translation of the *Montjoie!* interview in August, 1913, which prompted another indignant reply.[15] In a letter to *Muzyka*'s editor, Stravinsky claimed that the interview had been given "practically on the run," that the Russian translation was inadequate (the French version had been more "coherent"), that the information on the scenario was "inaccurate," and that the "style" of the essay was misleading; he requested that a revised version be published.[16] But Stravinsky's revised text, translated in the first volume of the recently published *Selected Correspondence,* does not substantially alter the original content.[17] The opening paragraphs are tamed somewhat, but his corrections are for the most part grammatical.

The final episode of this "affair" came some fifty-seven years later, in a communication to *The Nation*. Responding to a review of three publications on his music, Stravinsky claimed once again that the *Montjoie!* interview had been "con-

---

[13]Ibid., p. 525.
[14]Ibid., p. 524.
[15]*Muzyka*, No. 141, August 16, 1913.
[16]Robert Craft, ed., *Stravinsky: Selected Correspondence*, vol. 1 (New York: Knopf, 1982), p. 55.
[17]Ibid., p. 54.

cocted by a French journalist" and that he had "disavowed the essay not only at the time . . . but on later occasions as well."[18]

The signals here are contradictory. Yet behind the quibbling about accuracy, style, and translation seems to lie an early uneasiness with some of the aesthetic assumptions underlying the original production. Stravinsky is not explicit; he was perhaps unable to pinpoint the nature of his reservations. Possibly he felt that the claims of "primitivism," advanced with such insistence by the critics following the premiere, were too vehement and would distract the listener, inhibiting a thoughtful hearing and understanding of the music. Or Nijinsky's choreography may have seemed less than convincing, once memory of the very first performance, the only one attended by the composer himself in 1913, had dimmed.[19] But whatever the nature of Stravinsky's reservations, the extraordinary success of *The Rite* in the concert hall, crowned nearly a year later in Paris with Pierre Monteux once again at the podium, sealed its destiny. In a complete reversal of the riot that had accompanied its production as a ballet, *The Rite* became an overnight success on April 5, 1914; the composer, hoisted to the shoulders of a few bystanders, was led triumphantly from the hall of the Casino de Paris by an exuberant crowd of admirers. ("Our little Igor," Diaghilev mused, "now requires police escorts out of his concerts, like a prize fighter.")[20] Indeed, *Petrushka* underwent a similar transformation at this time, and one by no means fostered by the composer alone. Concerning his concert performances of *Petrushka* in March of 1914, Pierre Monteux wrote enthusiastically to the composer, "How much this music gains in concert performances; every detail is heard throughout the hall."[21] Stravinsky underscored these lines in red pencil.

Diaghilev's revival of the ballet in December, 1920, seven years after the premiere—after Stravinsky's traumatic break with Russia, and, perhaps above all, after *Pulcinella* (1919–20), his first fully developed neoclassical venture—was something quite different from the original. Léonide Massine composed the choreography, and apparently in accord with the composer's revised (or revisionist) wishes as expressed in another important interview at the time, "Les Deux *Sacre du Printemps*" in the journal *Comoedia*.[22] Stravinsky's comment that *The Rite* was neither "anecdotal" nor "descriptive" in character is consistent with earlier apparent objectives. Yet he went much farther than this, disavowing much of the pagan symbolism that had so obviously lain behind the original conception. His first idea, he now said, had been musical rather than visionary, and it was this idea that had

[18]"Stravinsky Replies," *The Nation*, August 3, 1970, p. 66.

[19]There were four subsequent performances in Paris on June 2, 4, 6, and 13. Stravinsky did not attend the July performances in London.

[20]Stravinsky and Craft, *Expositions and Developments*, p. 144.

[21]Robert Craft, ed., *Stravinsky: Selected Correspondence*, vol. 2 (New York: Knopf, 1984), p. 58. The letter is dated March 14, 1914.

[22]December 11, 1920. Reprinted in Lesure, *Le Sacre du Printemps: Dossier de presse*, p. 53. An English translation, "Interpretation by Massine," may be found in Minna Lederman, ed., *Stravinsky in the Theatre* (New York: Pellegrini and Cudahy, 1949), pp. 24–26.

spawned the image of a sacrifice in prehistoric Russia. In what appears to be an obvious allusion to the celebrated "Augurs of Spring" chord at no. 13 of the score, he announced that his first idea had been conceived "in a strong and brutal manner."[23] These claims are contradicted by all other available sources, which invariably cite the dream or "vision" as the trigger and as having been unaccompanied by musical ideas.[24]

Equally misleading in the *Comoedia* interview are statements describing *The Rite* as an "objective construction," claiming that its conception had proceeded as "a work of pure musical construction."[25] For although, as already noted, we have for some time now been able to appreciate *The Rite* both ways, as ballet and as "pure musical construction" (even if the "purity" on the formalist side of this equation will always remain something of an aesthetic puzzle), letters and sketches at the time leave no doubt as to the extraordinarily intimate terms of the collaboration, the degree to which the scenario and its stage action provoked and at times guided the musical invention. Roerich, Stravinsky's earliest collaborator on the scenario, is not mentioned in the *Comoedia* interview. Massine's choreography is preferred to that of Nijinsky because it ignored the "heavy-coated symbolism" of the earlier production and, more importantly, because it did not "follow the music note by note, or even measure by measure"; it "battled against the bar line" in realizing "a pure choreographic construction" to complement the "pure musical construction."[26] Many years later, in *Memories and Commentaries* (1960), Stravinsky's comments were much the same:

> [Nijinsky] believed that the choreography should re-emphasize the musical beat and pattern through constant coordination. In effect, this restricted the dance to rhythmic duplication of the music and made of it an imitation. Choreography, as I conceive it, must realize its own form, one independent of the musical form though measured to the musical unit. Its construction will be based on whatever correspondences the choreographer may invent, but it must not seek merely to duplicate the line and beat of the music. . . . I thought [Massine's choreography] excellent—incomparably clearer than Nijinsky's.[27]

And so *The Rite*'s career as an object of "pure musical delight" had begun. Henceforth all pronouncements by the composer and his adjuncts would up-

---

[23]Stravinsky, "Interpretation by Massine," p. 24.

[24]See, especially, Igor Stravinsky, *An Autobiography* (New York: Norton, 1962), p. 31. (First published as *Chroniques de ma vie* [Paris: Denoël et Steele, 1935].) The term *vision* appears on p. 31, while in *Expositions and Developments*, p. 140, the vision is referred to as a "dream."

[25]Stravinsky, "Interpretation by Massine," p. 26.

[26]Ibid., pp. 24–26.

[27]Igor Stravinsky and Robert Craft, *Memories and Commentaries* (Berkeley: University of California Press, 1981), pp. 37–42. (First published by Doubleday, 1960.)

hold the new doctrine of "objective construction." Performances of the Diaghilev revival in London in June, 1921, were duly launched with revisionist bulletins, an assignment performed in advance by Edwin Evans, who, seven years earlier, had lectured London audiences on the intricacies of the symbolic representation.[28] The critics reacted harshly. Those who had originally expressed mild support had tended to excuse the "hideousness" of the music by pointing to its "primitive" subject matter; in 1921 they merely ridiculed the aesthetic turnabout.[29] Stravinsky was a "faddist," a panderer to whims, an "abstract" cosmopolitan who had betrayed the spiritual origins of his work (cold, heartless, soulless, "abstract," mechanical Stravinsky—the beginnings of the image with which we have grown so familiar). But to no considerable avail. For the protests were by now reactionary and too clearly on the losing side; the autonomy of the music had taken hold too securely. (That the abstract, mechanical quality of *The Rite* might be linked to matters critical to the rhythmic organization was an issue left untouched, although it is one to which we shall be directing our attention in Chapters 3 and 4.) The peculiarly Russian features in the melodic, instrumental, and pitch construction were forgotten, as was, of course, the original scenic effect. As for Nijinsky as a choreographer, Stravinsky wrote in 1935: "What struck me then, and still strikes me most, about the choreography, was and is Nijinsky's lack of consciousness of what he was doing in creating it. . . . What the choreography expressed was a very labored and barren effort rather than a plastic realization flowing simply and naturally free from what the music demanded."[30] His remarks in 1960 were more explicit:

> My own disappointment with Nijinsky was due to the fact that he did not know the musical alphabet. He never understood musical meters and he had no very certain sense of tempo. You may imagine from this the rhythmic chaos that was *Le Sacre du Printemps,* and especially the chaos of the last dance where poor Mlle Piltz, the sacrificial maiden, was not even aware of the changing bars. Nor did Nijinsky make any attempt to understand my own choreographic ideas for *Le Sacre.* In the *Danses des Adolescentes* ["Augurs of Spring"], for example, I had imagined a row of almost motionless dancers. Nijinsky made of this piece a big jumping match.[31]

[28]See the reviews in *The Times, The Manchester Guardian,* and *The Daily Telegraph* as reprinted in Lesure, *Le Sacre du Printemps: Dossier de presse,* pp. 63–67.

[29]See especially Alfred Kalisch, "London Concerts," *The Musical Times,* July 1, 1921, and Ernest Newman, "The End of a Chapter," *The Sunday Times,* July 3, 1921, both reprinted in Lesure, *Le Sacre du Printemps: Dossier de presse,* pp. 72–75.

[30]*An Autobiography,* pp. 47–48.

[31]*Memories and Commentaries,* p. 37

The true high point of the revisionist spirit came in the early 1950s with the lengthy and superbly drawn studies by Pierre Boulez.[32] In both Boulez's celebrated critique of Stravinsky's music and his analysis of rhythm, there occurs not a single reference to *The Rite*'s scenic or choreographic design. And one suspects that the composer, flattered by the technically imaginative attention of so young, promising, and fanatical a serialist, must have felt supremely vindicated. In Boulez's new pantheon, the "Russian"-period works, stretching roughly from the very beginning to *Histoire du soldat* (1918), are still favored over the "decadent" neoclassical ones. But this is now because of their advanced craftsmanship, their superiority as musical (i.e., "technical") structures, and, above all, their rhythmic innovations, not because of their soulful ties to "Mother Russia," as earlier in the century.

In the wake of a series of remarkable developments in the past two decades, there has now been a shift in the opposite direction. Musicians, scholars, and critics have taken a renewed interest in the circumstances of the conception of *The Rite*. The developments sparking this reaction have been the appearance, after nearly half a century, of the long-lost sketchbook cited already above, published in facsimile with a commentary by Robert Craft (1969); the recovery, in 1967, of the four-hand piano score with choreographic annotations by the composer; the publication of numerous letters, documents, and photographs pertaining to the initial conception and production;[33] the publication of selected reviews of the 1913 premiere and of the 1920–21 revival in Paris and London, and of reviews of subsequent performances throughout Europe during the 1920s;[34] and, most recently, the publication of a *Selected Correspondence* in three volumes, edited by Robert Craft.[35] Most prominent of the recoveries is undoubtedly the sketchbook, a "find" which has already given students of Stravinsky's music a new look at *The Rite* and the intricacies of its creation. According to a dedication signed by the composer on the first page, the sketchbook was given to Diaghilev in October of 1920. It then passed to Diaghilev's heir, Boris Kochno, who retained it for some thirty years. André Meyer acquired it in 1961 and made it available for facsimile re-

---

[32]Reprinted in Pierre Boulez, *Notes of an Apprenticeship*, trans. Herbert Weinstock (New York: Knopf, 1968), pp. 61–62, 72–145, 150, 242–64.

[33]The most revealing of these are found in V. Stravinsky and Craft, *Stravinsky in Pictures and Documents*, and in the accompanying booklet to Stravinsky, *The Rite of Spring: Sketches 1911–1913*. See, in addition, Theodore Stravinsky, *Catharine and Igor Stravinsky, a Family Album* (London: Boosey and Hawkes, 1973); Irina Vershinina, *Stravinsky's Early Ballets*, trans. L. G. Heien (Ann Arbor: UMI, forthcoming); and the early Stravinsky correspondence in B. M. Yaroustovsky, ed., *I. F. Stravinskii: Stat'i i materialy* (Moscow, 1973), pp. 437–520. The last volume includes early letters on *The Rite*, dating from 1910 to 1914, to Andrei Rimsky-Korsakov, Alexandre Benois, N. F. Findeizen, and Maximilian Steinberg.

[34]As cited already, *Le Sacre du Printemps: Dossier de presse*.

[35]Cited above, Robert Craft, ed., *Stravinsky: Selected Correspondence,* 3 vols. (New York: Knopf, 1982, 1984, 1986.)

production several years later. The quality of the reproduction is stunning. The composer's red and blue markings are preserved in full color, and the impression it gives is very nearly that of the manuscript itself.[36]

Startling revelations have been accumulating. In a study dating from 1979, Lawrence Morton returned to the initial dream and claimed as its probable source a poem composed by the Russian modernist poet Sergei Gorodetsky.[37] This is not farfetched. There are no accounts of pagan sacrifice in standard Russian historical or anthropological literature, and Stravinsky's earlier "Two Melodies of Gorodetsky" (1907–08), opus 6, were composed to lyrics by this poet. *Staviat Iarilu, "They Are Building Iarila,"* the title of the poem cited by Morton, contains images of pagan ritual, wise elders, and the sacrifice of a virgin maiden. *Staviat Iarilu* appears in the same Gorodetsky volume as the two poems used in the earlier Stravinsky opus.[38]

More significantly, Morton examined the massive Juszkiewicz anthology of 1,785 Lithuanian folk songs known to have been in Stravinsky's possession at the time of *The Rite*—a formidable task, inasmuch as these melodies appear tediously in succession without title or harmonic realization.[39] Apart from no. 157 in this collection as the source of *The Rite*'s opening bassoon melody (the only borrowing previously acknowledged by Stravinsky), Morton unearthed three additional melodies with obvious ties to subsequent material in *The Rite*. These "source melodies," four in all, are listed in Examples 1–3, along with entries from the sketchbook and score that most closely approximate their contours.[40] Nos. 249 and 271, Examples 2a and b, are probable double sources for the tranquillo melody that frames the "Spring Rounds." Yet it should be noted that none of these "source melodies" is directly quoted in the sketchbook. Thus the melody at no. 46 in the "Ritual of Abduction" first appears on page 7 in the sketchbook with the shifting meter clearly in place (as shown in Example 3b); its source as no. 142 in the anthology, Example 3a, with the regular $\frac{2}{4}$ meter and E♭-major key signature, does not appear. Doubtless following a tip from the composer, André Schaeffner first published the information on the opening bassoon melody in his 1931 biography.[41] Much later

---

[36]In a prefacing remark to the publication, p. vii, François Lesure writes that the composer purchased the "exercize book" during "the winter of 1911–12" in Varese, a small Italian town near Lake Como. This date should read "winter of 1910–11."

[37]"Footnotes to Stravinsky Studies: *Le Sacre du Printemps,*" *Tempo* 128 (1979): 9–16. Other possible sources of the initial dream or vision are cited in Simon Karlinsky, "Stravinsky and Russian Pre-Literate Theater," *19th Century Music* 6, 3 (1983): 235.

[38]Sergei Gorodetsky, *Iar', Lyric and Lyric-Epic Verse* (St. Petersburg, 1907).

[39]Anton Juszkiewicz, *Litauische Volks-Weisen* (Kraców, 1900).

[40]Morton also identified no. 34 in the Juszkiewicz anthology as a possible source of the D♭–B♭–E♭– B♭ ostinato in the "Augurs of Spring." The problem here, however, is that the minor or Dorian tetrachord with a pitch numbering of (0 2 3 5), complete or incomplete (as in the "Augurs of Spring"), occurs with such frequency as a cohesive melodic unit in the Lithuanian songs and in Russian folk songs that any specific attribution is bound to seem suspect.

[41]*Strawinsky* (Paris: Rieder, 1931), plate XXI.

EXAMPLE 1

(a) Juszkiewicz, no. 157

(b) Introduction

EXAMPLE 2

(a) Juszkiewicz, no. 249

(b) Juszkiewicz, no. 271

(c) Sketchbook, p. 7

(d) "Spring Rounds"

EXAMPLE 3

(a) Juszkiewicz, no. 142

(b) Sketchbook, p. 7

(c) "Ritual of Abduction"

Stravinsky continued to insist that this had in fact been the only direct bor-rowing in *The Rite*: "If any of these ["Russian"-period] pieces *sounds* like ab-original folk music, it may be because my powers of fabrication were able to tap some unconscious 'folk' memory."[42]

Study of the sketchbook itself led to further discoveries of this kind. In a seminal study of recent years, Richard Taruskin identified the melody at the top of page 8 in the sketchbook (Example 4a) as a transposition of no. 50 in Rimsky-Korsakov's *One Hundred Russian National Songs* (1877), opus 24.[43] At first glance, the melody appears wholly unrelated to the material it prefaces on page 8 (the principal section of the "Spring Rounds"), or, indeed, any other material of *The Rite*. However, the F–C–F–G fragment at m.4 anticipates the

[42]Stravinsky and Craft, *Memories and Commentaries*, p. 98.
[43]"Russian Folk Melodies in *The Rite of Spring*," *Journal of the American Musicological Society* 33, 3 (1980): 512–13.

EXAMPLE 4

(a) Sketchbook, p. 8

(b) Sketchbook, p. 10

(c) "Spring Rounds" ("Vivo"), transposed

motive of the Vivo section in "Spring Rounds" (as shown above in Example 4b), and hence also the motive at nos. 37 and 46 in the "Ritual of Abduction," the latter in turn linking to no. 142 in the Juszkiewicz anthology. (In accord with the original order of the dance movements of *The Rite,* "Spring Rounds" and its concluding Vivo section were sketched before the "Ritual of Abduction." The "Ritual of Abduction" melody at no. 46, with its shifting meter, appears as a relatively isolated entry on page 7, which is otherwise devoted principally to "Spring Rounds.")

The additional sources cited by Taruskin are more tenuous, with their links to the score based on folk-derived prototypes rather than on individual, specific outlines. In fact, Taruskin's thesis is that Stravinsky was at this time alert not only to the authenticity of his folk-song borrowings but to their ethnological character as well; Stravinsky deliberately sought out material that, in seasonal and ceremonial character, seemed appropriate to the implications of the scenario. And there can in fact be little doubt that during and after his composition of *The Rite,* Stravinsky's preoccupation with genuine Russian folk sources was a good deal more intense and conscientious than his published—revisionist—statements suggest.[44] In one of the most striking pieces of evidence to date, a letter to his mother dated February 23, 1916, Stravinsky specifically requests that publications of the most recent, and hence most authentic, *phonographically* transcribed material be forwarded to his address in Switzerland:

> Send me please, and as quickly as possible (you'll find them at Jurgenson's), the folk songs of the Caucasian peoples that have been *phonographically* transcribed. Others, non-phonographic, you needn't pick up. And while you're at it, if Jurgenson has any other phonographically transcribed songs, get them as well. Keep in mind that I already have the first installment of "Great Russian Songs in Folk Harmonization" (as transcribed phonographically by Linyova). Have there been any further installments?[45]

It is not known whether the second volume of Linyova's anthology was forwarded. The first volume of twenty-three folk songs (evidently in Stravinsky's possession at this time) includes in its Introduction a highly revealing discussion of the irregular rhythmic-metric patterns in Russian folk songs and of the relationship of this irregularity to sung folk verse. The twenty-three folk songs are harmonized according to authentic polyphonic practice, not, as in the anthologies compiled by Rimsky-Korsakov, Tchaikovsky, and others, in the Westernized harmonic style. Unfortunately, it has not been possible to discover any of the specific outlines of these songs in the melodic material of Stravinsky's "Russian"-period works.

In a related study, Taruskin identified possible sources of the scenario, histories, and anthologies likely to have been known and consulted by Roerich.[46] They include a monumental study of peasant folklore and pagan prehistory by Alexander Afanasiev; a twelfth-century chronicle of early pagan customs entitled *The Primary Chronicle*; a description of the Scyths in *The Persian Wars,* book IV, by Herodotus; and a book of sixty lyric and epic poems by Sergei

---

[44]In light of these current findings, the earlier skepticism voiced by the present writer concerning the role of authentic folk songs in Stravinsky's "Russian"-period works ought perhaps be amended somewhat; see Pieter C. van den Toorn, *The Music of Igor Stravinsky* (New Haven: Yale University Press, 1983), p. 92. Still, the principal argument there concerning Stravinsky's transformation of source materials, his "simulation" and, in many instances, his indifference toward the question of authenticity or fabrication, remains valid.

[45]*I. F. Stravinskii: Stat'i i materialy*, p. 488. Quoted in Richard Taruskin, "Russian Folk Melodies in *The Rite of Spring*," pp. 507–8. The "first installment" referred to in this letter is Evgeniia Linyova, *Velikorusskie pesni v narodnoi garmonizatsii*, vol. 1 (St. Petersburg, 1904). The second volume was published in 1909. An English translation of the first volume was published as Eugenie Lineff, *The Peasant Songs of Great Russia* (St. Petersburg, 1905).

[46]"*The Rite* Revisited: The Idea and the Sources of Its Scenario," in Edmond Strainchamps and Maria Rika Maniates, eds., *Music and Civilization: Essays in Honor of Paul Henry Lang* (New York: Norton, 1984), pp. 183–202.

Gorodetsky. The latter is the book cited already as having inspired Stravinsky's original dream of ritual sacrifice and as the source of the two poems employed earlier by the composer in his "Two Melodies of Gorodetsky."

Remarkably, too, Stravinsky took an interest in the resurfacing of his original sources. In preparing the last 1967 edition of the score, he and Craft seem to have enjoyed the task of finding suitable English equivalents to the original Russian titles of the individual dance movements, a task that, for the composer, must inevitably have conjured up long-forgotten memories of the 1911–13 collaboration. In addition to the sketchbook, Stravinsky and Craft examined the newly recovered four-hand piano score with choreographic notation. The composer reported at length that, contrary to his earlier criticisms in *Comoedia* (1920) and *Memories and Commentaries* (1960), his annotations revealed choreographic accents and phrase units that were "seldom coterminous with the accents and phrases of the music"; the dance was "almost always in counterpoint to the music."[47] Thus, in the first climactic block of the "Augurs of Spring," at no. 28, the first eight measures, $\frac{2}{4}$ in the score, were to be counted "as if in $\frac{3}{4}$."[48] And in the concluding climactic block of this dance, the choreographic accents occur on the first beat of the $\frac{2}{4}$ measures at nos. 34–35, and on the second beat at nos. 35–36.[49]

Indeed, in his communication to *The Nation* cited above, Stravinsky urged that a revival be staged of the original Nijinsky realization, re-created from the recovered ballet score. Craft in turn proposed the New York City Ballet as the ideal company.[50] Although long at the forefront in the commission and production of Stravinsky's ballets, the company had never mounted a production of *The Rite*.

And so we arrive, in near full circle, at a brief moment of truth. Can these recoveries and the historical research they have already spawned lead to a revival of sorts, granting us the occasional luxury of actually experiencing *The Rite* both ways? Or, short of a revival, can the documentation newly illuminate the music and possibly transform our revisionist bent, our long-held perception of the work as indeed one of "pure musical construction"?

Clearly one problem is that the dynamics of revival, though intrinsically dependent on an historical record, are ultimately an aesthetic and hence supremely practical matter. Leaving aside the pull of sheer nostalgia (and there can surely be very little of this at the present time), an account of the symbolic origins of *The Rite,* however rigorously determined, can hardly be expected to govern contemporary matters of taste, fashion, or aesthetic appeal. One

[47]Stravinsky, "The Stravinsky-Nijinsky Choreography," p. 35.

[48]Ibid., p. 36.

[49]Ibid.

[50]V. Stravinsky and Craft, *Stravinsky in Pictures and Documents*, p. 514.

hopes that *The Rite* will continue to survive not as an historical document but as an artistic achievement that must work here and now. And surely no one, however much he may have distorted the record from time to time, could have been more acutely sensitive to these issues than Stravinsky himself. Indeed, the very distortions we have traced were symptoms of personally evolving aesthetic impulses and are as such no less genuinely legitimate than the assumptions that now appear to have governed the 1911–1913 conception and collaboration.

To take only one example: for listeners versed in Russian folk ways and folk songs, *Les Noces* has always seemed about as authentically Russian as could reasonably be imagined for a piece of this kind—indeed, in its folkish accent, far more Russian in spirit than the music of the so-called Mighty Five or of the more academically inclined post-Kuchkist tradition. Yet *Les Noces* contains far fewer direct musical borrowings than *The Firebird, Petrushka,* or *The Rite.* Stravinsky's insistence on his own uniquely devised "powers of fabrication" seems very much to the point here. For the libretto of *Les Noces* he borrowed extensively from Russian anthologies, but he reserved for himself the right to use this material "with absolute freedom."[51]

A restoration of Nijinsky's choreography of *The Rite* may well be in order, and few could remain indifferent to the prospect of a truly convincing dance complement to the music, one that could in addition stimulate the beginnings of a tradition in choreographic design which has for so long been lacking. However, visions of prehistoric Russia, at least as they appear to have been drawn in the original 1913 production, would almost certainly offer greater difficulty. Nor did the composer ever suggest a resurrection of this kind. His final argument was merely that Nijinsky's original composition had been dealt an "injustice."[52] There is no indication that he favored an abandonment of *The Rite*'s career in the concert hall or that his preference for the work as concert music was in any way affected. (The long-standing preference may well have been owing to the fact that *The Rite* was already very overtly "dance music" and that choreographic interpretations tended therefore to be redundant even when "in counterpoint to the music" and hence to degenerate into spectacle.)

Much of the criticism directed by present-day scholars at Stravinsky's revisionist stance during the neoclassical era is reminiscent of the criticism, sixty years earlier, of Massine's 1920 revival of the ballet. Critics of this effort had complained that the composer had forsaken the original scenic and choreographic trappings, components which for them had rendered the original production at least halfway intelligible. In a similar vein, Richard Taruskin, the

---

[51]Stravinsky, *An Autobiography*, p. 54.

[52]V. Stravinsky and Craft, *Stravinsky in Pictures and Documents*, p. 511. On his copy of Irina Vershinina's monograph on the early ballets (Moscow, 1967), the composer made a notation to the effect that criticisms of Nijinsky's choreography (including, presumably, his own) had always been "unjust."

most astute and knowledgeable of current scholars in the field of nineteenth-century Russian music and early Stravinsky generally, has chided Stravinsky for "busily revising his past" to suit his neoclassical preoccupations, his "fealty to the values of 'pure music.'"[53] He even construes André Schaeffner's revelation about *The Rite*'s opening bassoon melody as an attempt by the composer to conceal the increasingly unfashionable folkloristic origin of *The Rite*: "The clear implication," Taruskin writes, "was that this citation was the unique instance of its kind in the ballet."[54] Similarly, Truman Bullard has accused the composer of "attempting to rewrite the history of the work on the basis of its later success as a concert piece."[55]

There is no doubt that in *Comoedia* (1920), the *Autobiography* (1935), and *Memories and Commentaries* (1960), the composer forgot or sought deliberately to revise the circumstances of *The Rite*'s conception. (That he may have forgotten a great deal on each of these occasions should not be summarily dismissed. The 1920 revival came, as indicated already, seven years after the premiere, and Stravinsky attended only one of the 1913 performances. Moreover, his intense preoccupation with the here-and-now of his compositions, with his immediate artistic inclinations and objectives, is well documented.) But what is surprising is that his disenchantment with the 1913 production should have commenced not after the neoclassical shift, which began in earnest with *Pulcinella* in 1919–20, but almost immediately after the premiere. He encouraged and was undoubtedly greatly influenced by Monteux's concert performances in 1914. And his reasoning at the time could not have been entirely aesthetic. Surely he recognized the financial advantages of the concert option, respecting not only *The Rite* and *Petrushka* but, later in 1919, *The Firebird* as well.

But even on aesthetic grounds, were the composer's judgments necessarily "wrong"? Might he not have sensed that, by sidestepping its explicit symbolic confines, *The Rite* could attain, as music, the kind of universal appeal it has now for so long enjoyed? Furthermore, can the aesthetics of "musical abstraction," of "absolute" or "pure music," be isolated and depicted as a peculiarly Stravinskian inclination? These ideas have been with us for some time, at the very least since the late eighteenth century when there arose, as a defense against the stolid, virtuous tradition of "melody" and "the word," an attempt to fashion a new philosophical and critical basis on which to support the growing popularity and prestige of the new instrumental forms.[56] Taruskin and others might argue that this is precisely the point, that these ideas were

---

[53]"Russian Folk Melodies in *The Rite of Spring*," p. 502.

[54]Ibid.

[55]"The First Performance of Igor Stravinsky's *Sacre du Printemps*," Ph.D dissertation, University of Rochester, 1971, vol. 1, pp. 2–3. Quoted in Richard Taruskin, "*The Rite* Revisited," p. 184.

[56]The most detailed account of these developments is Carl Dahlhaus, *Die Idee der absoluten Musik* (Kassel: Barenreiter, 1978).

alien to the Russian symbolic climate in which *The Rite* was conceived and were adopted only later by the composer as part of his neoclassical volte-face. Yet here too one could argue quite differently. Considering the fate of much ballet, incidental, and program music during the past century, the concert-hall career of *The Rite* can hardly be deemed exceptional. For better or worse, the reality in modern times has been stubbornly one-sided: with opera as the exception, music has succeeded as musical structure (i.e., as "music") or it has barely succeeded at all. Indeed, so integrally a part of our musical consciousness have such concepts as "absolute" and "autonomous" music become that they have of late been seen as a threat to the authority of historical inquiry: giving "musical autonomy" free rein, of what use is the study of historical origins and contexts?[57]

For all the complexity of its implications, Stravinsky's formalist attitude was relatively straightforward. The notorious dictum that music was "powerless to express anything at all"[58] became, in *Expositions and Developments,* "music expresses itself"; music, being both "supra-personal and super-real," was "beyond verbal meanings and verbal descriptions."[59] The works of a composer might well embody his feelings, might express or symbolize these feelings. But "consciousness of this step does not concern the composer."[60] Stravinsky stressed the distinction between thinking *in* music ("perceptual") and thinking *about* music ("conceptual"). Modern-day thinkers to the contrary, the perceptual-conceptual, practice-theory, innate-learned, and doer-thinker dichotomies remained for him meaningful distinctions.

> (We do certainly love *talking* conceptually.) But the composer works through a perceptual, not a conceptual, process. He perceives, he selects, he combines, and is not in the least aware at what point meanings of a different sort and significance grow into his works. All he knows or cares about is the apprehension of the contours of form, for form is everything.[61]

Of course, these formalist convictions were closely aligned to aspects of musical structure, in particular to features of the rhythmic organization that required, for their proper apprehension, a clean, metronomic, "mechanical" approach, features entirely at odds with the Romantic and post-Romantic traditions. In succeeding chapters we shall be endeavoring to clarify the nature of these relationships. Suffice it to say here that these Stravinskian dicta are ones with which the present writer, on even a more general plane, can find no seri-

---

[57]For further discussion see Carl Dahlhaus, *Foundations of Music History*, trans. J. B. Robinson (Cambridge: Cambridge University Press, 1983), pp. 3–33.

[58]Stravinsky, *An Autobiography*, p. 53.

[59]Stravinsky and Craft, *Expositions and Developments*, p. 101.

[60]Ibid.

[61]Ibid., pp. 102–3.

ous disagreement. One need merely substitute *listener* for *composer* in the above quotations and the reasoning becomes impregnable.

Perhaps the second of the two possibilities mentioned above offers greater advantage for the immediate future: namely, that a study of the scenario and of the newly recovered source materials can in some fashion augment our understanding of the music. In the sketchbook itself, most of the individual movements are prefaced by Roerich's headings, and some of these include subheadings to cover the details of the stage action. On page 29, for example, a sketch for the material at no. 38 in the "Ritual of Abduction" is accompanied by an inscription identifying this as the moment at which, on stage, the tribal bride is "seized." Just below is Robert Craft's brief description of the "Ritual of the Rival Tribes" and the succeeding "Procession of the Sage," derived from a survey of the sketchbook and from the composer's later recollections of the original stage action.

> The ritual is a tribal war-game, a contest of strength as determined, for example, in a tug of war. Two sharply contrasted groups are identified, the first by heavy, comparatively slow figures in bass register (the first two measures at No. 57 and the brass chords before No. 59), the second by fast figures in treble register (the third measure of No. 57). The clash occurs (the fifth measure of No. 57) where the music of both is superimposed. The next event, the *Procession of the Oldest and Wisest One,* is heralded by the entrance of the tubas at No. 64. A clearing is prepared at the center of the stage and the Sage's arrival there, with the women of the tribe in his train, coincides with the first beat of No. 70, the orchestral tutti which signifies the gathering of all the people.[62]

All of this fits the musical discourse. The "Rival Tribes" at nos. 57–64 is in fact composed of three contrasting blocks of material which, shuffled and varied in length, are placed in repeated and abrupt juxtaposition. The first two of these blocks, at nos. 57 and 57 + 2, are highly dissimilar, and as such complement the individual movements of the two competing tribes; the third block, at no. 57 + 4, with its material borrowed from the two preceding blocks, is both musically and scenically a "clash." Finally, the music at no. 70 in the "Procession of the Sage" signifies the arrival of the Sage and "the gathering of all the people." And it is precisely here that the conflicting rhythmic-metric periods defined by the reiterating tuba and horn fragments at nos. 64–71 are brought within a stable synchronization, that the rhythmic-metric conflict of this section is resolved.

---

[62]Craft, "*The Rite of Spring:* Genesis of a Masterpiece," pp. 29–30. A slightly more detailed description of this stage action is given in Jann Pasler, "Music and Spectacle in *Petrushka* and *The Rite of Spring*," pp. 53–81 in Jann Pasler, ed., *Confronting Stravinsky: Man, Musician, and Modernist* (Berkeley: University of California Press 1986).

As indicated earlier in this chapter, much of *The Rite* was composed with images of the particular rites and ceremonies clearly in mind. Working now in the opposite direction, these same images can often clarify or at least confirm our perception of musical form. Whether, on the other hand, a study of the handful of individual Lithuanian and Russian "source melodies" can provide similar illumination seems more open to question. The lines of contact are here more remote, the bits and pieces of melody obscured by the reality of all that is indeed profoundly new. Stravinsky's extractions from the Lithuanian collection are no doubt of considerable interest, since they document an initial reliance which had earlier been thought nonexistent and in this way tie the piece to the two earlier ballets, placing it in the broader tradition of borrowing inherited from Stravinsky's immediate Russian predecessors. These extractions also point to fundamentals of the compositional process, to the composer's frequent dependence on borrowed, melodic "stuff" and his instinct for recomposing, simulating, "making his own" objects of practical or aesthetic appeal, all of which would eventually become as much a part of the neoclassical orientation as it was earlier of the "Russian." Yet there are fundamental differences between the use of folk songs in *The Rite* and the use of such material in *The Firebird* and *Petrushka*. In *Petrushka* it is revealing to compare Stravinsky's version of the Easter song at no. 5 in the first tableau to Rimsky-Korsakov's tonal adaption of the same melody, or to acknowledge how the instrumentation and harmony of "Elle avait un'jambe en bois" at nos. 13 and 15 ingeniously project the street flavor of this French chanson.[63] But there is nothing comparable to this in *The Rite*. The Lithuanian sources are without titles or harmony, and Stravinsky himself could scarcely have known all that much about their authentic character or function. The borrowings are of documentary interest only; musically, they are curiosities. Richard Taruskin has endeavored to pinpoint some of the ethnological implications of a number of melodic "prototypes," and with these possible Russian sources there is perhaps a greater certainty of the composer's familiarity. Yet even here, character, function, and outline are radically transformed, and in the end one is tempted to accept Stravinsky's plea of forgetfulness or indifference to the whole matter of borrowing. (On several occasions he confessed that the question of originality, of "fabrication or ethnological authenticity," was of no interest to him.)[64] What there is musically of a peculiarly Russian stamp in *The Rite* can better be pursued within the broader context of pitch structure, where many features, however much transformed by new techniques and rhythmic procedures, relate conspicuously to the preoccupations of Stravinsky's teacher Rimsky-Korsakov.

[63]For a discussion of the Easter song in *Petrushka*'s first tableau see van den Toorn, *The Music of Igor Stravinsky*, pp. 73–82, 91–95.

[64]See Robert Craft, "Commentary to the Sketches," Appendix I in the booklet accompanying Stravinsky, *The Rite of Spring: Sketches 1911–1913*, p. 16.

Then, too, even given the intimacy of Stravinsky's initial contact with Roerich's titles and ceremonies, it cannot be imagined that in the process of composition these materials were merely "set to music." Far more significantly, the detailed scenic action, once visualized, functioned as an ignition—as, earlier, the initial dream or vision had. It worked like a trigger that set the musical imagination in motion, performing much the same role as the syllables and words of the texts of Stravinsky's vocal works.[65] From this point on, the logic of the musical discourse inevitably took hold. (Stravinsky later recalled that the detailed stage picture did in fact often vanish "as soon as it had served its adjuvant purpose.")[66] Thus while images of "the old woman" in the "Augurs of Spring," of the seizing of the tribal bride in the "Ritual of Abduction," and of the two contending tribes in the "Rival Tribes" served as points of departure, the synchronization that eventually emerged between music and stage action is as likely to have sprung from the subsequent musical invention as from the initial picture itself.

The present inquiry sets off from the following propositions:

1. The "interdisciplinary" conception of *The Rite* was soon forgotten after the 1913 production, abandoned in favor of the "musical construction."
2. Recent recoveries of source materials have renewed an appreciation of the conditions attending *The Rite*'s conception as a ballet.
3. These sources, however enlightening as commentary, in no way undermine the integrity of *The Rite* as "musical construction."

In other words, merely by virtue of historical precedence, these recovered source materials in no way reveal a privileged conception of *The Rite*. Stravinsky's post-premiere attitudes are today no less valid than the assumptions that shaped the origin of this piece. And without in the least negating *The Rite*'s inception or continuing potential as ballet, it is with an ear and eye toward its musical significance that this discourse stakes its course. The music itself is the focus, and what may be examined of the initial collaboration, the choreography, and the scenario is weighed and acknowledged accordingly.

---

[65]See Igor Stravinsky and Robert Craft, *Dialogues* (Berkeley: University of California Press, 1983), p. 4. "When I work with words in music," Stravinsky commented, "my musical saliva is set in motion by the sounds and rhythms of the syllables." He conceded, however, that, once in motion, his musical train of thought often dictated verbal stress, a process which often led to unorthodox results. See the discussion of this in van den Toorn, *The Music of Igor Stravinsky*, pp. 246–51.

[66]Craft, "*The Rite of Spring*: Genesis of a Masterpiece," p. 32.

2

Sketches, Editions, and Revisions

The Sketchbook

As has often been told, the story of *The Rite* began with a dream or "vision" of pagan ritual "in which a chosen sacrificial virgin danced herself to death."[1] Unaccompanied by "concrete musical ideas," this came to the composer in March of 1910, as he was completing *The Firebird*. But it was not until July, following performances of *The Firebird* in Paris, that he confronted Diaghilev with ideas for a new ballet on the subject. Diaghilev's immediate reaction is not known. The impresario may have had other plans for his newly enshrined protégé, namely, a ballet based on the theme of Edgar Allan Poe's *The Masque of the Red Death*.[2]

Following his return to Russia that summer, Stravinsky contacted Nicolas Roerich, a painter, ethnographer, and specialist in the field of Russian pagan history. Several Stravinsky-Roerich letters survive from this period, two of which point to the existence of early sketch material.[3] Their working title at this time was

---

[1]Igor Stravinsky and Robert Craft, *Expositions and Developments* (Berkeley: University of California Press, 1981), p. 140.

[2]See the Stravinsky-Roerich letter, dated July 2, 1910 (New Style), in "Letters to Nicholas Roerich and N. F. Findeizen," Appendix II in the accompanying booklet to Igor Stravinsky, *The Rite of Spring: Sketches 1911–1913* (London: Boosey and Hawkes, 1969), p. 27. See also Vera Stravinsky and Robert Craft, *Stravinsky in Pictures and Documents* (New York: Simon and Schuster, 1978), pp. 77, 612.

[3]The two Stravinsky-Roerich letters that specifically mention early sketches are contained in Stravinsky, "Letters to Nicholas Roerich and N. F. Findeizen," pp. 27–29. Additional correspondence between Stravinsky and Roerich dating from 1910 has been published with annotations by Irina Vershinina in *Sovetskaia muzyka* 30, 8 (1966): 57–63.

"Great Sacrifice," and in a letter dated August 9, 1910, this is affectionately referred to as "our child": "I have started work (sketches) on the Great Sacrifice," Stravinsky wrote. "Have you done anything for it yet?"[4] Two drawings of Roerich's survive, but the sketch material has been lost.[5] Toward the end of September these plans were shelved as the composer became occupied with an entirely different project, a *Konzertstück* which would subsequently become the second tableau of *Petrushka*.

Nearly a year passed before the Stravinsky-Roerich collaboration was resumed. In Russia again after yet another triumphant appearance in Paris (this time with *Petrushka*), Stravinsky visited Roerich in mid-July of 1911 to work out the details of a scenario. Their work on this seems from the start to have been a cooperative effort. The division into two parts, representing day and night (with the "Sacrifice" itself shifted to Part II), was Stravinsky's idea, while the rites or ceremonies to be depicted by the individual dance numbers were in large part suggested by Roerich.[6]

To judge from Stravinsky's sketchbook, the original 1911 chronology of the movements and some of the titles as well differed in significant respects from the outline of the finished score. (The sketchbook is our only source of information on this: the earliest surviving descriptions of the scenario postdate the completed score, having been prepared during the period leading directly up to the premiere.) This is not to say that the simple sequence of ideas in the sketchbook is invariably reliable as a guide in these respects: inevitably, sketches for one dance overlap those of another. On page 7, for example, there are preliminary ideas for the "Ritual of Abduction" and the "Ritual of the Rival Tribes," although this page is ostensibly devoted to the "Spring Rounds."[7] It is apparent, moreover, that the movements of Part II were composed even less systematically than those of Part I. The sketches for Part II's Introduction and "Mystic Circles of the Young Girls" were composed more or less simultaneously on pages 50–66, while ideas for the following "Glorification of the Chosen One" are anticipated on pages 52, 59, 61, and 66, although not until page 67 does its composition get fully underway. Indeed, in one of the sketchbook's more curious anomalies, the "Ritual Action of the Ancestors" was at one point conceived as the concluding movement of *The Rite*. Prefacing the final

[4]Stravinsky, "Letters to Nicholas Roerich and N. F. Findeizen," p. 29.

[5]Of the three drawings sketched by Roerich in 1910, one was given to Stravinsky as a gift and was subsequently lost during the war along with the rest of his belongings at Ustilug. The other two were listed in a 1916 catalogue as belonging to Roerich's wife and B. G. Vlasiev. For further details see Richard Taruskin, "*The Rite* Revisited: The Idea and the Sources of Its Scenario," in Edmond Strainchamps and Maria Rika Maniates, eds., *Music and Civilization: Essays in Honor of Paul Henry Lang* (New York: Norton, 1984), p. 188.

[6]See Robert Craft, "*The Rite of Spring*: Genesis of a Masterpiece," *Perspectives of New Music* 5, 1 (1966): p. 23.

[7]The first entry on page 7 is the Tranquillo melody that frames the "Spring Rounds." As indicated in the preceding chapter (see Example 2), this melody was derived from the Juszkiewicz anthology of Lithuanian folk songs.

sketches for this dance on page 82, an inscription reads: "End of Part II of the *Sacre*" and, in parenthesis, "after the 'Sacrificial Dance.' "

Nonetheless, as shown in Table 1, an approximation of the early 1911 chronology and titles may be deduced, and, by way of the chronology, an account of the compositional progress itself from the "Augurs of Spring" on pages 3–6 to the end

TABLE 1: Chronology of the sketchbook

DATES	PAGES	HEADING/TRANSLATION	ENGLISH TITLE
Sept., 1911 (Ustilug)	3–6, 34	*Gadaniia na prutikakh* "Divination with twigs"	"Augurs of Spring"
	6–11	*Khorovod* "Round Dance"	"Spring Rounds"
Oct., 1911– Feb., 1912 (Clarens)	12–28	*Igra v goroda* "Game of the tribes"	"Ritual of the Rival Tribes"
	12–28	*Idut-vedut* "They are coming—they are bringing [him]"	"Procession of the Sage"
	15	*Potselui zemli* "Kiss of the earth"	"The Sage"
	7, 29–32	*Igra umykaniia* "Game of abduction"	"Ritual of Abduction"
Feb. 29, 1912 Part I completed. (Clarens)	35–39, 47–49	*Vypliasyvanie zemli* "The dancing-out of the earth"	"Dance of the Earth"
March 1–11, 1912, pp. 52–65 (Clarens)	50–51, 53–54, 62–65	[Introduction to Part II]	Introduction
	46, 50–51 53–62, 64–65	*Khorovody, Tainye igry* "Round dances; secret games"	"Mystic Circles of the Young Girls"
	52–59, 61, 66 67–72	*Velichanie-dikaia pliaska (Amazony)* "Glorification–savage dance (Amazons)"	"Glorification of the Chosen One"
	72–74	*Vzyvanie k praottsam* "Appeal to the ancestors"	"Evocation of the Ancestors"
	57, 66, 75–83	*Deistro startsev* "The act of the elders"	"Ritual Action of the Ancestors"
Nov. 17, 1912, p. 97. *The Rite* completed. (Clarens)	84–97	*Pliaska sviashchennaia* "Holy dance"	"Sacrificial Dance"

of the "Sacrificial Dance."[8] This chronology extends only to page 97, however, at which point there appear the by now celebrated lines: "Today 4/17 November, 1912, Sunday, with an unbearable toothache I finished the music of the *Sacre.* I. Stravinsky, Clarens, Châtelard Hotel."[9] The remaining pages of the total of 140 reproduced in facsimile consist of orchestral elaborations of sections from the "Sacrificial Dance," the Introduction to Part II, the "Augurs of Spring," and the "Ritual of Abduction."[10]

Ten principal Russian headings are included in Table 1.[11] Alongside these are literal English translations, the corresponding English titles from the 1967 edition, and the encompassing page numbers from the sketchbook. With the exception of *Vypliasyvanie zemli,* the headings are all Roerich's. *Vypliasyvanie* is Stravinsky's unique contribution to the titles, a neologism suggesting the stamping character of the sixth dance; it means, literally, the "Dancing-Out of the Earth" rather than the "Dance of the Earth." (Stravinsky later recalled imagining the dancers "rolling like bundles of leaves in the wind" at the beginning of this dance, while the rapid triplet figuration later suggested the stamping of Indians "trying to put out a prairie fire.")[12] There are two competing tribes in the "Ritual of the Rival Tribes," while the rhythmic turbulence of the "Glorification of the Chosen One" (or "Savage Dance"; see Table 1) at one time suggested an Amazonian scene. The Amazon idea was later abandoned as inappropriate and unworkable. The sketchbook lacks titles

[8]Page 3 is the first page of musical illustrations. The initial page bears the 1911 title *Vesna sviashchennaia* ("Holy Spring") and a dedication to Diaghilev that was added in October, 1920. The second page is a roster of instruments.

[9]The double-dating in the "4/17 November, 1912" inscription refers to Old Style (4 November) and New Style (17 November).

[10]Also included on pages 97–140 are sketches for *The Nightingale,* the *Souvenirs de mon enfance, Berceuses du chat,* and the first two of the *Three Japanese Lyrics.*

[11]The title "Divination with Twigs" is taken from the Stravinsky-Roerich letter of September 26, 1911, quoted in Chapter 1. The transliterations and translations in Table 1 are derived from Richard Taruskin, "*The Rite* Revisited," and from Simon Karlinsky, "The Composer's Workshop," *The Nation,* June 15, 1970, p. 732. Generally speaking, the translations by both Taruskin and Karlinsky are more explicit than many of those furnished by Robert Craft in his "Commentary to the Sketches," Appendix I in the accompanying booklet to Stravinsky, *The Rite of Spring: Sketches 1911–1913. Igra* means "game," although, in relation to both the scenario and composition of *The Rite,* "rite" or "ritual" is more appropriate. Karlinsky translates *Igra umykaniia,* the original Russian title for "Ritual of Abduction," as "Mock Abduction of the Bride," a title that conveys a good deal more of the original, primitive rite than either the more literal "Game of Abduction" in Table 1 or the Stravinsky-Craft rendition, "Game of Seizing the Girl," in "Commentary to the Sketches," p. 10. And *Idut-vedut,* which Craft transcribes as *eedoot-veedoot* and translates as "Leading-moving" ("Commentary to the Sketches," pp. 5–8), means, more literally and essentially apropos of the "Rival Tribes" and its succeeding "Procession," "they are coming—they are bringing [him]." In their own English translations in both the "Commentary to the Sketches" and the 1967 edition of the score, Stravinsky and Craft may have been torn between some of these more precise translations, the less precise but established French translations, and the practical need for short and concise titles. Stravinsky may also have forgotten some of the implications of the original scenario and stage action. The February 29, 1912, date for the completion of Part I in Table 1 derives from page 43 of the autograph of the full score, which is the last page of the "Dance of the Earth."

[12]Craft, "*The Rite of Spring*: Genesis of a Masterpiece," p. 30.

for the "Augurs of Spring," "The Sage," and the "Evocation of the Ancestors," yet the sketches on pages 3–6 and 73–74 for the "Augurs" movement and the "Evocation," respectively, clearly indicate that these dances were conceived as independent episodes.

It may be useful to compare Table 1 with the chronology and titles of the completed score, given below. The French translations in this chronology were reproduced in all editions of the score beginning with the 1913 publication of the four-hand piano version; the English titles are once again those of the 1967 edition.

PART I: *L'ADORATION DE LA TERRE*	ADORATION OF THE EARTH
Introduction	Introduction: nos. 0–13
Les Augures printaniers	Augurs of Spring: nos. 13–37
Jeu du rapt	Ritual of Abduction: nos. 37–48
Rondes printanières	Spring Rounds: nos. 48–57
Jeux des cités rivales	Ritual of the Rival Tribes: nos. 57–67
Cortège du sage	Procession of the Sage: nos. 67–71
Le Sage	The Sage: nos. 71–72
Danse de la terre	Dance of the Earth: nos. 72–79
PART II: *LA SACRIFICE*	THE SACRIFICE
Introduction	Introduction: nos. 79–91
Cercles mystérieux des adolescentes	Mystic Circles of the Young Girls: nos. 91–104
Glorification de l'élue	Glorification of the Chosen One: nos. 104–21
Évocation des ancêtres	Evocation of the Ancestors: nos. 121–29
Action rituelle des ancêtres	Ritual Action of the Ancestors: nos. 129–42
Danse sacrale (L'Elue)	Sacrificial Dance: no. 142–End

A synopsis of the final scenario may also prove helpful. There are three early accounts by Stravinsky, two of which were cited in Chapter 1: the synopsis sent to N. F. Findeizen in a letter dated December 15, 1912, and the description included in the controversial *Montjoie!* interview on the eve of the premiere. A third, sent to Sergei Koussevitsky as a program note for the latter's performance of *The Rite* in Moscow, February, 1914, reads as follows:

> *Vesna sviashchennaia* is a musical-choreographic work. It represents pagan Russia and is unified by a single idea: the mystery and great surge of the creative power of Spring. The piece has no plot, but the choreographic succession is as follows:

First Part: THE KISS OF THE EARTH

The spring celebration. It takes place in the hills. The pipers pipe and the young men tell fortunes ["Augurs of Spring"]. The old woman enters. She knows the mystery of nature and how to predict the future. Young girls with painted faces come in from the river in single file. They dance the spring dance. Games start ["Dance of the Abduction"]. The Spring Khorovod ["Spring Rounds"]. The people divide into two groups, opposing each other ["Ritual of the Rival Tribes"]. The holy procession of the wise old man ["Procession of the Sage"]. The oldest and wisest interrupts the spring games, which come to a stop. The people pause trembling before the great action. The old men bless the earth ["The Sage"]. *The Kiss of the Earth.* The people dance passionately on the earth, sanctifying it and becoming one with it ["Dance of the Earth"].

Second Part: THE GREAT SACRIFICE

At right the virgins hold mysterious games, walking in circles ["Mystic Circles of the Young Girls"]. One of the virgins is consecrated and is twice pointed to by fate, being caught twice in the perpetual circle. The virgins honor her, the chosen one, with a marital dance ["Glorification of the Chosen One"]. They invoke the ancestors ["Evocation of the Ancestors"] and entrust the chosen one to the old wise men ["Ritual Action of the Ancestors"]. She sacrifices herself in the presence of the old men in the great holy dance, the great sacrifice ["Sacrificial Dance"].[13]

Notice in Table 1 that the *Idut-vedut* in the sketchbook ("they are coming, they are bringing [him]," i.e., the Sage) became, at no. 67 in the final score, the "Procession of the Sage." Flowing into one another without interruption, the "Ritual of the Rival Tribes" and its succeeding "Procession" were in fact composed as a single, continuous unit, on pages 12–28. The sketches on the first of these pages are reproduced in Example 5; notice that the fourth entry on this page is already the G♯–G(F♯)–G♯–A♯–C♯ theme of the Sage, which, in the score itself, enters toward the end of the "Rival Tribes" at no. 64 and continues on through the entirety of the "Procession."[14] Moreover, while the note values of this theme are initially halved in relation to the final version, they are properly doubled in the remarkable sketch

---

[13]V. Stravinsky and Craft, *Stravinsky in Pictures and Documents*, p. 75. On p. 78 a facsimile of Stravinsky's original draft of this synopsis is misdated "1910. The libretto in Stravinsky's hand." A different translation of this synopsis appears on p. 526.

[14]Often enough in the sketchbook, Stravinsky seems to have been able to capture, in his initial sketches for a particular dance movement, the shape of the movement as a whole. For the "Sacrificial Dance," all the main ideas are sketched in preliminary fashion on pages 84–85.

EXAMPLE 5: Sketchbook, p. 12

(*continued*)

EXAMPLE 5 *(continued)*

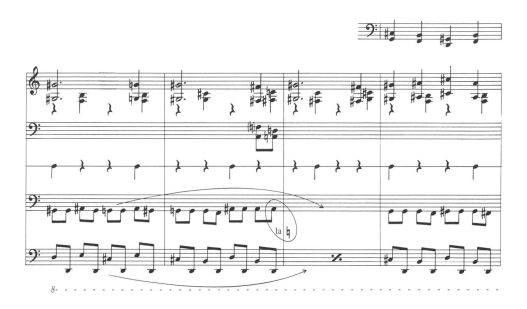

for no. 67 at the foot of page 12. Here, too, the accompanying three-against-four rhythm of the percussion, hypothesized just above, falls neatly into place.[15]

Indeed, while the first entry on page 12 is only a rough approximation of the beginning of the "Rival Tribes" (the blocks of material at nos. 57 and 57 + 4 are missing), the melody at m.3 in this entry, transposed to (G–F–E–D), is already superimposed over the Sage's theme in a development on page 13 (see Example 6). Of course, page 13 reverts to the theme's earlier "incorrect" halved rhythm. Yet the conditions of the theme's initial appearance at no. 64 are here firmly in place, and on page 16 the composer signals the end of this music with some remarkably accurate sketches for the conclusion of the "Rival Tribes." In the ensuing pages, 16–28, only the pitches of the new counter-theme in the horns, A–D–C–D in the final version, and the rhythmic coordination of this theme with that of the Sage would continue to pose problems.

A sketch of the quiet, four-bar interlude of "The Sage" appears on page 15

[15]The sketchbook scoring of this theme for muted horns instead of tubas is surprising, especially since, on pages 19 and 23, the new counter-theme is also scored for horns, *pavillon en l'air*. At some point Stravinsky must have realized that by scoring these two themes for different instruments (tubas and horns), the conflicting rhythmic-metric periods could more readily be brought to the fore.

EXAMPLE 6: Sketchbook, p. 13

EXAMPLE 7: Sketchbook, p. 15

(Example 7). This ends with a double bar and fermata and was clearly intended, early on in these sketches for the "Rival Tribes" and "Procession," to serve as a conclusion to these movements.[16] Only later was this episode given a name of its own, *Potselui zemli* or "The Kiss of the Earth," a title that Stravinsky preferred not only to *Le Sage* or "The Sage" at no. 71, but to "Adoration of the Earth" for Part I as a whole. In accord with the original stage action at this point, the Sage entered at no. 70, where, as was noted in Chapter 1, the rhythmic-metric conflict of the two

[16]In Example 7 the draft of the string chord on the far right (for the most part transposed up a half-step) was composed first. Despite obvious discrepancies between this initial sketch and the completed score, the accuracy of this anticipation on page 15 is striking.

reiterating themes, G♯–G(F♯)–G♯–A♯–C♯ and (D)–A–D–C–D in the tubas and horns, is resolved. The four-bar interlude was designed to accompany the Sage's benediction, the concluding string-harmonic chord his ceremonial "Kiss of the Earth."

But the real chronological shocker of the sketchbook entails the location in Part I of the "Ritual of Abduction." Originally, the "Abduction" followed "The Sage," while in the final score it comes immediately after the first dance, the "Augurs of Spring." The initial ordering is borne out musically in a number of interesting ways. For example, the C–B timpani fragment at no. 38 in the "Abduction" was derived from the C–B timpani-tuba motive that begins the "Rival Tribes" at no. 57 and was obviously intended to serve as an immediate link between the earlier "games" of the tribes and those of "abducting the bride."[17] Similarly, the climactic passage of the "Abduction" at no. 43 stemmed from the second motivic block of the "Rival Tribes" at no. 57 + 2.

It is not known precisely when the movements of Part I were arranged in their present order. But the reasons for the arrangement must have been both dramatic and musical. Scenically, the climax of Part I is the four-bar interlude of "The Sage"; coming after the feverish build-up of the "Rival Tribes" and the "Procession," it serves as a useful buffer, a brief, tranquil moment of release. To have returned after "The Sage" to yet another "game"—to have followed it by not one but two dance movements of considerable length and complexity, the "Ritual of Abduction" and the "Dance of the Earth"—would most assuredly have been anticlimactic. In addition, the rapid triplet figuration introduced at no. 75 in the "Dance of the Earth" (one quarter-note equals 168) bears too close and potentially too confusing or monotonous a correspondence with the rapid $\frac{6}{8}$ and $\frac{9}{8}$ meters of the "Abduction" (one dotted quarter-note equals 132).[18] And there are pitch correspondences between the "Augurs of Spring" and the "Abduction" which must at some point have come into play. The beginning of the "Abduction," at no. 37, returns to some of the same chords (the E♭ dominant seventh superimposed over (C–E–G), for example) and to some of the same referential implications as are found at the opening of the "Augurs of Spring." Still, the reshuffling might, at least initially, have come by way of a more chancy discovery. The first entry at the top of page 30 in the sketchbook is reproduced in Example 8. Following an incipient sketch of the music now at nos. 46 and 47, there are trills followed by the words "and the incantation," meaning, presumably, the Khorovod tune that frames the "Spring Rounds." Stravinsky might just at this point have realized that the change in tempo and pitch of the "Spring Rounds" (as composed on pages 7–11) formed an ideal consequence to the frenzied pace of the "abducting of the bride."

[17]On page 29 of the sketchbook, the C-B motive now at no. 38 was originally scored for timpani and tuba, as at no. 57 in the "Rival Tribes." Only after reshuffling these movements did Stravinsky decide to save the tuba for the "Rival Tribes."

[18]In the 1913 four-hand piano version, the marking for the "Dance of the Earth" was slightly faster: one quarter-note equaled 186.

EXAMPLE 8: Sketchbook, p. 30

Another curiosity of the sketchbook is the near-total absence of sketches that relate to the Introduction to Part I. There are three brief entries: a notation on page 3 of the chordal progression at no. 12 + 6 (shown in Example 58, Chapter 6), a sketch on page 5 of the clarinet piccolo melody at no. 9 + 2 (which is part of a draft for no. 21 in the "Augurs of Spring"), and an orchestral draft on page 117 of the eleven measures at nos. 1–2 (which looks odd because the continuation of the principal bassoon melody is missing). This neglect is but one of the many missing links that have inspired the widespread assumption that many other sketches and orchestral drafts must have existed at the time of the sketchbook, nearly all of which are presumably lost. For a time Stravinsky was thought to have retained his sketches for Part I's Introduction,[19] but a careful inspection of the *Nachlass,* undertaken by the New York City Library in 1983, uncovered no such items. In fact, as far as *The Rite* is concerned, the Stravinsky Archives proved something of a disappointment: a notebook dating from 1912 to 1918 contained just two pages of sketches for Part II's Introduction and "Sacrificial Dance," while a separate folder contained seven

---

[19]See Appendix C in Eric Walter White, *Stravinsky: The Composer and His Works* (Berkeley: University of California Press, 1966), pp. 553–54. Items 3b and 3c in this directory of manuscripts in Stravinsky's possession, compiled by Robert Craft in 1954, were for a while believed to contain sketches for the Introduction to Part I.

FIGURE 1: An early sketch of the music at no. 147 in the "Sacrificial Dance," taken from a small notebook dating from 1912 to 1918. The detailed instrumental cues appear to have been superimposed after the completion of the sketch. Notice the pizz-arco indication in the first and third measures. These markings would eventually find their way into the 1913 autograph, but they were deleted in the 1921 edition of the score and in the 1929 revised edition as well. Courtesy of the Paul Sacher Foundation.

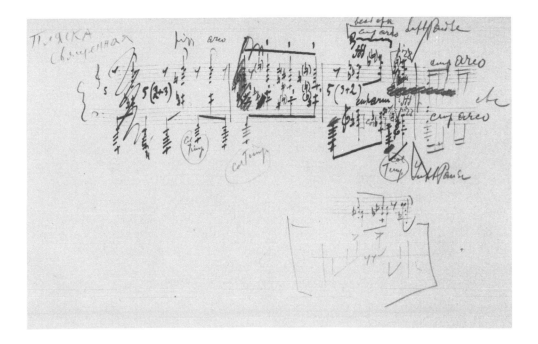

pages of an orchestral draft of the 1943 revision of the "Sacrificial Dance."[20] Much later, Stravinsky maintained that Part I's Introduction was composed after the other movements of this part had been completed.[21] There are no letters or documents that contradict this assertion.

---

[20]The results of this initial inspection, an inventory of the musical manuscripts in the Stravinsky Archives, are given in John Shepard, "The Stravinsky *Nachlass*: A Provisional Checklist of Music Manuscripts," *Music Library Association Notes* 40, 4 (1984): 719–50. In the notebook dating from 1912 to 1918, the first of the two pages includes a sketch of the music at nos. 147–49 in the "Sacrificial Dance." The sketch is very similar to the one on the second line on page 85 of the sketchbook of *The Rite* and may in fact have been composed at about the same time. There are detailed instrumental cues which appear to have been superimposed at a later date; many of these were eventually to find their way into the 1913 autograph. A facsimile of this sketch is reproduced in Figure 1. Sketches on the second of the two pages in the notebook pertain to the massive chordal progression at nos. 82 and 161 in the Introduction and "Sacrificial Dance" and are reproduced in Figure 4, Chapter 7.

[21]Stravinsky and Craft, *Expositions and Developments*, p. 141.

The sketchbook was begun during the summer of 1911, either before or soon after Stravinsky's visit with Roerich in mid-July. In August the composer traveled to Karlsbad, Warsaw, Lugano, and finally to Berlin to confer with his publisher, Russischer Musik Verlag. Craft cites the earliest notations for the "Augurs of Spring" on page 3 as having been composed either on or around September 2, after the composer's return from Berlin.[22] There is general agreement that the sketches for the "Augurs of Spring," "Spring Rounds," and possibly even portions of the "Ritual of the Rival Tribes" were composed at Stravinsky's summer residence in Ustilug, Russia.

In late September Stravinsky moved to a pension in Clarens, Switzerland, where the remaining movements of Part I were composed in the fall and early winter of 1911–1912. In January, while completing his sketches for Part I's concluding "Dance of the Earth," he may have received word of Diaghilev's decision to postpone production of *The Rite* until May of 1913. Sketches for the "Dance of the Earth" are interrupted on pages 41–45 for Act II of *The Nightingale,* and Stravinsky spent the greater part of February in London with the Ballet; neither the interruption nor the trip to London seems likely had he at this time still been pressed by the original performance dateline of June, 1912. The concluding sketches for the "Dance of the Earth" are on page 49, which includes an inscription heralding the "End of the Second Tableau." Apart from a brief anticipation on page 46, the first ideas for Part II are sketched on pages 50 and 51, and these refer to the Introduction and the "Mystic Circles of the Young Girls."

Dated March 1, 1912, an explosive sketch on page 52 for the section at no. 106 in the "Glorification of the Chosen One" (or "Savage Dance") may have coincided with the composer's return from London to Clarens. Following this, however, pages 52–65 return for the most part to the painstaking work of the Introduction and the "Mystic Circles." There are no fewer than seven separate notations for the Khorovod melody alone on these pages, and it is evident that the slow, chromatic lyricism of Part II's opening movements caused considerable difficulty. The explosive anticipations of the "Glorification of the Chosen One" on pages 52, 59, 61, and 66 doubtless convey the composer's impatience at this point, and the difficulty is all the more apparent when pages 52–65 are compared to some of the initial sketches for both the "Glorification" and the "Sacrificial Dance." These latter are almost fully developed and reveal great fluency. The comparison might seem paradoxical at first since these movements are faster and are metrically more irregular, hence more radical or "revolutionary" in appearance. Yet they are also composed in an idiom that even at this date may have come more naturally to the composer. In addition, the pianistic element in both the "Glorification" and "Sacrificial Dance" is conspicuous, and the sketches for these dances were undoubtedly prefaced by a considerable amount of keyboard improvisation. (Stravinsky composed *The*

---

[22]V. Stravinsky and Craft, *Stravinsky in Pictures and Documents,* p. 596.

Rite—indeed, nearly all his music—at the piano.)[23] Notice, in the opening sections of both dances, the rapid back-and-forth motion between the bass-timpani and *tutti* orchestra, a motion strikingly suggestive of the left hand–right hand alternation of the pianist. When rehearsing these passages during the 1920s and 1930s, the composer often recommended that bassists and timpanists visualize themselves as a pianist's left hand, the *tutti* orchestra as the same pianist's right hand. The tactic seems to have enhanced both the precision and the general rhythmic feel of this music.[24]

Following Part II's opening movements, the compositional pace slackened somewhat. Stravinsky worked only intermittently on *The Rite* during the remainder of 1912 and into 1913, his schedule now filled with appearances throughout Europe with the Ballets Russes. In April, 1912, he traveled to Monte Carlo for performances of *The Firebird* and *Petrushka,* and it was there that much of *The Rite* was unveiled for Diaghilev and Pierre Monteux. Monteux's recollection of this early audition is worth recounting, although his claim to have heard "the entire score" is improbable. Stravinsky may have omitted a great deal at the time or may simply have played through some of the as-yet-undecided passages in a quasi-improvisational fashion.

> With only Diaghilev and myself as audience, Stravinsky sat down to play a piano reduction of the entire score. Before he got very far I was convinced he was raving mad. Heard this way, without the color of the orchestra which is one of its greatest attractions, the crudity of the rhythm was emphasized, its stark primitiveness underlined. The very walls resounded as Stravinsky pounded away, occasionally stamping his feet and jumping up and down to accentuate the force of the music. Not that it needed such emphasis.[25]

The composer was in Paris in late May and June for ballet productions of Debussy's *L'Après-midi d'un faune* and Ravel's *Daphnis et Chloé,* and on June 9 he played through his four-hand piano arrangement of *The Rite* with Debussy. (This arrangement was probably complete to the end of Part I.[26] Debussy was a formidable reader at sight, and his amusement at some of the unaccustomed rhythmic difficulties of the new score has often been recorded.)[27] Dated November 17, 1912, the sketchbook's announcement heralding the completion of the music, "with an unbearable toothache," has been noted. Later in November Stravinsky traveled to

---

[23]"I am no mystic," Stravinsky wrote. "I need to touch music as well as to think it, which is why I have always lived next to a piano." (Igor Stravinsky and Robert Craft, *Themes and Conclusions* [Berkeley: University of California Press, 1983], p. 119.) For a brief discussion of the role of the piano in Stravinsky's inventive processes, see Pieter C. van den Toorn, *The Music of Igor Stravinsky* (New Haven: Yale University Press, 1983), pp. 204–6, 210–11.

[24]Craft, "Commentary to the Sketches," p. 17.

[25]"Early Years," in Minna Lederman, ed., *Stravinsky in the Theatre* (New York: Pellegrini and Cudahy, 1949), pp. 128–29.

[26]See V. Stravinsky and Craft, *Stravinsky in Pictures and Documents*, pp. 87, 613.

[27]Ibid., p. 87.

Berlin, where the first dance rehearsals of *The Rite* took place. The composer himself supervised several of these, using a two-hand piano version of Part I, and, as
with auditions in succeeding decades, these rehearsals left an indelible mark on several of the participants. It may be surmised that tempo and rhythmic precision were
major performance problems.

> Hearing the way his music was being played, [Stravinsky] blazed up, pushed
> aside the fat German pianist, nicknamed *"Kolossal"* by Diaghilev, and pro-
> ceeded to play twice as fast as we had been doing and twice as fast as we could
> possibly dance. He stamped his feet on the floor and banged his fist on the
> piano and sang and shouted.[28]

As will have been gathered, Stravinsky was preparing two-hand and four-
hand piano arrangements as he continued with his work on the instrumentation.
Nijinsky used the two-hand arrangement of Part I for his early rehearsals, including those conducted in London during February, 1913. Russischer Musik Verlag
began their printing of the four-hand arrangement in January of 1913, and this was
published in May, several weeks before the premiere.[29]

The full autograph of the orchestral score is dated and signed "completed in
Clarens, March 8, 1913."[30] But on March 29 Stravinsky inserted four additional
measures just before no. 86 in the Introduction to Part II (this may be the last music
to have been composed for *The Rite*),[31] while in early April he continued to revise

---

[28]Dame Marie Rambert, *Quicksilver* (London: Macmillan, 1972), quoted in V. Stravinsky and Craft,
Stravinsky in Pictures and Documents, p. 90.

[29]It was on a copy of this arrangement that the composer entered his notations for the choreography. A
facsimile of a page from the "Sacrificial Dance" may be found in V. Stravinsky and Craft, *Stravinsky in
Pictures and Documents*, p. 79. Stravinsky's original two-hand piano version of *The Rite* has been lost.

[30]Boosey and Hawkes acquired the autograph of the full score in 1947 from Russischer Musik Verlag.
In 1962, on his eightieth birthday, the manuscript was given to Stravinsky, at which time it was placed in a
bank vault in Geneva, Switzerland. In Zurich in October of 1968, the composer gave it to his wife, Vera
Stravinsky, who sold it in May, 1974, to Paul Sacher.

[31]This is Craft's guess in Robert Craft, ed., *Stravinsky: Selected Correspondence*, vol. 1 (New York:
Knopf, 1982), p. 398. Yet the issue remains complex. According to André Schaeffner, *Strawinsky* (Paris:
Rieder, 1931), p. 31, the eleven measures at nos. 86–88 in Part II's Introduction were the last to be composed. As evidence for the four bars that *precede* no. 86, however, Craft cites both the sketch for nos. 86–88
on page 63 of the sketchbook, already completed in March, 1912, and a letter from Monteux to Stravinsky
in Robert Craft, ed., *Stravinsky: Selected Correspondence*, vol. 2 (New York: Knopf, 1984), p. 54. Dated
April 15, 1913, the letter acknowledges receipt of "the four added measures." The controversy stems from
the curious pagination in the autograph of the full score for nos. 79–88. Page 43 in this manuscript is the last
page devoted to Part I. For some as yet unexplained reason, however, Stravinsky transferred the eleven
measures at nos. 86–88 to the back of this page, which is now numbered 44E. After this comes a title page
for Part II, and then two additional sheets numbered 44A, B, C, and D, which encompass the music now at
no. 79 to the end of no. 85. Directly underneath the final four bars of no. 85 on page 44D appears the controversial date March 29, 1913. A different interpretation is offered in Louis Cyr, "*Le Sacre du Printemps*: Petite
Histoire d'une grande partition," in François Lesure, ed., *Stravinsky: Etudes et témoignages* (Paris: Editions
Jean-Claude Lattes, 1982), pp. 104–5. According to Cyr, the March 29 date refers to all of the music on
pages 44A through D, while the eleven measures at nos. 86–88 were inserted at a still later date. The matter
is discussed at some length in Stephen Walsh, "Review Survey: Some Recent Stravinsky Literature," *Music
Analysis* 3, 2 (1984): 206–7.

the last section of the "Sacrificial Dance." Meanwhile, toward the end of March Monteux conducted his first orchestral rehearsals in Paris with an earlier first-draft score of Part I.[32] Two autographs of the orchestral score were thus in circulation at the time of the premiere, the first of these of Part I alone, the second of the score in its entirety: Monteux conducted his March rehearsals with the first of these manuscripts, while Stravinsky continued to work on his master draft of the entire work. A copy of the latter was subsequently made by "O.Th." in Leipzig and is dated May 1, 1913.[33] This is the score that bears the composer's "March 8, 1913" date and signature discussed above.

Directly following his first orchestral rehearsals, on March 30, 1913, Monteux wrote to Stravinsky advising the composer of a number of troublesome spots.

> You will have understood that, not having rehearsed in the hall of the Theatre [des Champs-Elysées], I cannot tell you what the *Sacre* will produce once the orchestra is in place. Nevertheless, and in comparison with *Firebird* and *Petrushka,* which I have rehearsed in the same hall, the *Sacre* sounds at least as good as your two elder children. The passages to which I refer and which perhaps will need to be slightly altered are the following:
>
> At 28, beginning with measure 5 (4-hand piano score, p. 22, first measure), I do not hear the horns loudly enough (unless the rest of the orchestra plays pp), and if I make a little crescendo, I do not hear them at all.
>
> At 37, measures 3 and 4 (4-hand piano score, p. 25, measure 3), it is impossible to hear a single note of the flute accompanied by four horns and four trumpets FF, and the first and second violins, also FF. The first flute plays the theme alone in the middle of all this noise.
>
> At 41, measures 1 and 2 (4-hand piano score, p. 27, measure 1), you have, first, the tubas, which, in spite of FF, produce only a very weak sound; second, the seventh and eighth horns, which one does not hear at all in the low register; third, the trombones, which are extremely loud; fourth, the first six horns, which one hears only moderately in comparison with the trombones. I have added the fourth horn to the seventh and eighth, but without achieving an equilibrium for the four groups. One hears: 1. mf; 2. nothing; 3. FF; 4. F. At 65, measure 3 (4-hand piano score, p. 39, measure 10), the first four horns have FF, but they play with mutes, and I can hear them only with difficulty.
>
> I think I have accomplished something with this work, and I will return to it. What a pity that you could not come to these rehearsals, above all for the *Sacre,* and that you did not attend the revelation of your work. I have thought

---

[32]See the correspondence between Stravinsky and Derzhanovsky in Craft, ed., *Stravinsky: Selected Correspondence,* vol. 1, pp. 53–56. This early draft score of Part I was sent to Nicolas Miaskovsky for corrections in mid-July of 1913 and then returned to the composer in August of that year. It is now part of the André Meyer Collection.

[33]Monteux apparently used this copy by "O.Th." for his 1913 performances in both Paris and London. It now belongs to the Paul Sacher Foundation in Basel, Switzerland.

about you a great deal and regretted your absence, but I know that you have much work to do.[34]

Stravinsky rewrote all four of the passages cited by Monteux, and these revisions were presumably among the very last to be entered prior to the premiere on May 29. For the original horn-viola rendition of the melody at no. 28 in the "Augurs of Spring" he substituted trumpets and three solo cellos, adding timpani, triangle, and antique cymbals at nos. 28–30 and changing many of the other orchestral parts as well. He added another flute and a piccolo to the principal flute melody at no. 35 in the "Augurs" movement, and then two horns to the three that Monteux had failed to hear at no. 41 in the "Ritual of Abduction." Finally, he dispensed with the mute for the A–D–C–D counter-theme in the horns at no. 65 in the "Rival Tribes." The original scoring of nos. 28–30 in the "Augurs of Spring" has been preserved and may be found in the holograph and in the copy of this made by "O. Th."[35]

Stravinsky's absence from Monteux's rehearsals in late March remains something of a mystery. No doubt the composer was preoccupied with last-minute changes, and with the scoring, in collaboration with Ravel, of parts of Mussorgsky's *Khovanshchina*.[36] Yet he had earlier interrupted work on several occasions to assist Nijinsky at dance rehearsals (in November and early December, 1912, in Berlin, for example, and in February, 1913, in London), and his travels with the Ballets Russes had no doubt awakened within him an awareness of the many novel technical and interpretive problems attending the performance of his music. Craft has speculated that Stravinsky might at this time have become apprehensive about the "actuality" of *The Rite,* preferring in these final months to work through Monteux, a trusted intermediary; *The Rite* was, after all, "unlike anything he (or anyone else) had ever wrought."[37] Yet the decision not to attend may have been a practical one. Monteux's rehearsals would almost certainly have stimulated the urge to revise further, and the composer, having labored for nearly a year and a half on the scoring of this music, may well have sensed that any tampering on the eve of the premiere (beyond that recommended by Monteux) would prove counterproductive and possibly unreliable. He may quite simply have deemed it prudent to wash his hands of the venture temporarily.

Not until May 13 did he arrive in Paris to supervise the final dance rehearsals with Nijinsky. The first rehearsals with full orchestra took place on May 26 and 27, the premiere itself on May 29.

---

[34]Craft, ed., *Stravinsky: Selected Correspondence,* vol. 2, pp. 52–54.

[35]Stravinsky's original scoring at nos. 28–30 has been transcribed and published by Volker Scherliess in his "Bemerkungen zum Autograph des 'Sacre du Printemps,' " *Musikforschung* 35 (1982): 234–50.

[36]Commissioned by Diaghilev, this project was completed in March and April of 1913. The first performance of the Stravinsky-Ravel version of *Khovanshchina* took place in Paris, June 5, 1913.

[37]V. Stravinsky and Craft, *Stravinsky in Pictures and Documents,* pp. 97–98.

The Revisions

If the making of *The Rite,* of its music, scenario, and choreography, is complex and difficult to reconstruct, the stream of corrections, emendations, outright rewritings and retractions that followed its initial performance is, regrettably, an even more tangled web of confusion, contradiction, and conflicting evidence.[38] No other work of Stravinsky's underwent such an extensive series of post-premiere revisions as *The Rite.* Here we can only hope to cover some of the highlights in the chronology, citing the more substantive changes in barring and scoring that will have a direct bearing on our analysis of rhythm and pitch structure.

To a large extent, the major changes can be examined simply by comparing the various editions of the score with one another and then by comparing these editions with the 1913 autograph, the 1913 four-hand piano version, and, in certain instances, orchestral drafts from the sketchbook. Unfortunately, such comparisons reveal only part of what is in the final analysis a much longer tale. Understanding when and under what circumstances specific alterations were introduced is an arduous task, and not all of the questions that subtly intervene are answered by studying the editions or the composer's own annotated copies of these, by consulting his correspondence with publishers and conductors (especially the letters to and from Ernest Ansermet during the 1920s), or by listening to his recordings of 1928, 1940, and 1960, and to those of Monteux and Ansermet. Stravinsky repeatedly changed his mind on a number of critical issues, and even after some of the more extensive revisions it is by no means always apparent just what his real or ideal intentions were; the role of the string pizzicato in the "Sacrificial Dance" is but one of the many cases in point. Often enough, adjustments were made as practical concessions to the difficulties encountered by specific performances.

Still, we can generally assume that the majority of the changes in barring and scoring were undertaken either to clarify the harmony and design (often by adjusting the orchestral balance) or, as indicated, to facilitate performance. Some of the more extensive rewritings do in fact coincide with celebrated performance dates. Thus, the Diaghilev revival of the ballet in December, 1920,

---

[38]Robert Craft has published three separate studies on *The Rite*'s revisions: "*Le Sacre du printemps*: The Revisions," *Tempo* 122 (1977): 2–8; Appendix B, "The Revisions," in V. Stravinsky and Craft, *Stravinsky in Pictures and Documents*, pp. 526–33; Appendix D, "*Le Sacre du printemps*: A Chronology of the Revisions," in Craft, ed., *Stravinsky: Selected Correspondence*, vol. 1, pp. 398–406. The most comprehensive and detailed survey of the source materials, autographs, editions, and revisions is Louis Cyr, "*Le Sacre du Printemps*: Petite Histoire d'une grande partition." A condensed version of this is Louis Cyr, "Writing *The Rite* Right," pp. 157–73 in Jann Pasler, ed., *Confronting Stravinsky: Man, Musician, and Modernist* (Berkeley: University of California Press, 1986). For a brief survey of the editions see Claudio Spies, "Editions of Stravinsky's Music," in Benjamin Boretz and Edward T. Cone, eds., *Perspectives on Schoenberg and Stravinsky* (New York: Norton, 1972), pp. 257–58.

prompted changes so extensive that the first edition of the score, dated 1921 but not published until 1922, deserves to be treated as a revision of the 1913 autograph, as has been noted by both Stravinsky and Craft.[39] Stravinsky's first appearance as conductor of *The Rite,* in February, 1926, was preceded by a host of additional adjustments, most notably in the barring of the "Evocation of the Ancestors" and of portions of the "Sacrificial Dance," many of which were subsequently included in the revised score of 1929. Performances and recordings in the United States during the early 1940s led the composer in 1943 to complete another revision of *The Rite*'s most obstinate thorn, the "Sacrificial Dance." A list of the major editions appears in Table 2.[40]

Conductors during the 1930s and 1940s were thus faced with at least two versions of *The Rite,* the first 1921 edition and its revision of 1929. The fact that the latter bore the same 1921 date and the same publisher's number (RMV 197) as its predecessor heightened the confusion.[41] Published by Associated Music Publishers in 1945, the 1943 revision of the "Sacrificial Dance" alone was intended by the composer to supersede all previous versions of this dance, and after its publication Stravinsky himself always conducted from this 1943 version. But this version did not subsequently become a part of the Boosey and Hawkes editions of 1948, 1965, and 1967. (The copyright, originally held by Russischer Musik Verlag, was assigned to Boosey and Hawkes in 1947. We might note that the *real* 1921 edition is now virtually inaccessible. The Boosey and Hawkes editions of 1948 and 1965 were essentially corrected reprints of the 1929 revised score.) Most conductors have ignored the 1943 revision of the "Sacrificial Dance," with the unfortunate consequence that it has come to figure as just one of many appendages in the long line of revisions from the 1913 autograph to the newly engraved Boosey and Hawkes score of 1967.

The printing of the orchestral score was begun as early as July, 1914. Stravinsky received two batches of proofs in December of that year, and these

[39]See Stravinsky and Craft, *Expositions and Developments*, p. 147, and V. Stravinsky and Craft, *Stravinsky in Pictures and Documents*, p. 527.

[40]For a list that includes the numerous pirated editions along with information on the engraving and revision of the orchestral parts, see Louis Cyr, "Petite Histoire d'une grande partition," pp. 98–101. Of the pirated editions, the widely circulated Kalmus edition of 1933 was a photocopy of the 1929 revised edition, RMV 197. Table 2 omits several reprints of the pocket score between 1951 and 1964. The new corrections and tempo indications of these reprints were for the most part included in the revised edition of 1965. Somewhat confusingly, the edition published by Boosey and Hawkes in 1948 became known as the "1947 revised version," that in 1965 as the "revised 1947 version." An oddity of the newly engraved 1967 edition, B & H 19441, is that the rhythm of the F♯–E–D♯ bass motive in the "Evocation" was changed from two eighths and a quarter to a triplet figure. With a metronome marking of 144 for the quarter-note, the practical implications of this distinction are minuscule. Moreover, the change obscures the motive's derivation from the preceding "Glorification."

[41]Outwardly, the two editions were distinguishable in two ways: the 1929 score bore the Paris address of the Russischer Musik Verlag—Edition Russe de Musique, 22 rue d'Anjou—and the name of an editor, F. H. Schneider. The latter was added in the hope of obtaining a copyright in the United States.

TABLE 2: Editions of *The Rite of Spring*

YEAR	EDITION	REMARKS
1913	RMV 196	Four-hand piano arrangement by Stravinsky. Barring of "Evocation" and "Sacrificial Dance" conforms to 1913 autograph, full score.
1921	RMV 197 RMV 197b (large and pocket scores)	First edition, released 1922. Barring of "Evocation" reverts to sketchbook version (pp. 73–74).
1929	RMV 197 RMV 197b	Second, revised edition. "Edited by F. H. Schneider" (p. 3, pocket score). 20 pages newly engraved to cover 1926 reorchestration and re-barring of "Evocation" and "Sacrificial Dance."
1945	Associated Music Publishers	Revised version of "Sacrificial Dance" completed in 1943. Major changes in orchestration, barring, and pitch. Unit of beat changed from 16th to 8th.
1948	B&H 16333 (large and pocket scores)	Corrected reprint of 1929 revised edition, RMV 197. Copyright assigned to B&H 1947.
1952	B&H 17271	Reprint of RMV 196 without modifications.
1965	B&H 16333	Corrected reprint of 1948 edition. "Revised 1947 version"; "Reprinted with corrections 1965" (p. 1, large score); "Revised 1947" (p. 3, pocket score).
1967	B&H 19441	Newly engraved edition. "Revised 1947. New edition 1967" (p. 1, large score); "Re-engraved edition 1967" (title page, pocket score).
1968	B&H 17271	Corrected reprint of 1952 edition. 11 pages newly engraved, primarily for "Evocation" and "Sacrificial Dance."

were promptly corrected and returned to the Russischer Musik Verlag in Berlin. The war delayed publication, however, as did Diaghilev's revival in December of 1920. Having heard the piece anew after an interval of seven-and-a-half years, the composer implemented numerous additional changes; not until February and May of 1922 did he receive his copies of the large and pocket versions of the published score (RMV 197 and RMV 197b). Before long, these, too, were blanketed with corrections and emendations.[42]

---

[42]A summary of the changes contained in these copies is given in Robert Craft, "A Chronology of the Revisions," in Craft, ed., *Selected Correspondence*, vol. 1, pp. 404–5. Changes in the composer's copy of the large score were made as late as April of 1940, and their precise dates are therefore difficult to determine. Other corrections and emendations prior to January of 1926 were sketched in two separate copies of the

Meanwhile, Ernest Ansermet, studying the newly engraved score during the summer of 1922 for performances in Berlin, compiled a list of errors along with a set of five "directions for the conductor." On August 9 he sent his *Erratumblatt* to Stravinsky, who acknowledged receipt on August 11 and replied in full a few days later:

> I have verified, added to, and corrected everything in the "Errata." I beg you to copy all of this *very carefully* because we are working with Germans who do not know, or pretend not to know, French. The directions for the conductor must be printed separately, for which reason I ask you to make a special sheet for them. . . . Make certain that I haven't made a new mistake in the timpani at [nos.] 57 and 58–59, since I could easily have slipped up there. Please send it to Oeberg [director of the Russischer Musik Verlag in Berlin] well copied and clear, since you . . . are the only one who can put everything in place and coordinate the parts.[43]

Included in this list of errors was an instruction regarding the suppression of the pizzicato markings in the "Sacrificial Dance" from no. 186 to the end of the score. The suppression and reinstatement of these markings would in due course become matters of considerable complexity.

As indicated by the parentheses in Example 12b, the 1913 autograph included pizzicato markings for some of the string chords at nos. 142–49 and in the corresponding sections at nos. 167–74 and 180. The 1921 edition eliminated these indications. It merely retained, from the 1913 autograph, the *pizz.-arco* alternation from no. 192 to the end of the score. Hence the instruction of the *Erratumblatt*, "verified, added to, and corrected" by the composer, was designed to ensure the total elimination of all pizzicati from the "Sacrificial Dance." The rationale behind these wholesale deletions can be found in another letter from Ansermet to Stravinsky, this one dated August 14, 1922.

---

pocket score, the first of these identified by markings in red ink and pencil, the second by markings in blue pencil (primarily for the bar lines of the "Evocation"). Alterations in the first of these scores were apparently made in 1922, since, according to a Stravinsky-Ansermet letter dated August 15, 1922 (*Selected Correspondence*, vol. 1, pp. 159–60), the score was sent to Ansermet in mid-August, 1922, to assist the conductor in his performances of *The Rite* in Berlin in November, 1922. Important changes in this score include the revision of the timpani parts at nos. 57 and 58–59 in the "Rival Tribes" and the transferral of the fermata from the first to the third sixteenth-note beat of the opening $\frac{3}{16}$ bar of the "Sacrificial Dance." A facsimile of the page containing the revision, in red ink, of the brass and timpani music at four measures before no. 59 is reproduced in V. Stravinsky and Craft, *Stravinsky in Pictures and Documents*, plate 4; the transferral of the fermata at the beginning of the "Sacrificial Dance" is shown in Examples 12a, 12b, and 12c. Alterations in the second of the two pocket scores were made between 1922 and January of 1926 and include the addition of a third trombone to double the G–D♯ figure in the lower strings at nos. 123, 124, and 128 in the "Evocation," and a re-barring of this latter movement that approximates the revision completed in January and February of 1926. As noted in Table 2, the 1921 edition had reverted to the lengthy $\frac{7}{4}$ and $\frac{8}{4}$ bars as found on pages 73–74 of the sketchbook, a matter to which we shall be turning presently.

[43]Craft, ed., *Stravinsky: Selected Correspondence*, vol. 1, p. 159.

Responding to Stravinsky's acknowledgment of the *Erratumblatt* (quoted above), Ansermet confessed to a number of reservations:

> I would like to come back to some correction details [in drawing up the errata list]. The corrections in the old proof score, which served as the basis for the present engraved score . . . were made during rehearsals and thus without the care one usually applies to correcting proofs. Thus, for the "Sacrificial Dance," it was decided to delete the pizzicati, and they were in fact eliminated, but not completely, as I notice that some still survive in the score after *192*. . . . But what bothers me the most are these pizzicati in the entire "Sacrificial Dance." They were deleted as a matter of principle: we were being rushed, there were few string players available, and even these were below average; we had enough trouble in coping with the rhythmic complexities alone. But now I am seriously wondering if we do right in sticking to that decision. After all, some day we'll be blessed with better performers and performing conditions. In that case, wouldn't writing the strings [alternately] *unisono pizz.* and *divisi arco* be the better solution? And won't the dryness of pizz. strings accompanying the oboes provide a more concise and clear-cut rhythm than any bowing ever could? Perpetual *arco* bowing seems to me (but I am only at the conductor's stand) to produce a sound that is constantly thick and undifferentiated, whereas intervening pizz. would provide clarity and definite contours to the music.[44]

These deletions, then, had been matters of practical convenience. But Stravinsky remained adamant. In his reply to Ansermet he again insisted on the removal of all pizzicati from the "Sacrificial Dance," since, as he put it, "orchestra players will always remain nitwits."[45] Nonetheless, the curious fact remains that the original 1913 pizzicati markings at nos. 186–89 and at no. 192 to the end of the score were reintroduced by the 1929 revision for all strings except double basses and that this reinstatement was in turn followed by another volte-face: the Boosey and Hawkes editions of 1948, 1965, and 1967 reverted to the total suppression as decreed by the 1922 *Erratumblatt*. Indeed, in adjusting to the new subdivisions in the barring of the "Sacrificial Dance," the 1929 revision introduced an added novelty: as shown in Examples 12b and 12c, some of the string chords at no. 142 and in the corresponding sections were doubled in length to a full eighth-note. (This distinction is rarely observed in performance.) Nor was this all. To complicate matters further, the 1943 revision of the "Sacrificial Dance" restored many of the pizzicato markings of the 1913 autograph and 1921 edition: pizzicato indications were

---

[44]See Louis Cyr, "Writing *The Rite* Right."
[45]Ibid.

added to the cello and double basses at nos. 142–49 and in the corresponding sections (nos. 1–9 in the 1943 score), while the *pizz-arco* alternation was reinstated for all strings *including* double basses at no. 192 to the end of the score (no. 53 + 3 in the 1943 revision).[46]

The 1922 "directions for the conductor" included a roster of instruments, a notification that the $\frac{4}{8}$ and $\frac{5}{8}$ bars at no. 39 in the "Ritual of Abduction" were to be combined as a single $\frac{9}{8}$ bar, and suggestions regarding the subdivisions of the $\frac{5}{8}$ and $\frac{7}{8}$ bars in the "Glorification of the Chosen One." These subdivisions were to be read 2 + 3 and 2 + 2 + 3 eighth-note beats respectively, and similar instructions were detailed for the "Evocation of the Ancestors" and portions of the "Sacrificial Dance."[47] As a final precaution, Stravinsky sent Ansermet his copy of the pocket score on August 15. "I have just sent to you by registered mail my pocket score of the *Sacre* with the corrections (not all of them!) marked in red ink and pencil—to make your work easier, in case you have any doubts. I beg you to hurry, and to send the corrections on to Berlin."[48]

All of these 1922 corrections, emendations, and "directions" were dutifully copied by Ansermet and forwarded to Berlin, as Stravinsky had requested. Curiously, however, the 1929 revision failed to incorporate many of the changes. It failed to unify the two bars at no. 39 into a single $\frac{9}{8}$ measure, and, in fact, the Boosey and Hawkes editions of 1948 and 1965 (which, as indicated, were essentially corrected reprints of the 1929 revision) merely printed the instruction as a prefatory remark. Only in the newly engraved edition of 1967 were these bars combined in the manner prescribed by the "directions for the conductor." Similarly, the 1929 revision did not print the revised timpani music at nos. 57–59, about which Stravinsky had cautioned Ansermet in his August, 1922, letter. This, too, would only later become a part of the printed score.

The next batch of revisions, too, came as the result of a celebrated performance date: Stravinsky conducted *The Rite* for the first time on February 28, 1926, with the Concertgebouw Orchestra in Amsterdam. Studying the score in January, he rewrote the whole of the "Evocation of the Ancestors" and portions of the "Sacrificial Dance." Both the harmony and the instrumentation were changed in numerous places, but it is in the re-barring of this music that these 1926 revisions are most conspicuous. Twenty pages were newly engraved for the revised score of 1929, and all of these pertain to the "Evocation" and the "Sacrificial Dance." It is in this 1929 revised form that *The Rite* has largely become known during the past forty or so years.

---

[46]For a detailed commentary and accompanying charts on these pizzicato revisions see Louis Cyr, "Petite Histoire d'une grande partition," pp. 120–26, or Louis Cyr, "Writing *The Rite* Right."

[47]These directions did not apply to nos. 174–79 and 181–85 in the "Sacrificial Dance."

[48]Craft, ed., *Stravinsky: Selected Correspondence*, vol. 1, pp. 159–60. The pocket score referred to here by Stravinsky, "with corrections . . . marked in red ink and pencil," is the first of the two annotated copies of RMV 197b mentioned above in note 42.

Some of the more prominent discrepancies in the barring of the "Evocation" are traced in Examples 9a–9c: Example 9a is from page 73 of the sketchbook, Example 9b is from the 1913 autograph of the score,[49] while Example 9c is drawn from the 1929 revision. (Only the first twelve or so measures of the "Evocation" are reproduced by these examples. The sketchbook version is fully transcribed in Example 9a, but Examples 9b and 9c allow for a considerable condensation of the score.)

The initial sketchbook version, in Example 9a, seems to have aimed first and foremost at simplicity. Seven quarter-note beats are inferred as a kind of steady, background periodicity, which is confirmed above all by the successive repeats of the F♯–E–D♯ motive in the $\frac{7}{4}$ bars at mm. 1, 4, and 6. The fermata at m.6 eases the rigidity of the scheme somewhat but points as well to its eventual breakdown: in the 1929 revision, shown in Example 9c, the spans that encompass the successive repeats of the F♯–E–D♯ motive are extended well beyond the limits of the conventional fermata—in Example 9a the initial F♯–E–D♯ statement spans four quarter-note beats (with a fermata underneath the D♯), in Example 9b seven quarter-note beats, in Example 9c twelve. The proportions vary in these versions, and the changes must inevitably have been linked to an altered conception of the dance as a whole. As the smaller dimensions of the sketchbook version yielded to the more expansive ones of the 1929 revision, the rationale behind the governing $\frac{7}{4}$ periodicity presumably gave way. (Note that the unit of pulsation—one eighth-note equals one quarter-note in relation to the preceding "Glorification of the Chosen One"—is acknowledged by the sketchbook.)

The "Evocation" conforms in general outline to a type of block structure that is typical not only of *The Rite* but of Stravinsky's music generally. Two distinct blocks of material are placed in abrupt juxtaposition with one another, the first of these blocks spacing or marking off successive appearances of the second, principal block. (The F♯–E–D♯ motive, which is derived from the preceding "Glorification of the Chosen One," identifies the first block. The second block enters at m.2 in Example 9a.) At the same time, development within such a structure has principally to do with the changing lengths of the two interacting blocks: upon successive repeats, the motivic reiteration within one or both is lengthened or shortened. In the sketchbook version of the "Evocation" (Example 9a), appearances of the second, principal block are spaced by the first, whose stable duration is one $\frac{7}{4}$ bar (seven quarter-note beats). Set against the relative stability of this spacing, the motivic reiteration within the second block is constantly varied, lengthened or shortened. Thus, too, a kind of rhythmic play develops as a consequence of this modification.

---

[49]The barring in the 1913 four-hand piano version is identical to that of the autograph except that in the piano version there are no fermatas over the opening $\frac{6}{4}$ measure or over the D♯ in the $\frac{4}{4}$ measure at no. 122. The barring in the autograph is given in Scherliess, "Bemerkungen zum Autograph," pp. 241–42.

EXAMPLE 9: "Evocation of the Ancestors"

(a) Sketchbook, p. 73

(continued)

EXAMPLE 9 *(continued)*

(b) 1913 Autograph

(c) 1929 Revision

FIGURE 2: Early sketches of the "Evocation of the Ancestors," page 73 of the sketchbook of *The Rite*. The version transcribed in Example 9a begins at the third line with the $\frac{7}{4}$ signature. *The Rite of Spring (Le Sacre du Printemps) Sketches, 1911–1913,* © copyright 1969 Boosey & Hawkes Music Publishers Ltd. Reprinted by permission of Boosey & Hawkes, Inc.

73

For although the barring of a particular motive may remain constant, this constancy may not always be felt as primary. Upon successive repeats, a motive may assume a changed rhythmic-metric identity, which hinges in turn on the felt presence of a second (concealed) meter.

Much later, in *Expositions and Developments* (1962), Stravinsky explained that with the longer measures in his earlier versions of both the "Evocation" and the "Sacrificial Dance" he had sought "to measure according to phrasing," but that later on, in 1921, his performance experience had led him "to prefer smaller divisions"; the "smaller divisions," he averred, "proved more manageable for both conductor and orchestra and they greatly simplified the scansion of the music."[50] But as can readily be seen in Examples 9a–9c, the different proportions that distinguish the three versions of the "Evocation" could hardly have been matters of practical convenience. Even if they had, *method* would presumably have intervened at some point. Observe that the "smaller divisions" of the 1913 autograph in Example 9b are quite different from those of the 1929 revision in Example 9c. Indeed, while the later subdivisions doubtless proved, for conductor and orchestra alike, "more manageable" than the $\frac{7}{4}$ and $\frac{8}{4}$ measures of the sketchbook version, this could only have been true in relation to the changed and expanded dimensions. For the sketchbook version of the "Evocation" is in truth a far simpler piece. Notwithstanding its cumbersome $\frac{7}{4}$ and $\frac{8}{4}$ measures, the barring is less sophisticated and reveals little of the intricacy in motivic reiteration that vividly marks, in particular, the 1929 revision. Stravinsky's remarks betray considerable (and quite understandable) confusion about the dates of his revisions. He seems to have forgotten, when writing *Expositions and Developments,* that the "smaller divisions" were not a later conception in the "Evocation" but were already a part of the 1913 autograph, if in somewhat different form than in the revision of 1929. His confusion may have stemmed from another of those remarkable reversals in the chronology of the revisions: although it is not shown here, the 1921 edition actually returned to the longer measures and fermatas of the original sketchbook version!

All the same, Stravinsky's recollection of having measured the "Evocation"'s longer bars "according to phrasing" is revealing. The problem here, however, is that the "smaller divisions" of the 1913 and 1929 versions are really no different in this respect. They, too, are a form of phrasing, even if the conception of this phrasing is different from that of the original sketchbook. Indeed, all three versions of the "Evocation" in Examples 9a–9c introduce the same startling departure in rhythmic-metric design: as in so many of Stravinsky's block structures with irregular or shifting meters, meter and phrasing (or *grouping*) coincide. On at least one hierarchical level, meter becomes a form of phrasing while phrasing becomes meter or "measure."

---

[50]Stravinsky and Craft, *Expositions and Developments*, p. 147.

The absence of phrase markings in the "Evocation" is to be remarked, as is, throughout *The Rite* generally, the absence of phrase markings that contradict the bar lines. A more conventional phrasing is found in certain passages of Part II's Introduction and "Mystic Circles"—and it was of course precisely the slow, chromatic lyricism of this music, its evidently non-idiomatic, Debussy-like character, that when compared to the more rhythmically active material of the initial sketches of the "Glorification," "Evocation," and "Sacrificial Dance" proved uniquely difficult for the composer.

What in turn saves this one-dimensional rhythmic-metric approach from sterility are the differing lengths of the juxtaposed blocks upon successive appearances, the lengthening or shortening of the motivic reiteration within these blocks, and the resulting play in rhythmic-metric identity which, although frequently concealed by a shifting meter which graphically preserves identity, lies at the heart of the invention.

Examples 10a–10c further condense the opening measures of the three "Evocation" versions. In Example 10b the subdivisions of the 1913 autograph are closely related to the original $\frac{7}{4}$ periodicity of the sketchbook version: as indicated by the brackets, these divisions merely slice up the earlier sevens into smaller units of $4 + 3$ or $3 + 4$ quarter-note beats. And so here Stravinsky's reasoning seems very much to the point: in the 1913 autograph, the prime objective may well have been to render the earlier sevens "more manageable for both conductor and orchestra." Observe that the second of the two $4 + 3$ units in Example 10b merely reproduces the first; that is, while the motivic reiteration is actually shortened by two beats at m.4 (as enclosed by the brackets), Stravinsky bars the second of the two $4 + 3$ units at mm.3–4 as if, metrically speaking, it were a carbon copy of the first at mm.1–2. Thus, too, the rhythm at m.1 is preserved at m.3, leaving a motivic reiteration metrically exposed. The willingness of listeners to accept this constancy, to accept m.3 as a repeat of m.1, will naturally hinge on how attuned they are to the unorthodox design of the sevens. If doubt and uncertainty prevail at m.3, then the repeat will be found to embody a contradiction in rhythmic-metric identity, which in turn points to the felt presence of a second (concealed) meter.

In contrast to the 1913 autograph in Example 10b, the "smaller divisions" of the 1929 revision in Example 10c are a radical departure. Here, the earlier sevens, to which the subdivisions of the 1913 autograph closely adhere, are obscured beyond meaningful apprehension after the first two measures. The rhythm at m.1 is not preserved at m.3 as it is in the 1913 autograph, and the $4 + 3$ subdivision at mm.1–2 is not merely reproduced at mm. 3–4. Rather, the $4 + 3$ subdivision at mm.3–4 is now $2 + 3$, which means that the shifting meter will actually *record* the shortening of the motivic reiteration. Hence, too, the termination of the shortened reiteration occurs on the downbeat at m.5, which will now parallel the downbeat at m.3. Yet the chief distinction of this 1929 revision is its introduction of the half-note beat as a unit of pulsation,

EXAMPLE 10: "Evocation of the Ancestors"

(a) Sketchbook, p. 73

(b) 1913 Autograph

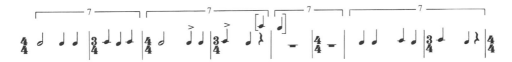

(c) 1929 Revision

which partially replaces the prevailing quarter-note beat of the earlier versions. This is naturally consistent with the enlarged dimensions of this revision, as discussed above. Then, set against the half-note pulse, the $\frac{3}{4}$ bar is now consistently exploited as the disruptive element. (The $\frac{3}{4}$ bars in the "Evocation" bear a resemblance in this respect to the $\frac{3}{8}$ bars in the opening March of *Histoire du soldat* (1918), a context to which we shall be turning in Chapter 3.) There are other implications that warrant consideration apropos of Example 10c, but these can perhaps best be pursued within the broader context of Chapters 3 and 4.

Stravinsky's conception of "phrasing" seems again very much to the point in the sketchbook version of the second section of the "Sacrificial Dance." As in the preceding illustrations, three versions of the opening measures of this section are cited: Example 11a is from pages 90–91 of the sketchbook,[51] Example 11b follows all editions of the full score beginning with the

---

[51]The entry on pages 90–91 of the sketchbook is actually a full orchestral draft of the music. This is condensed in Example 11a in order to focus more closely on the barring.

1913 autograph, while Example 11c is from the 1943 revision of the "Sacrificial Dance" alone. As in the three versions of the "Evocation," here the early sketchbook version is characterized by longer measures (or longer "phrases") which in subsequent editions are sliced up into "smaller divisions" (or smaller "phrases"). But notice that the longer groupings of the sketchbook version

EXAMPLE 11: "Sacrificial Dance"

(a) Sketchbook, pp. 90–91

(b) 1913 Autograph

EXAMPLE 11 *(continued)*

(c) 1943 Revision

are preserved in subsequent editions by means of beams that cross the bar
lines. The 1943 revision in Example 11c retains the subdivisions but opts for
"an easier-to-read unit of beat," which, as Stravinsky later explained, was designed to facilitate performance.[52] Quite simply, eighth-notes become quar-
ters. Yet the disadvantage of the 1943 revision is that the earlier, longer groupings are ignored. Single beams over the bar lines could have preserved some of
the earlier connections, but these, too, are sacrificed, presumably in the interests of facility or simple legibility. (The longer groupings or "rhythmic cells"
of Examples 11a and 11b are the ones upon which Pierre Boulez based his
rather extensive analysis of this passage.)[53]

The idea behind the music at nos. 149–54 in the "Sacrificial Dance" is
quite simple. In accord with a single beat or unit of pulsation (the quarter-note
in Example 11c), a single chord is punctuated one, two, or three times in succession. These punctuations or successions of punctuations are always sepa-
rated by a single unit of rest. To a large extent, the metrical subdivisions in
Examples 11b and 11c reflect this smaller and simpler conception: the downbeats of these subdivisions coincide with the beginnings of these smaller

---

[52]Stravinsky and Craft, *Expositions and Developments*, p. 147.
[53]Pierre Boulez, *Notes of an Apprenticeship*, trans. Herbert Weinstock (New York: Knopf, 1968), pp.
84–88.

groupings. The exception occurs at the third and fourth measures in Examples 11b and 11c, which, to accord with the simpler conception, should have been combined as a single $\frac{4}{8}$ or $\frac{4}{4}$ measure. In Example 11c the changing meter would thus have read: $\frac{3}{4}, \frac{2}{4}, \frac{4}{4}, \frac{2}{4}, \frac{2}{4}, \frac{3}{4}, \frac{4}{4}, \frac{2}{4}, \frac{3}{4}$, etc. Yet in practical application, difficulties arise when attempting to rationalize the constant reshuffling in the horizontal alignment of the smaller groupings or when attempting to explain the (at least graphically suggested) cohesion of Stravinsky's longer groupings or "rhythmic cells" as defined by the meter in Example 11a and by beams in Example 11b.

The one-dimensional approach noted above applies in all three versions of Examples 11a–11c: with or without subdivisions, meter and phrase coincide, are here wholly "in phase" (to borrow a term from the recent work of Lerdahl and Jackendoff).[54] And the rhythmic play that develops occurs precisely at those points where the groupings are reproduced. In the 1943 revision of Example 11c, the groupings at mm. 3–5 are reproduced at mm. 8–10. Is this metrically exposed repeat heard as such? If not, then we are again dealing with a metrical scheme not graphically in evidence.

As a final illustration, four different versions of the opening measures of the "Sacrificial Dance" are cited in Examples 12a–12d. Once again the sketchbook begins with longer measures which in subsequent versions are subjected to "smaller divisions": the $\frac{5}{8}$ bar in Example 12a is split into groupings of $2+3$ and $3+2$ in the 1929 and 1943 revisions, respectively. (The $2+3$ subdivision of the 1929 revision was re-barred in this manner in January and February of 1926 and had of course been anticipated much earlier by the 1922 "directions for the conductor.") The very odd history of the pizzicato markings in this dance has been surveyed briefly. Most astonishing in Examples 12a–12d, however, is the "easier-to-read unit of beat" of the 1943 revision, which had been anticipated by the original sketchbook version, reproduced in Example 12a.

The 1943 revision also changed the harmony of the very first chord. It began at the outset with the (E♭–D♭) or (E♭–C♯) unit and eliminated the earlier B♭ altogether. As can be seen in Example 13, this pervasive *"complex sonore"* derives from the celebrated "Augurs of Spring" chord at no. 13 of the score, and, as is readily apparent, the B♭ actually strengthens the correspondence. The B♭ points as well to the chords just ahead at no. 144, where (E♭–B♭) and (E♭–G♭–B♭) become fixed elements in relation to the changing chords in the bass and treble parts.

As was indicated above, the 1943 revision of the "Sacrificial Dance" did not become a part of the now widely used 1948, 1965, and 1967 editions of the score. Had a settlement been possible between Associated Music Publishers

<hr>

[54]Fred Lerdahl and Ray Jackendoff, *A Generative Theory of Tonal Music* (Cambridge, Mass.: MIT Press, 1983), p. 30.

EXAMPLE 12: "Sacrificial Dance"

(a) Sketchbook, p. 84

(b) 1913 Autograph

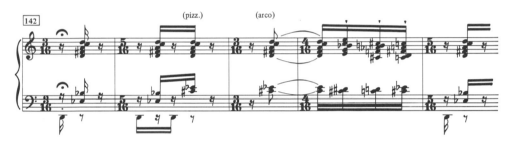

(c) 1929 Revision

(d) 1943 Revision

EXAMPLE 13: "Sacrificial Dance"

Sketchbook, p. 84   1913 Autograph   1943 Revision

and Boosey and Hawkes in the late 1940s and had Stravinsky been willing and able to continue with his revisions for the remainder of *The Rite*, something like a "final version" might well have emerged as a convenient cap to several decades of incessant tampering. The absence of such a version is to be regretted, all the more since it has placed the 1943 revision of the "Sacrificial Dance" in an awkwardly peripheral position.

Here again Stravinsky no doubt had his reasons. As he later explained, he preferred composing anew to merely recomposing the old: "I would go on eternally revising my music . . . were I not too busy composing more of it."[55] Yet the turbulent history of *The Rite*'s revisions suggests a nagging dissatisfaction with certain particulars of the music itself. (Stravinsky remained dissatisfied with the final chord of the piece even after the substantial alterations of the 1943 revision.) With so many notes, and with such variety of structure for such a large orchestra, *The Rite* may have seemed burdened by problematic details that were beyond any conclusive formulation. In the end, Stravinsky may have been put off by the futility of a "definitive" effort.

All versions and editions of *The Rite* will be taken into consideration in the present inquiry. Ultimate authority rests with the newly engraved 1967 edition of the full score and with the 1943 revision of the "Sacrificial Dance." Yet the earlier versions, especially when in substantial disagreement with the later ones, offer considerable insight into Stravinsky's methods. They will remain points of reference.

---

[55]Stravinsky and Craft, *Expositions and Developments*, p. 147. See also V. Stravinsky and Craft, *Stravinsky in Pictures and Documents*, p. 531, where Craft prints Stravinsky's notations on the margin of a letter from Edwin Stein dated September, 1948. Stein, editor at Boosey and Hawkes, had inquired about the numerous errors in the existing scores of *The Rite*, to which the composer replied: "Have no time for it. I prefer to compose a new music rather than losing time on this old one."

3

Stravinsky Re-barred

Music Criticism

The idea that in passages of metric irregularity meter and phrase might often coincide in some characteristically Stravinskian fashion (that, in other words, the barring might here often represent a localized form of phrasing or grouping) is not especially new. Well before publication of the composer's recollections in *Expositions and Developments,* critics had come to roughly the same conclusions about the rhythmic phenomenon. The difference, however, was that these earlier conclusions were drawn up in the form of an indictment. The one-dimensional implications of this meter-phrase coincidence were viewed as an impoverishment.

It need hardly be remarked in this connection that the opinions of critics such as Cecil Gray and Constant Lambert are today of little or no consequence. Certainly the general tone of this early English commentary is pompous in the extreme. While Lambert's *Music Ho! A Study of Music in Decline* (1934)[1] is at times subtle and entertaining, and a good deal more compelling than Gray's earlier *A Survey of Contemporary Music* (1924),[2] both Lambert and Gray project a puffy, know-it-all image that is difficult to shake. Nor are the musical heroes of these critics—Delius for Gray, Sibelius for Lambert—likely to inspire confidence, especially as these affections come at the expense, in devastating detail, of nullities such as Debussy,

[1](London: Faber and Faber; 3d ed. 1966).
[2](Oxford: Oxford University Press, 1924).

Schoenberg, and Stravinsky. Of course, *verdicts* in music criticism need not count for much—"opinions are mostly worthless," as Virgil Thomson once observed.[3] Listeners familiar with the music and musical issues at stake are more likely to be taken by the descriptive details of an argument than by its judgemental bias; often enough, details pursued on behalf of a negative assessment can just as easily be weighed in favor of the sympathetic vote, and the very traits isolated and decried by the detractors can become the ones that admirers most admire. What is interesting is that Gray and Lambert erected a critical edifice that has in one way or another served as a point of departure for nearly all subsequent critiques of Stravinsky's music. Even Theodor Adorno, intellectually a more acceptable figure nowadays, can add little to the general impression of the music as conveyed by Gray and Lambert. Most appropriately, all three critics—Gray, Lambert, Adorno—are not in the least hesitant about directing their attention to that single dimension in which Stravinsky's impact has most readily been felt, namely, that of rhythm.

As a general premise, rhythmic "effect" is seen as a net loss, since it disrupts the balance of the classics, an idealized equilibrium between melody, harmony, rhythm, and timbre. An emphasis on one of these components can come only at the expense of the others.

> Although it is often convenient for the purposes of criticism and analysis to speak of musical language as if it were made up of three or four separate and independent elements in combination—melody, harmony, rhythm, and possibly . . . color—we must be careful not to think of it as such. As long as we make use of these terms in order to define more accurately certain qualities in certain works, they are quite legitimate and sometimes even necessary, but that is all. In actual fact it is impossible to conceive of one without the others. They are interdependent and indissoluble. . . . Not only, however, are these component elements inseparable from each other, but each is at its highest when they are all in complete equilibrium, when one does not predominate over the others. In the music of the greatest masters . . . one will find this perfect balance and equipoise; you cannot say of this music that it is "harmonic," "rhythmic," or "melodic"; it is all and it is none. But the moment that one element grows at the expense of the others the perfect concord is broken or impaired.[4]

Melody is the first casualty. In Gray's words, Stravinsky's melodic style, "short and monotonous," consists in the main of "a ceaseless alternation between two or three notes."[5] (The "Evocation of the Ancestors," Examples 9 and 10 in Chapter 2, comes readily to mind, as do the opening pages of *Les Noces*. Years later, apropos of a few measures from the *Elegy to J. F. K.* (1964), Stravinsky him-

[3]*A Virgil Thomson Reader* (Boston: Houghton Mifflin, 1981), p. 187.
[4]Cecil Gray, *A Survey of Contemporary Music*, pp. 137–41.
[5]Ibid., p. 143.

self acknowledged the two- or three-note alternation as "a melodic-rhythmic stutter characteristic of my speech from *Les Noces* to the *Concerto in D* [1947], and earlier as well—a lifelong affliction, in fact.")[6] More to the point, for Gray the emphasis on rhythm led not only to "an impoverishment of melody and harmony, but to
the loss of the very quality to which [Stravinsky] sacrificed the other two—
rhythmic vitality." Divorced by sheer "effect" from its sister components, rhythm
stiffened into design or pattern; it "degenerated into meter."[7]

> The moment [rhythm] is divorced from the other constituent elements of mu-
> sical speech it changes its character; it stiffens, petrifies, and becomes lifeless—
> *becomes meter.* In much the same way that formal design and rhythm when they
> cease to be representative tend, inevitably, automatically, to become mere geo-
> metrical pattern, as in a wallpaper or carpet, so musical rhythm, divorced from
> melodic implications, also becomes inert, lifeless, mechanical, *metrical.*[8]

> So Stravinsky's obsession with rhythm in the *Sacre* has led, not only to the
> impoverishment of both harmony and melody, but to the loss of the very
> quality to which he sacrificed the other two—rhythmic vitality. The *Sacre du
> Printemps,* so far from being the triumphant apotheosis of rhythm, the act of
> restoration to its rightful supremacy of the most important and essential ele-
> ment of musical expression, is the very negation and denial of rhythm. In sa-
> crificing everything to it, Stravinsky has, with admirable poetic justice, lost it,
> along with its companions, as well. *Rhythm has here degenerated into meter.*[9]

Gray follows this with an account of the "Sacrificial Dance."

> Even those sections of the *Sacre* which give the impression of complexity, such
> as the final dance of the Elect, in which every musical interest is sacrificed to
> rhythmical purposes, are very primitive in construction. The time-signature
> changes constantly from bar to bar, but the music itself does not; it is only the
> eye and not the ear which perceives the changes. There is nothing there but the
> incessant reiteration of the same insignificant metrical phrase in slightly vary-
> ing quantities. . . . Strip the music of the bar-lines and time-signatures which
> are only loincloth concealing its shameful nudity, and it will at once be seen
> that there is no rhythm at all. Rhythm implies life, some kind of movement or

---

[6]Igor Stravinsky and Robert Craft, *Themes and Episodes* (Berkeley: University of California Press,
1983), p. 58. Many other contexts could be cited in this connection, but see, in *The Flood* (1962), the C♯–D♯
alternation at mm.7–45 which bears such a close resemblance to nos. 35–40 and 82–87 in *Les Noces*. A
number of pitch-relational implications of these half-step or whole-step alternations are discussed in Pieter
C. van den Toorn, *The Music of Igor Stravinsky* (New Haven: Yale University Press, 1983), pp. 152–54,
182–91, 280–81, 439–40.

[7]C. Gray, *A Survey of Contemporary Music,* p. 140.

[8]Ibid., p. 139. (Italics added.)

[9]Ibid., p. 142. (Italics added.)

progression at least, but this music stands quite still, in a quite frightening immobility. It is like a top or gyroscope turning ceaselessly and ineffectually on itself, without moving an inch in any direction, until, in the last bars of the work, it suddenly falls over on its side with a lurch, and stops dead.[10]

The description here of paradox, of seeming "rhythmic vitality" that conveys an overall impression of stasis or "frightening immobility," is entirely apropos. So, too, is the sense of futility that accompanies the conception of "a top or gyroscope turning ceaselessly and ineffectually on itself." A rhythm that, outwardly restless, conveys little overall sense of "movement or progression" is in fact one of the more striking aspects of Stravinsky's invention, acknowledged in these terms by countless critics on both sides of the fence, and a topic to which we shall eventually be returning for further discussion. An early admirer of Stravinsky's music, André Schaeffner, likewise pointed to "the rigid, solemn, priestly, petrified, or gilded" aspect of Stravinsky's art, to "a fixed, hieratic, mummified quality" that seemed "so paradoxical in a musician whose richness of rhythmic invention is undeniable."[11]

Many of Gray's arguments are rephrased by Lambert. There is, initially, the sense of a "dissociation" of rhythm "from its melodic and harmonic components," leading in turn to a "short-winded" melodic style.[12] Indeed, for Lambert it is "the lack of a melodic faculty," the apparent inability of this composer to chisel a melodic substance of his own (to create "a typical Stravinskian tune"), that provoked the stylistic upheaval of neoclassicism, the abrupt move from the borrowed or fabricated folk tunes of the "Russian" era ("monotonous peasant fragments") to the comic rewriting of Pergolesi in *Pulcinella*.[13] And here, too, rhythmic "effect" and its consequent "dissociation" tend merely "to restrict the development of the specific element" favored.[14] Rhythm deteriorates into meter or "mathematical groupings."

---

[10]Ibid., pp. 142–43.

[11]André Schaeffner, "On Stravinsky, Early and Late," *Modern Music* 12, 1 (1934): 2–3. See also, in this connection, André Schaeffner, *Strawinsky* (Paris: Rieder, 1931). Two equally sympathetic accounts were published at the time of Schaeffner's biography: Boris de Schloezer, *Igor Stravinsky* (Paris: Editions Claude Aveline, 1929), and Paul Collaer, *Strawinsky* (Brussels: Editions Equilibres, 1930). Eric Walter White, *Stravinsky's Sacrifice to Apollo* (London: Hogarth Press, 1930), should be mentioned as an early enthusiastic appraisal on the other side of the channel.

[12]Lambert, *Music Ho*, p. 91. Following Gray and Lambert, the idea that Stravinsky lacked a "melodic gift" became a proverbial lament among detractors. Humphrey Searle dubbed the composer "a poor melodist" in *Twentieth Century Counterpoint* (London: Williams and Norgate, 1954), pp. 29–30, while Donald C. Mitchell, although on the whole an enthusiast, pointed similarly to "a crisis in melody," in *The Language of Modern Music* (New York: St. Martin's Press, 1963), p. 144. For a brief rebuttal see van den Toorn, *The Music of Igor Stravinsky*, pp. 237–38.

[13]Lambert, *Music Ho*, pp. 97–98.

[14]Ibid., p. 49.

> Stravinsky's rhythm is not rhythm in the true sense of the term, but rather "meter" or "measure." In many sections of *Le Sacre* the notes are merely pegs on which to hang the rhythm.[15]

> *Histoire* consists almost entirely of an objective juggling with rhythm, or rather meter, for there can be no true rhythm where there is no melodic life. Like Gertrude Stein, Stravinsky chooses the drabbest and least significant phrases for the material of his experiments, because if the melodic line had life, dissection would be impossible. . . . The melodic fragments in *Histoire* are completely meaningless in themselves. They are merely successions of notes which can conveniently be divided up into groups of three, five, and seven, and set against other mathematical groupings.[16]

In most if not all of these particulars, Adorno follows suit. True, the argument acquires a Marxist and Freudian rationale. Yet, here too, Adorno's comments are not altogether new. Gray also complained about the "infantilism" of some of the shorter "Russian" pieces such as the *Berceuses du chat* and *Pribaoutki* and portrayed the composer's celebrated wit and irony as something "wholly negative," a kind of "grin" which, when compared to "the ghastly inhuman laughter of Schoenberg's *Pierrot Lunaire*," was "mere cynicism," an empty, "meaningless dog-laugh."[17] And he ridiculed the aesthetics of "abstraction" along with the composer's "absurd feats of austerity" (which for Adorno became "renunciation" or "a perverse joy in self-denial"),[18] referring the reader for further study "to Professor Sigmund Freud's treatise on the 'Resemblances between the Psychic Life of Savages and Neurotics.' "[19] Here follow Adorno's comments on Stravinsky "the rhythmist," where reference is again made to the element of "dissociation" and its adverse consequences.

> Stravinsky's admirers have grown accustomed to declaring him a rhythmist and testifying that he has restored the rhythmic dimension of music—which had been overgrown by melodic-harmonic thinking—again to honor. In contrast it has been rightly asserted by the Schoenberg school that the rhythmic concept—for the most part manipulated much too abstractly—is constricted even in Stravinsky. Rhythmic structure is, to be sure, blatantly prominent, but this is achieved at the expense of all other aspects of rhythmic organization. Not only is any subjectively expressive flexibility of the beat absent—which is always rigidly carried out in Stravinsky from *Sacre* on—but furthermore all

---

[15]Ibid., pp. 49–50.
[16]Ibid., p. 93.
[17]Gray, *A Survey of Contemporary Music*, pp. 133–34.
[18]Theodor W. Adorno, *Philosophy of Modern Music*, trans. Anne G. Mitchell and Wesley V. Bloomster (New York: Seabury Press, 1973), p. 145.
[19]Gray, *A Survey of Contemporary Music*, p. 145.

rhythmic relations associated with the construction, and the internal compositional organization—the "rhythm of the whole"—are absent as well. *Rhythm is underscored, but split off from musical content. This results not in more, but rather in less rhythm than in compositions in which there is no fetish made of rhythm;* in other words, there are only fluctuations of something always constant and totally static—a stepping aside—in which the irregularity of recurrence replaces the new.[20]

Note the allusion here to the mechanical character of the invention, to the fact that it does not admit "any subjectively expressive flexibility of the beat," a matter to which we shall likewise be returning for additional comment. Crucial to Adorno as well is the static nature of rhythm's "dissociation," its splitting-off "from musical content." For whether the shifting accents occur within periods of metric regularity or whether, in passages of irregular barring, the material is dissected or sliced up into smaller "melodic cells" that are in turn reshuffled and varied in length, a true sense of progress or development is replaced by "mere repetition."[21] "There are only," as he says, "fluctuations of something always constant and totally static."

> The most elementary principle of rhythmic variation—which is the basis of repetition—is that the motif be constructed in such a way that, if it immediately reappears, the accents of their own accord fall upon notes other than they had upon first appearance (for example, "Jeu de Rapt" in *Sacre*). Frequently, not only are accents shifted, but length and brevity are interchanged as well. In all cases, the differentiations derived from the motivic model appear to be the result of a simple game of chance. In this perspective, the melodic cells seem to be under a spell: they are not condensed, rather they are thwarted in their development.[22]

> The school rooted in Stravinsky has been called motoric. The concentration of music upon accents and time relationships produces an illusion of bodily movement. This movement, however, consists of the varied recurrence of the same: of the same melodic forms, of the same harmonies, indeed of the very same rhythmic patterns. Motility . . . is actually incapable of any kind of forward motion.[23]

Most serious in this indictment is the charge of arbitrariness. "The modifications of accents . . . could in all cases just as well be fixed in another way."[24] In this

[20]Adorno, *Philosophy of Modern Music*, pp. 154–55. (Italics added.)
[21]Ibid., p. 164.
[22]Ibid., p. 151.
[23]Ibid., p. 155.
[24]Ibid.

sense they are "abstract irregularities" that, "void of traditional meaning," constitute a kind of "arbitrary game," a "game of chance." (Gray pictured them as "geometrical pattern, as in wallpaper or carpet," while for Lambert the "abstract" patterns defined by the irregular or shifting accents were "rhythmical jigsaw puzzles.") Thus, too, pursued as ends in themselves (because "dissociated" or "split off from musical content"), the shifting accents were unprepared, and were therefore apt to be experienced as a series of "convulsive blows or shocks." And while the notion of shock is acknowledged as fundamental to much modern music, its implications in Stravinsky are "dehumanizing." Unable to apprehend the logic behind the "abstract irregularities" and hence unable to *participate* (to anticipate, resist, or absorb), the listener, as if under a spell, became the hapless victim of a kind of barrage. The composer's complicity is termed "sadistic" or "sado-masochistic."[25]

> In the "sacrificial dance," the most complicated rhythmic patterns restrain the conductor to puppet-like motions. Such rhythmic patterns alternate in the smallest possible units of beat for the sole purpose of impressing upon the ballerina and the listeners the immutable rigidity of convulsive blows and shocks for which they are not prepared through any anticipation of anxiety.[26]

> Everything depends upon the manner in which music deals with the experience of shock. The works of Schoenberg's middle years take up a defensive position by portraying such experiences. In *Erwartung* . . . the gesticulation recalls a man gripped by wild anxiety. Psychologically speaking, however, the man is saved by his anticipation of anxiety: while shock overcomes him, dissociating the continuous duration of traditional style, he retains his self-control. He remains the subject and, consequently, is able to assert his own constant life above the consequence of shock experiences which he heroically reshapes as elements of his own language. In Stravinsky, there is neither the anticipation of anxiety nor the resisting ego; it is rather simply assumed that shock cannot be appropriated by the individual for himself. The musical subject makes no attempt to assert itself, and contents itself with the reflexive absorption of the blows. The subject behaves literally like a critically injured victim of an accident which he cannot absorb and which, therefore, he repeats in the hopeless tension of dreams.[27]

Arbitrariness—"abstract" design or pattern that is "void of traditional meaning"—is an impression shared by all three critics. And what may have induced this shared response can perhaps be traced to two interrelated factors: (1) the absence, during periods of acute metric irregularity, of an acceptable *tactus* (that is to say, an

---

[25]Ibid., p. 159.
[26]Ibid., p. 155.
[27]Ibid., pp. 156–57.

acceptable marking for the beat or unit of pulsation),[28] and (2) the fact that the shifting accents which accompany the irregularity (or which, during periods of regular metric periodicity, disrupt the periodicity) severely compromise melodic identity. In other words, the difficulty seems to have arisen not so much from the absence of a steady meter as from the fact that in the most disruptive cases the irregularity occurred at a subtactus level, at a level below that of a standard (and in some instances preestablished) pulse. One of Adorno's complaints is that the rhythmic patterns in the "Sacrificial Dance" involved "the smallest units of beat," thus restraining the conductor to a series of mechanical, "puppet-like motions." In tonal music, of course, irregularity may routinely be inferred at the hypermeasure levels of metric structure, and even at the level immediately above that of the measure; in Stravinsky's music, irregularity occurs routinely at the level of the measure, coming by way either of the tactus or, as indicated already, note values or "units of beat" below that of a standard or prearranged pulse.

For example, at nos. 37 and 40 in the "Ritual of Abduction," the principal melody of this movement is introduced within a $\frac{9}{8}$ metrical framework where the tactus is unmistakably the dotted quarter-note with a marking of 132. Subsequently, at no. 46, the melody is dissected or sliced up into smaller metrical units of $\frac{3}{8}$, $\frac{5}{8}$, $\frac{5}{8}$, $\frac{3}{8}$, $\frac{4}{8}$, $\frac{5}{8}$, and $\frac{6}{8}$, forcing the listener at some point to abandon the dotted quarter and to adjust, if possible, to the rapid eighth-note as the "common denominator." (See Examples 14a and 14b. The irregularity at no. 46 will eventually *force* listeners to make at least an attempt at the eighth-note, although their initial efforts will most likely be directed at attempts to reconcile the abrupt "break-up" with the prearranged dotted quarter-note pulse. The situation is somewhat similar at the beginning of the "Evocation of the Ancestors," where the half-note pulse of the 1929 revision is challenged almost immediately by disruptive $\frac{3}{4}$ bars.) Moreover, the disruption of the tactus is all the more ferocious at no. 46 since it comes at the expense—comes by way of the mutilation—of a previously established metric identity, namely, that of the principal melody as first introduced at nos. 37 and 40. Hence, in this and similar passages throughout *The Rite,* the impression gained by all three critics of a rhythm "dissociated" or "split off from musical content" and of a melody sacrificed in the interests of "rhythmic effect."

More subtly, the disruption at no. 46 brings to the foreground those elements, meter and pulse, which in past tonal music are apt to be taken more or less for

---

[28] *Tactus* and *pulse* (or *unit of pulsation*) are here used interchangeably. Both refer to that particular level of metrical structure where, in past tonal music, regularity is most stringent, and in accord with which batons are commonly waved, floors are tapped, and steps are danced. *Tactus,* a Renaissance term, encompasses both the notion of pulse and a standard marking of 70 beats per minute; in past tonal music, the rate has commonly been between 40 and 160 beats. In Fred Lerdahl and Ray Jackendoff, *A Generative Theory of Tonal Music,* p. 71, these terms are introduced in the following manner: "Musical intuitions . . . clearly include at least one specially designated metrical level . . . the *tactus.* This is the level of beats that is conducted and with which one most naturally coordinates foot-tapping and dance steps. When one wonders whether to 'feel' a piece 'in 4' or 'in 2,' the issue is which metrical level is the tactus. In short, the tactus is a perceptually prominent level of metrical structure."

EXAMPLE 14: "Ritual of Abduction"

granted on a background, nearly subconscious level of perception. In other words, in first establishing and then disrupting these ingrained levels of metrical structure, passages such as those at no. 46 have the effect of momentarily intensifying their presence. Hence, too, for the above critics, the shared impression of a rhythm that had mechanically stiffened into design, that had "degenerated into meter." The metric irregularity at no. 46 could have come by way of the tactus, the dotted quarter–note at nos. 37–46, and hence by way of extensions or contractions of the $\frac{9}{8}$ meter to, say, $\frac{12}{8}$ or $\frac{6}{8}$. And although all three critics would doubtless have reacted similarly to this alternative, the disturbance is far less wrenching, as perceptual adjustments at this level are made with greater ease. A good comparison would be to nos. 57–64 in the "Ritual of the Rival Tribes," where, by way of the quarter-note as tactus, the meter alternates among $\frac{6}{4}$, $\frac{5}{4}$, $\frac{4}{4}$, $\frac{3}{4}$, and $\frac{2}{4}$. Only if the irregularity had ventured into the realm of the eighth-note, a subtactus unit, would the disruption here have rivalled that at no. 46 in the "Ritual of Abduction."

Unable, then, to identify these elementary terms of reference, unable to rely on the crutch of a steady meter or uniform pulse, critics were understandably at a loss in locating a grain against which the invention could in some meaningful fashion be heard and understood. Nor, by the same token, could they appreciate the contradictions or reversals in the metric identity of the reiterating fragments, chords, configurations, or "cells," since such "displacement" hinges necessarily on these automatic, background terms of reference. Whether acknowledged or unacknowledged by the meter, the patterns defined by the shifting accents or stresses were thus interpreted as "abstract" design, "as in wallpaper or carpet." As music such design was, quite literally, meaningless.

In a curious way, too, all three critics would have found confirmation for their arguments in the analytical excursions of Pierre Boulez.[29] For while Boulez is an admirer of *The Rite*—while, for Boulez, *The Rite* is a piece in which rhythm had in fact finally been given its due—his more technical accounts tend merely to document the earlier vision of abstract design and pattern.

Boulez's analysis of the passage at no. 46 in the "Ritual of Abduction" is shown in Example 14b.[30] The outline here is useful because it scans the characteristic block structure prominently in evidence. Two blocks of material, labeled B and A respectively, are placed in an abrupt juxtaposition with one another; Block B, which consists of an F-punctuation spanning a single $\frac{3}{8}$ bar, marks off successive appearances of Block A, the principal block, whose durations vary in length and are hence "mobile." (Recall the similar construction examined in connection with the "Evocation of the Ancestors" in Chapter 2, a setting to which we shall be returning in due course.) Yet Boulez's commentary never strays beyond the design itself, beyond the measurements and proportions as defined in Example 14b; it never confronts the meaning or significance of these measurements and hence the experienced reality of the passage as a whole. This is not to suggest that the design is irrelevant to perception, but only that the irregularity at no. 46 cannot be removed from the conditions of periodicity that precede it. For it is only with reference to these prior conditions of periodicity, pulse, and melodic identity that the disruptive effect of the passage, its explosive sense of timing and suspense (and so its "mean-

---

[29]Indeed, leaving aside Gray and Lambert as points of departure in music criticism, many of Adorno's descriptions of pitch structure in *The Rite* come close to those of Boulez. In his *Philosophy of Modern Music*, p. 151, Adorno emphasizes the "contradiction between the moderated horizontal and the insolent vertical," between the "antiquated" diatonic fragments of the horizontal plane and the harsh dissonance of the vertical. Similarly, in Pierre Boulez, *Notes of an Apprenticeship*, trans. Herbert Weinstock (New York: Knopf, 1968), p. 74, *The Rite* is described as a piece in which a "horizontal diatonicism" stands in opposition to a "vertical chromaticism." This is an issue to which we shall be turning in Chapters 5 and 6.

[30]Boulez, *Notes of an Apprenticeship*, p. 98.

ing"), can properly be gauged. The element of disruption is entirely absent from the carefully enumerated graph of Example 14b.

At the heart of many of these problems is the fact that, like earlier critics, Boulez takes the irregular or shifting meters at face value. Indeed, his extensive analysis of rhythm in *The Rite* includes no mention at all of the role of steady metric periodicity, even though steady meters govern much of the music in Part I with, by and large, their traditional hierarchical implications intact. Like his predecessors, Boulez tends therefore to ignore the grain against which the disruptive effect of the invention is felt. Rhythm may not here have reached a state of impoverishment, but it remains a one-dimensional affair nonetheless. Attention is drawn to the irregularity and reshuffling of the individual "melodic" or "rhythmic cells," which, acknowledged or unacknowledged by the meter, form the basis of the kinds of designs illustrated in Example 14b. Indeed, all four critics, Gray, Lambert, Adorno, and Boulez, are "radical" interpreters of Stravinsky's music, in the sense in which this term was first introduced by Andrew Imbrie several years ago.[31] What this means is that, in analytical review and hence presumably in perception, they tend to readjust their metrical bearings "radically" at the first signs of conflicting evidence. On the other hand, the instinct of the more "conservative" listener is to cling to an established regularity for as long as possible, and often with the consequence that the effect of conflict or disruption is all the more acutely felt. Thus, too, for the conservative listener, the one-dimensional implications of the meter-phrase coincidence often prove deceptive. For while the irregular barring might indeed often represent a localized phrasing or grouping, the other side of this coin is that it might not in fact reflect the full extent of metrical awareness. It might harbor a preestablished or readily inferable periodicity which guarantees the apprehension of contradiction in metric identity—indeed, that very "displacement" that commentators have been prone to invoke when confronting Stravinsky "the rhythmist."

In contrast to the irregularly barred passage at no. 46, the rhythmic pattern of the celebrated "Augurs of Spring" chord at no. 13 is introduced in a steady $\frac{2}{4}$ setting. Boulez's analysis of this eight-measure stretch, shown in Example 15, marks off the individual measures as independent "rhythmic cells" that are in turn linked to longer two-measure "cells" labeled A, B, and B1.[32]

[31]See Andrew Imbrie, " 'Extra' Measures and Metrical Ambiguity in Beethoven," in Alan Tyson, ed., *Beethoven Studies* (New York: Norton, 1973), pp. 45–66. In Beethoven, however, the radical-conservative dichotomy entails reactions to irregularity and disturbance at levels of structure above that of the measure. The notion is reintroduced in Lerdahl and Jackendoff, *A Generative Theory of Tonal Music*, pp. 23–25, in reference to the opening measures of Mozart's G Minor Symphony. At the two-measure level, the first movement begins with accents on the downbeats of the odd-numbered measures, a formula that is clearly reversed with the restatement of the principal theme at m.20. The authors conclude that the conservative listener might hold on to the established framework until m.14, while the radical one might promptly readjust with the first signs of conflict at m.9. These alternatives are labeled "Interpretation A" and "Interpretation B."

[32]Boulez, *Notes of an Apprenticeship*, p. 91.

EXAMPLE 15: "Augurs of Spring"

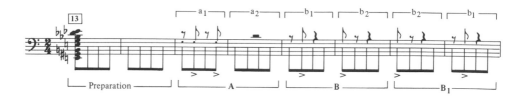

EXAMPLE 16: "Augurs of Spring"

His intent is to trace the reappearance and reordering of these "cells" in the varying contexts that lie ahead, and what emerges from his account is the clear sense of a "rhythmic theme," a rhythmic pattern that is in fact "split off from musical content" and that gradually acquires an independent life of its own. The passage of transition at no. 30, although overlooked by Boulez, serves as illustration. Shown in Example 16, the entire eight-measure pattern is lifted from its initial setting at no. 13 and applied to the bridge leading directly to the movement's climactic block at nos. 31–37.

Example 17 shows an even more radical approach. Here the analysis marks off the groupings as defined by the shifting accents, so that in opting for the irregular meter, the analyst (or composer) may be imagined as having "jumped the fence." The eight-measure stretch is split up into irregular bars of $\frac{9}{8}$, $\frac{2}{8}$, $\frac{6}{8}$, $\frac{3}{8}$, $\frac{4}{8}$, $\frac{5}{8}$, and $\frac{3}{8}$. Note the extreme irregularity of the design as here defined, which even obscures the retrograde implications of cells B and B1 as noted by Boulez. This re-barring may seem a bit farfetched, but it is in fact

EXAMPLE 17: "Augurs of Spring"

seen not to be so if, as in Example 17, a reiterating fragment, taken from no. 46 in the "Ritual of Abduction," is applied.

Missing from these accounts, however, is an appreciation of the role of the steady $\frac{2}{4}$ meter. In fact, the "Augurs of Spring" chord at no. 13 is a classic example of the typical Stravinskian set-up: as is shown in Example 18, the passage is preceded by a clear definition of the governing $\frac{2}{4}$ periodicity, here coming by way of a Db–Bb–Eb–Bb ostinato whose duple implications are unmistakable. (The preparation figures as a kind of bait. Boulez's "preparation," marked for the initial two measures of no. 13 in Example 15, comes much too late.) The impression of $\frac{2}{4}$ periodicity is likely to persist at least through the fifth bar of no. 13, where, up to this point, the shifting accents occur regularly on the offbeats of the $\frac{2}{4}$ scheme. Doubt may arise at m.6, however, where this accentual identification is contradicted. The stress is shifted to the beat, and from this point on the effect of disruption is similar to that of the irregularly barred passage at no. 46; it materializes in the form of a systematic attack on the prevailing meter and tactus (here the quarter-note with a marking of 100). In other words, at some point in this display onbeats become indistinguishable from offbeats and, in terms of both the meter and pulse, the listener becomes "lost." So, too, in establishing and then disrupting these familiar crutches, their automatic, background character breaks down and they are momentarily thrust to the surface of musical consciousness. Yet perhaps just at the initial point of disorientation (or perhaps at the point where the tactic, pursued at greater length, would have become tedious and hence counterproductive; the timing here is crucial), the Db–Bb–Eb–Bb ostinato reappears at no. 14 and restores, retroactively, the $\frac{2}{4}$ "feel" to the section as a whole. Nor are the longer two-, four-, and eight-measure units irrelevant to this conception. Indeed, in light of the initial regularity of these hypermeasures, it seems not in the least whimsical to apply dots in the Lerdahl-Jackendoff manner indicating the levels of a conventional metric structure—the levels of the quarter-

EXAMPLE 18:   "Augurs of Spring"

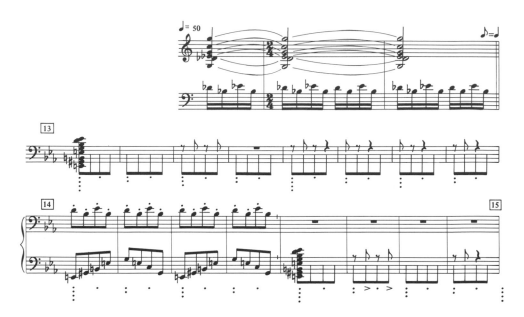

note (tactus), measure, and the two- and four-measure units (see Example 18).[33]

Of course, the purpose of these introductory remarks is not to squeeze the variety of rhythmic structure in *The Rite*—or, indeed, in Stravinsky's music generally—into a single barrel of uniformity. On the contrary, steady meters often imply a construction that, in harmonic, melodic, and instrumental detail, differs fundamentally from that implied by irregular meters, so that a central concern in these chapters will be the identification of two prototypes of construction based on these distinctions. The kind of construction presupposed by the steady meters of "Procession of the Sage" and "Dance of the Earth" is quite different from the block structures that accompany the shifting

---

[33]In Lerdahl and Jackendoff, *A Generative Theory of Tonal Music*, p. 18, beats are conceived not as durations but as points in time (analogous to geometrical points in space) which, strongly or weakly accented, are organized hierarchically in a manner that is independent of grouping or phrasing. Hence in their analyses, as here in Example 18, dots are used to represent beats at various levels of a metrical structure. The conception of beats as durationless points in time stems from Arthur J. Komar, *Theory of Suspensions* (Princeton: Princeton University Press, 1971), p. 52, and from Imbrie, " 'Extra' Measures and Metrical Ambiguity in Beethoven," p. 53; the spatial analogy is Imbrie's. It should be added, however, that in *A Generative Theory*, pp. 19–21, meter is viewed as "inherently periodic" and as "a relatively local phenomenon"; Lerdahl and Jackendoff contend that at higher levels of structure, where the formulation is seldom regular, the sense of meter, of a strong-weak alternation, dims and gives way to large-scale grouping and "thematic parallelism." In contrast, Imbrie's conception of meter allows for greater irregularity, so that in their independent, interacting roles, meter and grouping continue to coexist at higher structural levels.

meters of "Ritual of Abduction" and "Evocation of the Ancestors." And irrespective of the imposed irregularity of Example 17, there are reasons for the steady $\frac{2}{4}$ design at no. 13, just as there are reasons for the notated irregularity at no. 46 in the "Ritual of Abduction." Yet, as should by now be equally apparent, correspondences between these essential types are no less obvious and of no less consequence. Our argument has in fact been that in passages of metric irregularity, contradictions or reversals in the metric identity of reiterating fragments often impose themselves by way of a concealed periodicity. Readers will doubtless detect the conservative bias of this perspective. Yet, without some measure of conservatism, it is difficult to imagine how a perception of this music can avoid the impression of arbitrariness, of "abstract" design and pattern, as stingingly portrayed in the accounts of all four critics cited. If the shifting accents or stresses are to have meaning, then this can come only to the extent that the resultant patterns are tied to regularity, and often, as noted, to hidden implications of steady periodicity.

Les Noces (1914–23)

When Stravinsky himself first drew attention to the coincidence of meter and phrase in certain passages of irregular barring in *The Rite* (recalling that in many such instances he had sought "to measure according to phrasing"), he had in mind rather specifically the lengthy, irregular measures of the early sketchbook and printed versions of "Evocation of the Ancestors" and "Sacrificial Dance." Clearly, however, the logic of this coincidence extends to the later application of "smaller divisions" as well. Nor is the progression from large to small confined to the composition and revision of *The Rite*. An early draft of *Les Noces*, scored for mezzo soprano, woodwinds, and double string quintet, exhibits the same symptoms in relation to this work's final version of 1917–23.[34]

Labeled A and B, the opening two blocks of *Les Noces* are reproduced in Examples 19 and 20; Example 19 is from the draft (where the two blocks are set apart by a change in tempo), and Example 20 is condensed from the final version. The earlier version features longer measures of seven, six, and five eighth-note beats that were subsequently sliced up into "smaller divisions" of two and three beats. Nor does the correspondence end here, for the proportions in these two versions of *Les Noces* are quite different. Just as with the several versions of the "Evocation" examined in Chapter 2, the opening material of *Les Noces* underwent a process of expansion: Block A is considerably

---

[34]This early *Noces* draft is now a part of the Paul Sacher Foundation in Basel, Switzerland. A facsimile of the first page appears in Vera Stravinsky and Robert Craft, *Stravinsky in Pictures and Documents* (New York: Simon and Schuster, 1978), p. 144.

EXAMPLE 19: *Les Noces* (early draft)

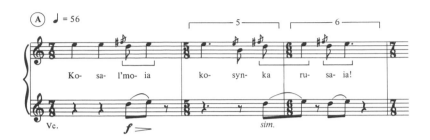

EXAMPLE 20: *Les Noces*

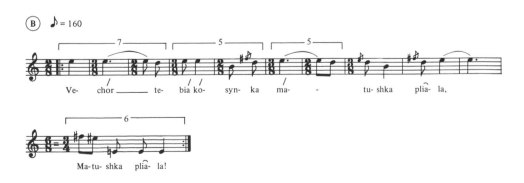

shorter in the earlier version, while Block B, although very nearly intact, misses the final arrangement by a quarter-note beat. The brackets in Examples 19 and 20 mark off the longer measures of the earlier sketch which, in subdivisions, were retained by the final version.

More critical distinctions between these two *Noces* texts relate to motivic identity, pulse, and tempo. Notice that the two $\frac{5}{8}$ and $\frac{6}{8}$ bars that conclude Block A in the early draft were among those retained, with subdivisions, in the finished score. And of special note in this retention is the concluding $\frac{6}{8}$ bar with its quarter–eighth–dotted quarter rhythm for the E–D–E segment. For it appears that in making the transition to the expanded dimensions of the later version, this particular figure was at some point singled out for emphasis. Its triple implications are underscored by the later $\frac{3}{8}$ subdivision, where, transferred to the opening of the piece, it serves as a motivic point of departure and return for the block as a whole. Hence, from within a seemingly random series of pitch inflections ("a ceaseless alternation between two or three notes," as Gray observed), there emerged the beginnings of a coherent repeat structure. Seized upon as a motivic focal point, E–D–E became a metrically fixed element, a *constancy*.

Some of these implications are detailed in Example 21, where the two versions of Block A are placed in vertical alignment. The retained $\frac{5}{8}$ and $\frac{6}{8}$ bars are marked by dotted lines, while an arrow points to the later insertion of E–D–E at the opening of the piece. The two versions appear to be distinguished also by what little may be inferred as to long-range periodicity—or, in view of the successive $\frac{3}{8}$ bars for the E–D–E motive, by what may perhaps already be sensed as a commitment, on the part of the finished score, to a triple mold. For in the early draft the quarter-note is assigned the metronome marking, a stipulation obviously at odds with these later implications. Still, as shown in Example 21, $\frac{3}{8}$ and $\frac{6}{8}$ meters may be imposed from the start of the early draft, and these arrive on target with the concluding $\frac{6}{8}$ bar and its E–D–E segment.

EXAMPLE 21: *Les Noces*

More eventful from the standpoint of fixed metric identity is the tiny D–E segment. Marked off by brackets underneath both versions of Block A in Example 21, D–E is a part of E–D–E and of subsequent extensions of this motive as well. Returns to E invariably come by way of D, and the succession is stressed by a doubling in the cello in the early draft (see Example 19) and by octave doublings in Pianos I and III in the final version (see Example 23). Notice, however, that in accord with the longer measures of the early draft, D–E is barred differently on each occasion, while, in the finished score, D–E is always barred as an over-the-barline succession; irrespective of the notated irregularity, D–E assumes the same metric identity. Hence, just as with the E–D–E motive, the finished score latches on to a fixed element or constancy, here in the form of the smaller but more pervasive D–E component. In addition, E, as the registrally fixed pitch of departure and return, always falls on the first beats of the irregular measures. Indeed, as can now readily be seen, the notated irregularity of the final arrangement is in large part determined by these metrically fixed components; they tend, as it were, *to regulate the irregularity*. The shifting meter seeks, at least in part, to *preserve* fixed identity in repetition.

A summary of these conclusions appears in Example 22, where a hypothetical scheme further demonstrates just how regular the irregularity is. Observe how the shifting meter revolves around the fixed components, and in particular the over-the-barline identity of D–E. Indeed, according to the hypothesized version, Block A contains only three motivically defined metrical units: a $\frac{3}{8}$ bar for E–D–(E), another $\frac{3}{8}$ bar for the dotted quarter-note E, and a $\frac{5}{8}$

EXAMPLE 22: *Les Noces*

bar for E–D–B–D. And if we omit the dotted quarter-note, the scheme reduces to only two such units: E–D–(E) and an extension in the form of E–D–B–D–(E). (In the fifth bar of the hypothetical version, the dot of the quarter-note must yield to D as an eighth-note [marked by parentheses] to allow for complete motivic correlation.) So, too, there are only $\frac{3}{8}$ and $\frac{5}{8}$ bars or "phrases": four $\frac{3}{8}$ bars with a total of twelve eighth-note beats, and three $\frac{5}{8}$ bars for a total of fifteen beats. (The implications of three as common denominator will be discussed just below.) And since a $\frac{3}{8}$ bar with the E–D–(E) motive serves as a point of departure and return for the block as a whole, the $\frac{5}{8}$ bars are recognized as extensions of the latter (or as metrical troublemakers): each $\frac{5}{8}$ bar delays, by two beats, the return of D, the inflection, to E.

Notice, too, that the natural stresses of the Russian syllables underscore D–E as a metrically fixed unit in the final version.[35] As is shown by the stress markings for Block A in Example 20, these stresses coincide with the (musically) stressed D of the D–E unit for all D–E repeats except the final two. In contrast, the repeats of D–E in the draft (Example 19), although doubled by a solo cello, lack this support. In view of the tradition of flexible accentuation in the singing of Russian popular verse, the coincidence here of natural stress and musical accent (for the upbeat D of the D–E unit) takes on an obvious significance.[36] A peculiarly Stravinskian trait in these opening passages is the stutter effect, the repeat, in the fourth and fifth measures of the final version, of the individual syllable *ko* of *Kosal'*, meaning "braid." Within the framework of a bride's ritualized lament, the stutter suggests a sob or sigh.

Up to this point the logic of the barring has been pursued solely from the standpoint of metrically fixed elements. What may be termed the opposite

[35] A translation of the two lines of Blocks A and B runs as follows: "Braid, my dear little blond braid!/ Yesterday my mother braided you, my dear little braid, my mother braided you!" Most of the libretto of *Les Noces* was adopted from P. V. Kireevsky's anthology of peasant wedding verses: V. F. Miller and M. N. Speransky, eds., *Pesni sobrannye P. V. Kireevskim, Novaia seriia*, vol. 1 (Moscow, 1911). I am indebted to Simon Karlinsky for his assistance in the translation and transliteration of the above text.

[36] An early discussion of the flexible or "movable" accent in Russian folk songs is contained in the Introduction to Eugenie Lineff, *The Peasant Songs of Great Russia*, vol. 1 (St. Petersburg, 1905), pp. xvi–xvii. In Igor Stravinsky and Robert Craft, *Expositions and Developments* (Berkeley: University of California Press, 1981), p. 121, the composer recalled that his own conscious recognition of this feature had come as a "rejoicing discovery" while working on the libretto of *Renard*: "One important characteristic of Russian popular verse is that the accents of the spoken verse are ignored when the verse is sung. The recognition of the musical possibilities inherent in this fact was one of the most rejoicing discoveries of my life." It need in this connection hardly be reiterated that this folk-song tradition of flexibility in verbal stress is analogous to the musical technique of displacement, of shifting the accentual identity of a reiterating fragment, and that the latter may well have had the former as its origin. At the same time, and as will presently be made clear, the technique of displacement always carries with it the opposing force of fixed metric identity, an element which lies at the root of metric irregularity in Stravinsky's music. Both the flexible stress in Russian popular verse and its implications in Stravinsky's early vocal music are pursued in illuminating detail in Richard Taruskin, "Stravinsky's 'Rejoicing Discovery' and What It Meant: Some Observations on His Russian Text-Setting," in Ethan Haimo and Paul Johnson, eds., *Stravinsky Retrospectives* (Lincoln: University of Nebraska Press, forthcoming).

side of this rather elaborate coin—the opposite side, that is, of fixed metric identity or constancy—is "displacement," the notion of a "modification of accents," as Adorno expressed it—presumably, metrical accents. For, as can readily be seen from the irregular barring of the finished score, displacement is not here graphically a part of the invention. On the contrary, and as suggested, each of the designated components assumes, in relation to the shifting meter, a fixed identity: E–D–(E) is barred as a $\frac{3}{8}$ bar, D–E as an over-the-barline succession, while E falls on the downbeats of the measures in question. But the notion of *displacement* implies just the opposite of what is here notationally evident, namely, a *change* in the metric accentation of a reiterating component, fragment, chord, or configuration. And while references in this connection have frequently been made to the mere shifting of accents, at times to the shifting merely of "phenomenal accents" or stresses[37] and at other times merely to the resultant design or pattern, the implications for the listener are in truth far more dramatic. They materialize more immediately in the form of a shift in the metric identity of a component; while interval order and note values remain intact, metrical placement is altered. (To emphasize accent or pattern at the expense of motivic identity is to emphasize cause at the expense of perceived effect.) Moreover, displacement is irrevocably linked to steady metric periodicity, since shifts of this kind can be perceived only with reference to a periodic grain. So, too, these shifts materialize in the form of up-beat-downbeat (weak-strong) or offbeat-onbeat contradictions. A reiterating component, introduced on the upbeat, is contradicted by a subsequent down-beat appearance (or vice versa), while another such component, introduced off the beat, is contradicted by a later onbeat appearance (or vice versa).

There is little difficulty in rearranging the opening blocks of *Les Noces* accordingly. As is indicated by the brackets in Example 23, a $\frac{3}{8}$ meter is inferred from the E–D–E motive of the opening measures and is imposed on the block as a whole. It is with reference to this background periodicity that displacements in the metric identity of the reiterating components materialize.

Thus, in the opening two measures, the stressed D–E succession falls on the third beat of the $\frac{3}{8}$ bar, with D–E assuming its over-the-barline, upbeat-downbeat identity. But subsequent repeats contradict this identity, for, in terms of the $\frac{3}{8}$ periodicity, the D in this succession falls on the second beat at m.3, and then on the first beat at m.6. Hence a carefully patterned cycle of displacement is exhibited: the D of the D–E succession is introduced on the third beat, is subsequently displaced to the second and first beats, and then, in the completion of the cycle, is displaced yet another notch back to the original third beat, at which point D–E resumes its over-the-barline identity in con-

[37]In Lerdahl and Jackendoff, *A Generative Theory of Tonal Music*, p. 17, the term *phenomenal accent* is used to distinguish local stresses such as sforzandi, long notes, and leaps from metrical and structural accents. Earlier, in Grosvenor Cooper and Leonard B. Meyer, *The Rhythmic Structure of Music* (Chicago: University of Chicago Press, 1960), p. 8, *stress* is defined as "a dynamic intensification of the beat."

junction with the return of the E–D–E motive in the final bars of the block. Moreover, the $\frac{3}{8}$ meter emerges on target with the foreground irregularity in these final measures. The two conflicting meters are aligned as the block draws to a close. This serves to intensify the "feel" of the steady $\frac{3}{8}$ periodicity, along with the displacements which, as indicated, depend for their apprehension on this presence.

EXAMPLE 23: *Les Noces*

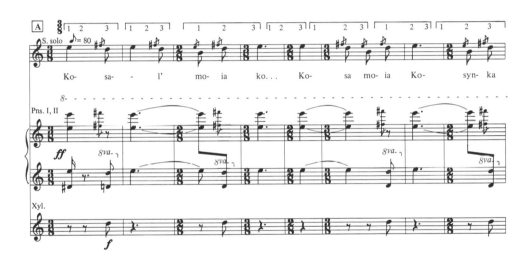

(continued)

EXAMPLE 23 *(continued)*

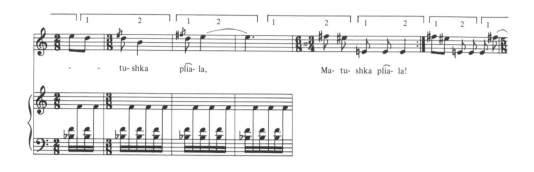

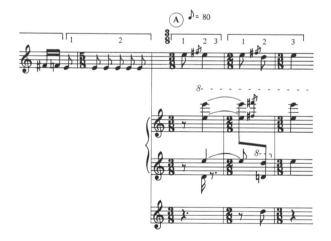

Similar inferences may be drawn from the material of Block B. Here, however, the periodicity is duple rather than triple. Moreover, the foreground irregularity comes by way of a subtactus unit, while in Block A it surfaces by way of the tactus. In other words, while Stravinsky doubles the marking for the eighth-note from 80 to 160 at Block B, the listener is far more apt to hold on to the marking of 80, which becomes the marking for the quarter-note (as tactus). And with the eighth-note relegated to a subtactus unit (and given, as well, the brevity of Block B in relation to Block A), the $\frac{2}{4}$ meter becomes far more conspicuous than is the $\frac{3}{8}$ scheme in Block A. Notice also that, just as with Block A, the steady meter arrives on target with the foreground irregularity, a circumstance that here, too, heightens the sensation of periodicity.

With Block C the dotted quarter-note is given the marking of 80, which in turn stipulates a triple division of the retained pulse. And while the stressed F♯–E♯ figure falls on the downbeat of the first bar, F♯–E♯ is more readily heard as a stressed upbeat to the punctuating E; in both Blocks A and B, the inflection is stressed as an upbeat to E as the point of departure and return. Observe, too, that the $\frac{2}{4}$ periodicity of Block B favors this alternative, since, as outlined by the brackets, an extension following the repeat sign emerges at Block C with an extra eighth-note beat to spare. Further along, the invention follows a familiar path. Subsequent repeats of F♯–E♯–(E) are irregularly spaced, a circumstance that tends gradually to undermine the inferred $\frac{6}{8}$ periodicity. (The irregular spacing nonetheless comes closest to a $\frac{6}{8}$ scheme, which, in view of the $\frac{2}{4}$ periodicity of Block B, would in any case have been the "preferred" reading.) The result here is a kind of tension between the implied $\frac{6}{8}$ mold and the irregular spacing of the F♯–E♯–(E) repeats, which usually miss a $\frac{6}{8}$ or $\frac{3}{8}$ delineation by one or two eighth-note beats. Contradictions similar to those noted in connection with Block A could in fact have been plotted on behalf of F♯–E♯–(E). Moreover, the irregularity emerges on target with the $\frac{6}{8}$ meter at the conclusion of Block C. Block C is then followed by slightly varied repeats of Blocks A and B.

Example 24 re-bars the material of Blocks A and B in accord with the $\frac{3}{8}$ and $\frac{2}{4}$ periodicities bracketed in Example 23. The brackets underneath Block A refer to the stressed D–E succession whose patterned cycle of displacement was noted just above.

EXAMPLE 24: *Les Noces* (re-barred)

Histoire du soldat (1918)

Other contexts can illuminate the present perspective more fully. Most compelling among these are passages of irregular barring in which a steady meter, as forcibly applied to the opening blocks of *Les Noces,* surfaces more explicitly in the guise of an ostinato, generally in the bass. Such passages abound in Stravinsky's music, of course. The opening "Soldier's March" of *Histoire du soldat* is a particularly apt example, if only because the habit of applying "smaller divisions" had by the time of its completion reached a decisive formulation. Moreover, the disruptive $\frac{3}{8}$ bars of the March closely parallel the $\frac{3}{4}$ bars of the 1929 revision of the "Evocation of the Ancestors" (which, as was indicated in Chapter 2, was actually completed in 1926). Indeed, the renewed conception of the motivic repeat structure of the "Evocation" could have come—it seems fair to suggest—only as a consequence of contexts such as *Les Noces* (1914–23), *Renard* (1916), *Histoire* (1918), and the *Octet* (1924). Quite apart from the changed dimensions in the successive revisions of the "Evocation," the re-barring of 1926 reflects a new interpretation of fixed metric identity.

The disruptive content of *Histoire*'s March can be traced to the marching tune's B–C#–D upward sweep, which, as shown in Examples 25a–25d, is barred throughout as a $\frac{3}{8}$ unit. In opposition to this barring, a steady $\frac{2}{4}$ meter is imposed at the outset by a G–E/D basso ostinato whose connecting beam invariably crosses the bar line during stretches of foreground irregularity. The contradictions to which the B–C#–D sweep are subjected can be apprehended by examining the alignment of subsequent repeats with the G–E/D ostinato pattern. In Examples 25a–25d these repeats are duly aligned and then marked with a series of dotted lines.

Similar implications can be applied to the terminating E of the sweep which, like the E in the opening blocks of *Les Noces,* functions as a melodic point of departure and return. Indeed, there is an obvious correspondence here between the over-the-barline D–E succession of *Les Noces* and the B–C#–D–(E) sweep of the March: E, as termination of B–C#–D, always falls on the downbeats of the irregular measures. Yet, while B–C#–D–(E) is the focal point in this display, the effect of dislocation is felt well beyond its immediate confines.

This is especially true of the climactic passage at mm.50–57, as shown in Example 25d. In Example 25a, these motivic components are introduced with a minimum of disturbance. Here metric identity is first established in relation to the ostinato's $\frac{2}{4}$ periodicity and is not as yet subject to displacement. The $\frac{3}{8}$ bar of the B–C#–D sweep is followed by another $\frac{3}{8}$ bar that immediately cancels the threat to the quarter-note tactus. Moreover, with the earlier $\frac{3}{4}$ bar at m.14, the two $\frac{3}{8}$ bars are effectively cancelled out at m.18. Hence the $\frac{3}{8}$ bar at m.16 figures merely as a potential troublemaker. And the terminating E

EXAMPLE 25: *Histoire du soldat*

at m.17 is likely to be heard as an offbeat element, a syncopation pursuant to the steady $\frac{2}{4}$ framework of the ostinato.

Moreover, at mm.45–46 in Example 25b, this identity is not markedly affected. For while B–C♯–D is shifted to the second, "weak" beat of the $\frac{2}{4}$ frame of reference, E retains its syncopated, offbeat identity. But further along, at mm.49–50 in Example 25c, this identity *is* contradicted. For in accord with the $\frac{2}{4}$ meter, the sweep now falls off the beat, which means that its terminating E will assume an onbeat, not, as earlier, an offbeat identity. Hence a contradiction is forged, and here of the conspicuous offbeat-onbeat variety. Notwithstanding the preserved $\frac{3}{8}$ bar of the B–C♯–D–(E) sweep, the initial offbeat identity of its terminating E is contradicted by an onbeat appearance.

Finally, at mm.50–57 in Example 25d these conflicting identities are presented successively in a final, tutti summation. In the first occurrence, at mm.52–53, the initial offbeat identity of the terminating E is restored; in accord with the $\frac{2}{4}$ meter, E resumes its initial syncopated identity. But instead of an immediate cancellation of the first $\frac{3}{8}$ bar, as earlier at mm.16–17 in Example 25a, a resolution of the $\frac{3}{8}$ troublemaker is delayed to mm.56–57, where B–C♯–D–(E) reappears in its displaced, contradicted version. Yet it may be prior to this final contradiction, already at m.53 in fact, that giddy doubt and uncertainty arise. Indeed, the contradiction at mm.56–57 may not even be felt as such. For the reversals have now become so persistent and the highly irregular stresses in the percussion (not shown in Example 25d) have wrought such additional havoc that the steady $\frac{2}{4}$ periodicity of the ostinato itself is challenged. Listeners seeking to hold on to the initial onbeat identity of the B–C♯–D sweep might here begin to question the stability of the ostinato's $\frac{2}{4}$ meter.[38]

In other words, the sense of a "true" metric identity for the B–C♯–D–(E) fragment is temporarily lost, as its point of departure can no longer be distinguished from subsequent displacement. And with the loss of such identity comes the simultaneous loss of periodicity and pulse (here the quarter-note with a marking of 112); offbeats are for a moment no longer distinguishable from onbeats. True, order is eventually restored as the climactic stretch draws to a close at m.57; the foreground irregularity emerges on target with the background $\frac{2}{4}$ meter. Yet the overall effect differs little from that noted earlier in connection with the "Augurs of Spring" chord and other contexts as well. Identity is first established in relation to a steady periodicity, which (1) is subsequently displaced; (2) leads climactically to a temporary state of disorientation where the periodicity and tactus are disturbed; and (3) is followed by a resolution of the conflict as the foreground irregularity and background periodicity emerge on target.

Nonetheless, in direct opposition to displacement, the irregular barring

---

[38]Also missing from Examples 25c and 25d is the clarinet fragment, which, at mm.45–47 and 57–59, is likewise subjected to onbeat-offbeat reversals in relation to the $\frac{2}{4}$ frame of reference of the ostinato.

stubbornly *preserves* fixed metric identity. In *Histoire*'s March, B–C♯–D is always barred as a $\frac{3}{8}$ unit, while its terminating E always falls on the first beats of the succeeding measures. And that Stravinsky was conscious of this counteraction seems indicated by the stress and slur markings at m. 49 in Example 25c. These are introduced precisely at the point where the initial onbeat identity of B–C♯–D is first contradicted by an offbeat placement. Consequently, in opposition to the strong current of displacement, these markings attempt to hold B–C♯–D's initial onbeat identity as introduced at mm. 16 and 45.

The double edge here is critical. On the one hand there is a form of displacement, an effort to contradict the accentual identity of a reiterating fragment (which presupposes steady metric periodicity, even if of the concealed, background type as bracketed or re-barred in the preceding examples), and, on the other hand, there is an effort to counter this displacement by pressing for a fixed metric identity in repetition. And if the strategy does in fact entail an element of "sadism," this can perhaps best be heard and understood as it relates to counteraction, to the attempt to press for a sameness in the repetition of a fragment (and often, in effect, a static, downbeating kind of sameness), to compose, indeed, as if the repetition were metrically genuine.

Still, questions may linger about the ultimate effectiveness of counteraction, of fixed metric identity in repetition and as it here entails the integrity of the preserved $\frac{3}{8}$ bar in *Histoire*'s March. At m. 16 in Example 25a, for instance, just how authentic is the $\frac{3}{8}$ "feel"? Obviously, the character of the $\frac{3}{8}$ bar is quite different from what it would have been had it been situated within a $\frac{3}{8}$ periodic mold—or, as might here have been more likely, within a $\frac{6}{8}$ mold. Given the strong $\frac{2}{4}$ current in "The Soldier's March," the irregular barring takes on the "feel" of a self-conscious counting, which replaces the automatic sense of a steady periodic undertow; in a conventional context, the March's $\frac{3}{8}$ bar would undoubtedly have been replaced by stress and slur markings. (Gray, Lambert, and Adorno would all have concurred, of course, citing the "disintegration" of rhythm into meter and the consequent "abstract" character of the metric design.) Yet a change in character does not here signal an absence of purpose. A respect for the preserved $\frac{3}{8}$ bar is essential if the element of counteraction is to be observed properly. This is important in a performance of this music, where a strict, metronomic, percussive approach is required. For the point of the invention, of its displacement and fiendish counteraction, is lost if subjected to any fluctuation of the beat, to "any subjectively expressive flexibility of the beat," in Adorno's words. Indeed, it is from this kind of an angle that Stravinsky's "formalist" convictions can perhaps best be understood—not merely as philosophy, but as a reaction to the special articulative demands of the music, demands patently at odds with the articulative conventions of nineteenth-century symphonic literature. The March leaves little room for interpretation along conventional lines. If counteraction is applied, then this can come only by way of a strictly mechanical reproduction of the metrically fixed elements. Hence, too, the re-barring of Stravinsky hazarded in this chapter is analytical, designed to uncover the concealed side of the double edge, not to serve as a substitute for the printed page.

Indeed, as is in this respect sufficiently evident, Stravinsky himself was a radical interpreter of his music. And as a conductor he favored a strict adherence to the bar line, a fact borne out today by a number of recorded rehearsals[39] and by the following excerpt from *Conversations with Stravinsky*. Here, of course, *accent* means phenomenal accent or stress.

> R. C.: Meters. Can the same effect be achieved by means of accents as by varying the meters? What are bar lines?
>
> I. S.: To the first question my answer is, up to a point, yes, but that point is the degree of real regularity in the music. The bar line is much, much more than a mere accent, and I don't believe that it can be simulated by an accent, at least not in my music.[40]

Yet it seems inconceivable that he could have been oblivious to the contradictions in the metric identity of the reiterating components that, hinging on a steady periodicity, lie concealed beneath the imposition of a foreground irregularity. The shifting meter can acknowledge only one side of the coin, only one side of the double edge, namely, counteraction, the effort to render the repetition as metrical sameness. And such an effort can be appreciated only in relation to the current against which it is directed. The surface of this music may be radical, but its meaning is subject to a deeply conservative grain of musical thought.

A passage from *Oedipus Rex* (1926) serves as a final illustration. Shown in Example 26, a melodic fragment is introduced at no. 139 and is then repeated at no. 140. Of course, as in previous examples, the repeat harbors a contradiction. For in accord with a concealed $\frac{3}{4}$ periodicity, the initial statement begins off the beat while the repeat begins on the downbeat. Yet the high point of this passage comes later, at no. 144, where the concealed $\frac{3}{4}$ meter is brought to the surface and the irregular subdivisions are replaced by stress and slur markings. From the standpoint of the initial irregularity, the later conception exposes the background periodicity, while from the standpoint of the later periodicity, the earlier irregularity dissects or slices up a periodic conception in accord with its stress and slur articulation. Here, then, at nos. 139 and 140, meter and a localized type of "phrasing" coincide.

---

[39]Especially apropos in this regard is a private recording, made in the 1940s, of the composer rehearsing the *Symphonies of Wind Instruments* (1920). Stravinsky's insistence on a very close reading of the shifting $\frac{2}{8}$ and $\frac{3}{8}$ bars of the opening pages eventually tried the patience of a number of the musicians, who retaliated by mimicking some of the composer's idiosyncrasies. I am indebted to Richard Taruskin for lending me his tape of the original recording.

[40]Igor Stravinsky and Robert Craft, *Conversations with Stravinsky* (Berkeley: University of California Press, 1980), p. 21.

EXAMPLE 26:   *Oedipus Rex*

"Evocation of the Ancestors"

It will be remembered that the "Evocation" consisted of two alternating blocks of material, the first of which spaced or marked off successive appearances of the second, principal block. Attention will here be focused primarily on the second of these two alternating blocks, henceforth designated Block B.

At issue arc (1) fixed metric identity and (2) displacement. These, of course, are the twin sides of the double edge or coin referred to above. However, in the "Evocation" the second of these edges surfaces with an inconvenient hitch: at strategic points of arrival and departure, the background periodicity upon which felt displacement hinges does not, as in the previous illustrations, flatten out the foreground irregularity. Except for the initial statement of Block B at no. $121+3$, the periodic grain that may be inferred does not as a rule arrive on target with the shifting meter as subsequent Block B statements are concluded. At the same time, the "feel" of periodicity is inescapable. In the 1929 revision the half-note is initially the tactus with an assigned marking of 72. And with the half-note–quarter–quarter motive of Block B's initial bar, a $\frac{2}{2}$ meter may be inferred, in relation to which the subsequent $\frac{3}{4}$ bars assume the by now familiar role of disruptive troublemakers. Indeed, the "play" of the "Evocation" derives in large part from the stimulation of long-term periodic expectations and the stubborn, counteracting refusal of fixed metric identity, as defined by subsequent repeats of the initial motives and submotives of Block B, to comply.

This, of course, is the familiar twist of the double edge. Yet for the reasons indicated already, hidden periodicity seems here at a greater disadvantage than in the passages examined from *Les Noces* and *Histoire,* so that, in turn, displacement in the metric identity of the reiterating motives may not be as acutely felt. With subsequent repeats of Block B's initial motives, the listener is more apt to readjust his/her metrical bearings than to persevere with the diminishing traces of a prevailing periodicity. Hence the opposing forces of fixed identity and displacement are placed in a more balanced relationship. For the conservative listener, the radical implications of the shifting meter are more persuasively brought to the fore.

Shown in Examples 27a–27c are three versions of Block B's initial statement at no. 121 + 3. These are drawn from page 73 of the sketchbook, the 1913 autograph, and the 1929 revision. As reported earlier, the sevens of the sketchbook version were carved up into two units of 4 + 3 quarter-note beats in the 1913 autograph. Highlighted in particular in the autograph is the underlying repeat structure of the initial B statement. For while motive a7 is shortened by two notes at m. 4, the initial 4 + 3 unit is retained. (The deleted notes are bracketed in Example 27b, where the a7 label is retained for the repeat.) Hence, motivically speaking, modified restatements of Block B derive in their entirety from the single motive a7 and its 4 + 3 subdivision. All subsequent extensions, contractions, and reorderings materialize with reference to this single motivic point of departure.

EXAMPLE 27: "Evocation"

(a) Sketchbook, p. 73

(b) 1913 Autograph

(c) 1929 Revision

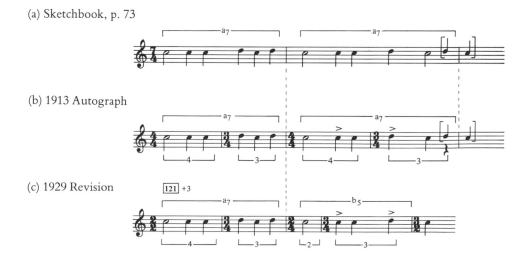

In contrast, the barring of the 1929 revision records the actual shortening of motive a7 at mm.3–4. As shown in Example 27c, the final C falls on the downbeat at m.5. And since the downbeat here coincides with the return of Block A, the C is placed in a parallel relationship with the earlier C at m.3. This in turn underscores a more separately realized identity for the repeat (labeled b5 in Example 27c), whose 2 + 3 subdivision will in turn differ from that of a7. In addition to a $\frac{2}{4}$ bar for the half-note C, a disruptive $\frac{3}{4}$ bar will now accommodate C–C–D as well as D–C–D. Moreover, as barred in Example 27c, the a7–b5 succession will serve as the somewhat lengthier motivic point of departure according to which subsequent modifications in Block B statements are gauged.

This does not suggest, of course, that the repeat structure of a7 followed by b5, as graphically exposed by the autograph version, is entirely obscured. On the contrary, a7 still contains b5, while, as boxed off in Example 28, a single inflection, the D, acts as a kind of pivot in distinguishing subsequent repeats of the two motives. Indeed, by including the final C in the motivic definition, the boxed-off D in Example 28 divides Block B into two equal units of six quarter-note beats.

And in this way, too, the "Evocation" emerges as yet another illustration of that earlier noted addiction to pitch-stutter, to "a ceaseless alternation between two or three notes," here in the reduced form of a punctuation of C and its inflection D. Correspondences with the above-noted passages need hardly be cited in this connection. Yet perhaps especially in the "Evocation," the very idea that so much could in fact have been made of so little presses itself on the imagination to a degree quite without equal among the many other, similarly disposed passages in this *oeuvre*.

Two restatements of Block B are shown in Examples 29 and 30. These feature extensions and reshufflings of the original a7–b5 motivic order as introduced at no. 121 + 3. In addition, there are hinges in these lengthier statements, slight infractions in terms of C–E♭–D and G–F♯–E that occasionally extend the motivic repeats by three quarter-note beats. Additional variety is achieved by deleting the initial half-note C of motive a7, so that a7 becomes a5.

EXAMPLE 28: "Evocation"

EXAMPLE 29: "Evocation"

EXAMPLE 30: "Evocation"

Most extensive among these restatements, however, is that at nos. 125–27 + 1. Shown in Example 30, this begins with a recapitulation of the original a7–b5 order, which is followed by a b5/a7 overlap; the barring here of b5 conceals the longer a7 repeat, which is then extended by the C–E♭–D hinge. The latter hinge adds refinement and "tease" to the balancing act of these measures. Yet, as recomposed in Example 31, the omission of these hinges in the form of an a7–b5–a7–a7–b5 succession would not have made for an entirely improbable B statement. That Example 31 could indeed have figured as a semi-respectable alternative is at least partially owing to the fact that, following the a7–b5 recapitulation, the motivic order is reshuffled. Still, the pe-

EXAMPLE 31: "Evocation" (hypothetical version)

culiar tension of these measures cannot be said entirely to reside in the repetition of a string of unchanging motives. For instance, at nos. 125–26 in Example 30, to what extent is the second of the two successive b5's heard and understood as a "true" repeat of the first? Or in the recomposed version in Example 31, in what sense is the second of the two successive a7's perceived as a straightforward repeat of the first? The point seems to be that these repeats raise expectations of periodicity that, in a delicate balance between compliance and forced readjustment, are subtly either affirmed or rebuffed by subsequent motivic placement.

As was mentioned already, similar inferences may be drawn from the initial a7–b5 succession itself at no. 121 + 3. For with the half-note as the tactus, the opening bars initiate a $\frac{2}{2}$ periodicity in relation to which the $\frac{3}{4}$ bars are the disruptive troublemakers. Hence the tension of the repeat motive b5 relative to a7 may be traced (1) to the fact that seven misses eight by one, and (2) to the fact that b5 can in this sense be heard and understood as a syncopation in relation to a7—that, in other words, b5 becomes an offbeat contradiction of the onbeat identity of a7.

Here again the exposed repeat structure of the autograph version is instructive. As outlined in Examples 32a and b, the two sevens and their 4 + 3 subdivisions are a condensation, by one quarter-note beat for each 4 + 3 unit, of a square metrical scheme of two eights with subdivisions of 4 + 4. In other words, with the initial motive a7, a square periodic 4 + 4 unit is squeezed into an "irrational" one of 4 + 3; at m.3, the shortened repeat of a7 arrives one quarter-note beat too soon. And with the shrinkage of this 4 + 4 unit to 4 + 3, pressure tends to accumulate precisely at the juncture of the motivic repeats, that is, at the half-note C that invariably initiates repeats of both a7 and b5. (Note that the half-note C always falls on the downbeats of the irregular measures.) Thus while the initial C at m.3 serves first and foremost as the start of

EXAMPLE 32: "Evocation"

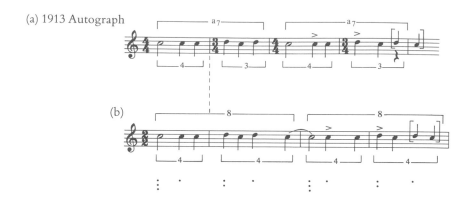

the shortened repeat motive, it never entirely severs its ties to a7 as a terminating element; at m.3, a7 is cut short and remains in this respect unfulfilled. (The impact of the condensation could be represented by an interminable succession of elision loops at the juncture of all a7/b5 repeats.) Hence the motivic repetition of Block B assumes, built in from the start, a tight, breathless quality. Always arriving a bit too soon, the repeats within a particular succession appear hurried and impatiently realized, always lacking the sense of a true rhythmic finality or resolution.

The second of the two factors mentioned above concerns b5 as a contradiction of a7. For with the trimming of $4 + 4$ to an "irrational" count of $4 + 3$, the shortened b5 repeat at m.3 assumes, in relation to a7, a syncopated identity. In accord with the $\frac{2}{2}$ periodicity as inferred from a7's opening $\frac{2}{2}$ bar, and in direct opposition to the fixed metric identity of the reiterating motives as defined by the shifting meter, the initial onbeat identity of motive a7 is contradicted by an offbeat placement at mm.3–4. These conclusions are outlined in Examples 33a and 33b, where brackets outline the background $\frac{2}{2}$ meter for the autograph and 1929 versions, and according to which the block is re-barred in Example 33c. And so, once again, fixed metric identity stands in opposition to displacement, the latter relying for its apprehension on a steady background frame of reference. Note that with the initial Block B statement at no. $121 + 3$, the concealed periodicity arrives on target with the foreground irregularity as the block is concluded four measures later.

A final step in this analysis is to situate these findings within the wider context of the two alternating Blocks A and B. Shown in Example 34, the total quarter-note count for Block B is twelve. And Block B is flanked by A

EXAMPLE 33: "Evocation"

(a) 1913 Autograph

(b) 1929 Revision

(c) Re-barred

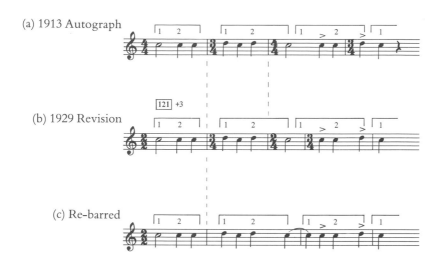

EXAMPLE 34: "Evocation"

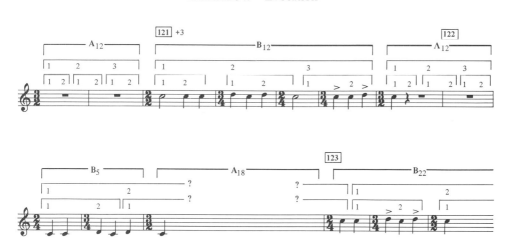

statements whose $\frac{3}{2}$ divisions likewise total twelve quarter-note beats. Almost immediately, however, this initial regularity is subjected to disruption. For in the echo statement of Block B at no. 122 + 1, the initial half-note C of motive a7 is dropped, a7 becoming a5. And in accord with the prevailing $\frac{2}{2}$ arrangement, the second half of a7's $\frac{2}{2}$ bar falls on the first or "strong" beat rather than on the second, as earlier at no. 121 + 3. Moreover, the $\frac{2}{2}$ scheme fails to coincide with the foreground irregularity at the conclusion of the echo statement; indeed, with the entrance of a5 at no. 123, the original $\frac{2}{2}$ "feel" has disappeared altogether. For at this point—indeed, perhaps already at the beginning of the echo statement—the initial fixed identity of a7 in its a5 condensed form holds sway, forcing the listener to readjust his/her periodic bearings. And the "play" of the "Evocation" thus unfolds in the manner described above. A7's initial bar stimulates expectations of periodicity which, with each displaced motivic repeat, are continually thwarted and then renewed in a kind of back-and-forth motion. This, in a nutshell, is the crux of the balancing act.

Of course, it could easily be argued that at the higher level of structure in Example 34, the 1–2–3 triple count of Block B at no. 121 + 3 is inherently unstable. For quite apart from the many psychological and physiological points that have traditionally been raised in support of the thesis of an innate duple preference in situations of this kind, Block B is an abbreviation of a conventional duple scheme.[41] As was shown already in Examples 32a and 32b, the 7 + 7 and 7 + 5 schemes of the autograph and 1929 revision are a condensation of a square 8 + 8 scheme, so that, at the higher level in the 1929 revision, a potential 1–2–1–2 count shrinks to 1–2–3. Yet a duple alternative at this level at no. 121 + 3 would not appreciably have altered the disruptive effect as sketched in Example 34 on behalf of the triple mold. Beginning with the downbeat at no. 121 + 3, the entrance of a5 in the echo statement at no. 122 + 1 would still have fallen "incorrectly" on a first, "strong" beat.

In Example 35 these implications are applied to the lengthy B statement at nos. 125–27 + 1. Here, a 1–2 duple scheme is pursued at two levels of structure while, underneath the excerpt, the brackets indicate the motivic repeats and hinges as surveyed in Example 30. And as is evident, the first major point of reckoning comes with motive a7 in the $\frac{3}{2}$ bar at no. 126 + 2, just after the a7/b5 overlap and the C–E♭–D hinge. For in accord with the prevailing $\frac{2}{2}$ meter, a7's half-note C enters "incorrectly" on the second, "weak" beat rather than on the first. Here again, however, the listener is likely to switch metrical gears, opting in favor of a7's fixed identity. But these implications are also short-lived. For the consequence of this readjustment is that b5 enters "incorrectly" on the beat at no. 127, a contradiction which in turn fails to arrive on

[41]Reflections on binary intuition can be traced back to the Renaissance theorist Franchinis Gafurius (1451–1522), *Practica Musicae*, trans. Irwin Young (Madison: University of Wisconsin Press, 1969). More recently, correspondences have been drawn between the binary count and automatic functions such as breathing and walking. Schenker invoked "the principle of systole and diastole inherent in our very being" as part of his argument regarding the "natural" two-ness of metrical structures. See Heinrich Schenker, *Free Composition (Der Freie Satz)*, trans. Ernst Oster (New York: Longman, 1979), p. 119. In Lerdahl and Jackendoff, *A Generative Theory of Tonal Music*, p. 101, the duple bias is introduced as a "metrical preference rule" regarding higher levels of structure in tonal music. It is discussed briefly and then dismissed in a different context in David Lewin, "Some Investigations into Foreground Rhythmic and Metric Patterning," in Richmond Browne, ed., *Music Theory: Special Topics* (New York: Academic Press, 1981), pp. 101–3.

EXAMPLE 35: "Evocation"

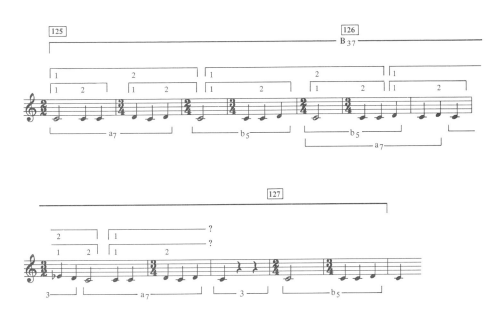

target with the irregular barring as the entire block draws to a close two measures later.[42]

As a final illustration, an outline of the "Evocation" as a whole is sketched in Chart 1. Here, of course, the design is similar to those introduced by Boulez in his extensive discussion of *The Rite*.[43] Note the sequential character of the format; within the alternation between Blocks A and B, principal statements of B alternate with the shorter echo statements. In addition, the echo statements retain a stable duration of five quarter-note beats for the condensed motive a5, while the remaining, principal statements expand from twelve to twenty-two and finally to thirty-seven beats in the lengthy block surveyed in Example 35. But as should by now be apparent, the perceptual implications of these measurements are far from "abstract." Heard and understood with reference to the double edge of fixed metric identity and displacement, they take on a lively sense of the "play" of this invention, its true *raison d'être*.

---

[42]Actually, the fixed metric identity of a7, and in particular of its initial $\frac{2}{2}$ bar, is likely to force readjustments in the $\frac{2}{2}$ periodicity as traced at the half-note level in Example 35. Accordingly, the Block B statement at no. 125 divides into three sections, defined motivically in terms of a7–b5, a7(+3), and a7(+3)−b5. Thus, too, the total count of thirty-seven quarter-note beats divides into three sections of twelve, ten, and fifteen beats.

[43]Boulez, *Notes of an Apprenticeship*, pp. 72–145. The most detailed analyses are those of the "Dance of the Earth," the "Glorification of the Chosen One," and the "Sacrificial Dance." Boulez ignored the "Evocation" altogether.

CHART 1: "Evocation"

A12   ┌──── B12 ────┐   A12   ┌─B5   (echo) ─┐
                            a7   b5   a5

A18   ┌──── B22 ────┐   A3   ┌─B5   (echo) ─┐
                           a5 a7 3 7   a5

A12   ┌──── B37 ────┐   A10   ┌─B5   (echo) ─┐
                       a7 b5 a7 3 a7 3 b5   a5

"Sacrificial Dance"

The kind of repeat structure that initiates Block B in the "Evocation" is by no means unique to this single movement. Similar configurations are found in the opening two bars of the "Ritual of the Rival Tribes," in the first two $\frac{5}{8}$ bars of the "Glorification of the Chosen One," and in the initial eight bars of the first section of the "Sacrificial Dance." Indeed, in the "Sacrificial Dance," a hidden $\frac{2}{8}$ meter leads to a higher-level 1–2–3 triple count, similar to that at no. 121 + 3 in the "Evocation," and in which connection similar implications of instability arise.

In Example 36 attention is drawn to the two principal motives a and b (labeled *cells* by Boulez).[44] And, as in Example 25 from the March of *Histoire,* subsequent repeats of these two units are aligned vertically and then marked off by dotted lines. Thus, too, fixed metric identity imposes itself along familiar lines. For notwithstanding the irregular $\frac{2}{16}$ and $\frac{3}{16}$ measures of the tiny submotives, a punctuation of D or a sixteenth-note rest always falls on the downbeats of these irregular measures, while the reiterating chord itself follows on the second sixteenth-note beat. Hence, as earlier, fixed identity or constancy tends to regulate the irregularity. But neither, of course, are these graphics strictly "mechanical" in conception, for the irregularity reflects an intent to retain a second beat "feel" for the reiterating chord—or, in relation to the eighth-note, an offbeat "feel."

Still, with the eighth-note inferred initially as the tactus with an assigned tempo marking of 126, a concealed $\frac{2}{8}$ periodicity emerges with little resistance, especially in view of the immediate, verbatim repeat of the a5–b7 succession and its higher-level (and "targeted") 1–2–3 count. Indeed, with subsequent repeats of motive b7, the details of displacement are similar to those pursued on behalf of the B–C♯–D–(E) sweep in *Histoire*'s opening March. Here, an

---

[44]Ibid., pp. 124–27.

EXAMPLE 36: "Sacrificial Dance"

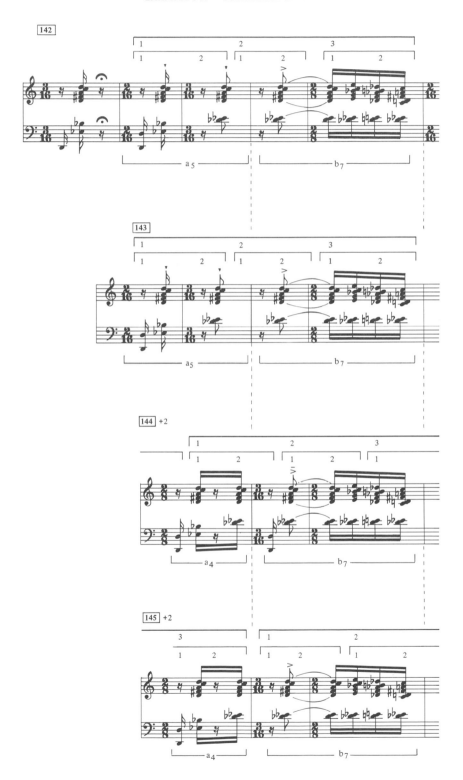

initial identity is established for motive b7 at nos. 142 and 143, which at no. 144 + 4 is displaced by an eighth-note beat, the reversal thus coming by way of the tactus. Finally, at no. 145 + 4 the displacement surfaces more conspicuously in the form of an offbeat-onbeat contradiction, and from this point on the struggle of fixed metric identity and displacement assumes its relentless and by now celebrated disposition.

Of course, the "Sacrificial Dance" does not have the convenience of a basso ostinato. And without question the impact of the disruption, of a periodicity constantly lost to the modification and reshuffling of the metrically fixed elements, is ultimately far more severe, far more disorienting. Yet the strategy itself remains unchanged. Even the more active role of the percussion in the climactic section at nos. 146–48 can revealingly be compared to the climactic stretch at mm. 50–57 in *Histoire,* as examined and discussed apropos of Example 25d.

A Conclusion

As a final suggestion it should again be noted that the "play" or double edge of Stravinsky's invention is not as new or as exceptional as might at first be imagined. For if, in past tonal music, measures were routinely added or deleted at higher levels of metrical structure with expectations of periodicity, disruption, and readjustment, then it can be seen that in Stravinsky's case these same processes were merely shifted to different and more immediate structural levels. Thus, to take a famous example already cited, in the first movement of Mozart's G Minor Symphony thematic statements are introduced at m. 1 and m. 20, so that, at some point in these first twenty measures, the two-measure module is broken as the accents at this level shift from the odd- to the even-numbered measures.[45] And in the first movement of Beethoven's Piano Sonata in D Major, Op. 10, No. 3, the repeat of the entire exposition can be heard and understood as embodying a similar contradiction or reversal at the two-measure level, with the accents at the even-numbered measures shifting to the odd-numbered measures at some point during the exposition.[46]

To be sure, the invention with Stravinsky presumes a new concept of motivic repetition, of harmony and formal outline. Yet the relationship here is important, because it points again to underlying assumptions of conventional dance periodicity. So, too, the radical-conservative dichotomy in perception shifts to another level of metrical structure.

[45]See Lerdahl and Jackendoff, *A Generative Theory of Tonal Music,* pp. 23–25.
[46]See Imbrie, " 'Extra' Measures and Metrical Ambiguity in Beethoven," pp. 45–51.

4

Rhythmic Structure

Prototypes

Most of the music examined thus far conforms to what has loosely been termed a *block structure*. Within such a framework, two or more blocks of relatively heterogeneous content are repeatedly and often abruptly juxtaposed. A simple illustration—simple as design only—can serve here as a useful departure.

In Example 37 the opening section of *Agon*'s "Bransle Gay" is reproduced in condensed form. As is apparent, the general outline corresponds to that at no. 46 in the "Ritual of Abduction" and, indeed, to the more extended format of the "Evocation." Two blocks, labeled A and B, alternate with one another, the first of these pacing successive appearances of the second. Here, of course, each block remains stable in duration. But even within the limitations of such a framework, the modification is subtle and typical. At m. 4, motive a7 is shortened to a5, while in the restatement of Block B at mm. 7–10 the motivic succession is reshuffled, a5–c7 now preceding a7–b5.[1] Of special note is the fixed registral and instrumental identity of

---

[1]The reasons for this reshuffling in motivic order can be traced to register and to a transposition of the hexachordal set. At the end of Example 37, the flute enters with a tight articulation of the set's C–G–F–B♭–A♭–B order, where the framing pitches C and B relate registrally to the C–B span between the first bassoon and second flute parts of motive b5. Note also that the steady $\frac{3}{8}$ meter arrives on target with the foreground irregularity as successive Block B statements are brought to a close. Still, a steady $\frac{2}{8}$ meter seems equally convincing for Block B and, indeed, the higher-level implications of this $\frac{2}{8}$ alternative, a 1–2–3 count for each of the two motivic orders a7–b5 and a5–c7, seems more plausible.

EXAMPLE 37:   *Agon* ("Bransle Gay")

each block or motivic unit: upon successive repeats, content remains fixed. And this is true even when, at mm. 7–10, the initial motivic order is reshuffled.

Nearly all the dance movements of *The Rite* conform in one way or another to the features and implications of this construction. Most conspicuous in Part I are the "Ritual of Abduction" and the "Ritual of the Rival Tribes" (both presently to be discussed), and, in Part II, the "Glorification of the Chosen One," along with the "Evocation" and the opening section of the "Sacrificial Dance" (as discussed already). The underlying principles of this structure, henceforth designated rhythmic Type I, may be summarized as follows.

1. Foreground metric irregularity; an irregular or shifting meter.
2. Two or more blocks of contrasting material alternate with one another in constant and often rapid juxtaposition. A block may consist of a single measure (which will correspond to the repeat of a single motivic unit or "cell") or of several measures (which will reflect the subdivision of a lengthier strand of material into smaller motivic units or "cells").
3. The irregular meter records the diverse lengths of the blocks, their internal "cellular" subdivisions, and subsequent extensions and contractions.
4. Upon successive restatements, blocks and their internal subdivisions remain stable in content. Moreover, within each block the horizontal lines or parts share the same rhythmic-metric periods (cycles or spans) as defined by the shifting meter; they proceed *en masse*, as it were, with no imitative dialogue or exchange. Thus, too, sharing the same periods as defined by the meter, these lines or parts are synchronized unvaryingly in vertical or harmonic coincidence; from one statement or repeat to the next, the vertical disposition is always the same. Blocks thus convey little internal sense of harmonic progress, such progress being possible only *between* blocks. And even the latter requires qualification, since, within the larger dimensions of a juxtaposition, the same blocks, modified or reordered, are always preceding or succeeding one another.
5. It follows from the above that the invention presupposed by Type I is fundamentally rhythmic in conception. A sense of "development," of progress, change, or movement, derives in large part from the lengthening, shortening, or reshuffling of the blocks and their internal subdivisions upon successive repeats.

A second type of construction, henceforth designated rhythmic Type II, is, in contrast, most often characterized by a steady meter. Structures adhering to this second type tend often to emerge as separate blocks at the end of extended movements, as with the passages at nos. 28–30 and 31–37 in the "Augurs of Spring," where reiterating fragments are brought together in a climactic fashion. Thus, too, the whole of the "Procession of the Sage," conforming in all particulars to Type II, surfaces without interruption as the climactic section of the preceding "Ritual of the Rival Tribes." On the other hand, the "Dance of the Earth" is an independently realized Type II structure, one of the lengthiest of its kind in Stravinsky's music. The general features of Type II are as follows.

1. Foreground metric regularity; most often, a steady meter.

2. The construction consists of a superimposition of two or more motives that repeat according to periods, cycles, or spans that are not shared but vary independently of, or separately from, one another. The periods of these re-iterating fragments may be stable (a motive whose duration is always four quarter-note beats, for example), or unstable (always changing in duration). (Pauses or rests that follow the repeat of a motive are always counted as part of its period.) As noted, the construction may emerge as one of the several blocks within a larger block structure or, in climactic fashion, as the concluding section to an extended movement.

3. The steady meter generally records the stable periods of one of the superimposed, reiterating fragments. In the "Procession of the Sage" at nos. 64–70, the $\frac{4}{4}$ scheme reflects the metric organization of the tuba fragment, whose periods, although irregularly spaced, project a steady $\frac{4}{4}$ periodicity. And in the "Dance of the Earth," the $\frac{3}{4}$ meter reflects the quarter-note motion of the F♯–G♯–A♯/C–D–E basso ostinato, in relation to which the periods defined by the reiterating fragments above are unstable or "mobile," being of unequal duration. Occasionally, a shifting meter is applied to a Type II construction, which will in turn reflect the unstable or "mobile" periods of one of the several reiterating fragments. In the climactic block of the Introduction to Part II at nos. 87–89, the $\frac{5}{4}$, $\frac{4}{4}$, and $\frac{3}{4}$ bars record the irregularly spaced entrances of the compound fragment in the clarinets and horns.

4. As with Type I, the reiterating fragments remain fixed registrally and instrumentally, with no imitative or developmental dialogue or exchange. But since, as indicated, these fragments repeat according to periods that vary independently of one another, they produce a vertical or harmonic co-incidence that is inconstant, constantly changing. But here, too, there are static implications, since this inconstancy in vertical coincidence is effected by reiterating fragments which, although repeating to independent periods, remain fixed in content.

5. It follows from the above that the invention presupposed by Type II is fundamentally rhythmic in conception. A sense of "development" has in large part to do with the synchronization and non-synchronization of the stable or unstable periods as defined by the reiterating fragments and with the vertical or harmonic implications of these shifts in alignment.

The true distinction between these types of rhythmic structure can best be gauged as it relates to the motivic or fragmental repetition. With the first of these two types, the individual motives, lines, or parts share the same irregular periods, as defined by the shifting meter. They proceed, as indicated, *en masse* and are hence synchronized unvaryingly in vertical or harmonic coincidence. Thus, in the opening block of *Les Noces* (Example 23 in Chapter 3), all the parts move in unvarying synchronization with the stressed, over-the-barline D–E succession, while the xylophone punctuates always, and only, the one particular D that, over the bar line, is succeeded by E as the point of departure and return. And with the initial B statement in the "Evocation" (Examples 27–34 in Chapter 3), all the parts unvaryingly coincide with the punctuation of C and its inflection D—or, in chordal terms, with the punctuation of (A--C–G–A–C–E) and its (G–D–G–B♭–D–E) inflection. On the other hand, with the second of these types the individual motives repeat according to periods that are not shared but vary independently of one another. These motives thus effect a vertical or harmonic coincidence that is constantly changing or shifting.

Even more critical from the standpoint of these distinctions is the play of fixed metric identity and displacement, the theme to which the present discussion has in large part been devoted. Actually, both types partake of the play or double edge. The difference is that with Type II felt displacement is graphically a part of the invention. The steady meter immediately exposes changes in the metric identity of the reiterating fragments, changes which, with Type I, are concealed by the foreground irregularity. On the other hand, the opposite side of this coin, fixed metric (or rhythmic) identity in repetition, is equally a part of Type II. But in place of Type I's shifting meter, fixed stress and slur markings are applied to the repeats of a reiterating fragment, which intone a counteracting sameness in identity irrespective of placement or subsequent displacement in relation to the steady meter. An account of the "Ritual of the Rival Tribes" and its succeeding "Procession of the Sage" can further explain these interactions.

"Ritual of the Rival Tribes"

As is shown below in Chart 2, the uninterrupted stretch that begins with the "Rival Tribes" at nos. 57–67 and extends through the whole of the "Procession" to "The Sage" at no. 71 divides into three large sections. As is evident, the construction in the first of these sections adheres to Type I; four contrasting blocks of material are

CHART 2: "Rival Tribes"/"Procession"

Section I:	nos. 57–62	II. nos. 62–64	III: nos. 64–71
	A B C B C A B A B D B D	C and E	D (Type II)

placed in abrupt juxtaposition to one another.[2] Indeed, in the original stage action, Blocks A and B accompanied the individual movements of two contending tribes, while Block C accompanied a type of tribal "clash." In Section II, extended repeats of Block C alternate with a new (E♭–A♭–C)–(D–F–A) chordal punctuation, labeled Block E in Chart 2. A gradual crescendo leads to the climactic Section III, which, beginning at no. 64 in the "Rival Tribes," runs through the whole of the "Procession." The latter is a single block conforming to Type II; at no. 64 the lyrical fragment of Block D is superimposed over a new reiterating fragment in the tubas, the theme of the Sage. Here the original scenario called for a gradual dispersal of the tribal "games" in anticipation of the arrival of the Sage. The Sage entered at no. 70 and blessed the earth with a "Kiss" to the accompaniment of the string-harmonic chord at no. 71.

The block structure of Section I is outlined in Example 38. In quarter-note beats, the brackets record the varying lengths of the four alternating blocks, their internal subdivisions, and subsequent modifications in block succession. Note the prolonged absence of Block C at nos. 58(+6)–62; it is eventually reclaimed at no. 62 as the principal block of Section II. Block D is in turn ignored in Section II, with its principal fragment retrieved at the beginning of Section III.

Attention in Example 38 is focused primarily on Block B and its two motivic units, a and b. There are five B statements in Section I, the first of which, at no. 57 + 2, introduces an a4–b3 motivic order as a point of departure. This is modified at no. 58 by a 4 + 2 delineation, which is reinforced at no. 59 by back-to-back 4 + 2 statements, the second of which features a transposition by a major third. The initial 4 + 3 division returns at no. 59 + 5 but is then followed, after an extended introduction of the new lyrical Block D, by a 4 + 4 + 2 statement. The specifications are summarized in Chart 3.

Obviously, the invariant element in these B statements is motive a, which retains the stable duration of four quarter-note beats. In contrast, motive b, varying between three and two beats, is mobile and as such determines the modification of subsequent B statements. Moreover, the mobility of motive b is in no way patterned. Yet, following the back-to-back 4 + 2 statements at no. 59, the restoration of its original 4 + 3 count at no. 59 + 5 may be felt as a welcome return to its—at this point—nearly forgotten point of departure.

Notice, too, that upon successive restatements, the horizontal motives, lines, or parts are fixed registrally in relation to one another. In accord with most structures adhering to Type I, these parts share the same irregular periods as defined by the shifting meter, so that the vertical disposition—the harmony or vertical alignment—remains unchanged from one statement to the next. (The disposition for Block B is given only for the initial two statements in Example 38; subsequent reentries do not deviate from this model.)

---

[2]The block labeled D in Section I refers to the passage at no. 43; the material here is derived from Block B in the "Rival Tribes." Recall that, according to the chronology of the sketchbook, the music of the "Rival Tribes," "Procession," and "Sage" was composed before that of the "Abduction."

EXAMPLE 38: "Ritual of the Rival Tribes"

CHART 3: "Rival Tribes"

no.57 + 2	B7	a: 4	b: +3
58	B6	4	+2
⌈ 59 ⌉	B6	4	+2
⌊ 59 + 1 ⌋	B6	4	+2
59 + 5	B7	4	+3
60 + 4	B10	4 + 4	+2

In Section I, the quarter-note is the tactus, with a tempo marking of 168. And since the meter shifts throughout by way of the tactus, perceptual adjustments are made with greater ease than in those instances where, as examined earlier, a dissection by smaller units of beat leads to an actual disruption of the pulse. Nonetheless, that Block B's initial 4 + 3 count at no. 57 + 2 might be heard and understood as an abbreviation of a "rational" 4 + 4 count (with, in other words, Block C entering a quarter-note beat too soon at no. 59 + 4) seems by no means farfetched. For it does appear that, pursuant to the higher-level duple implications of a steady $\frac{4}{4}$ periodicity beginning at no. 57 + 2, the downbeat at Block C at no. 58 + 2 acquires emphasis. In other words, the "irrational" sevens might here, as earlier, in the "Evocation," suggest the shrinkage of "rational" or "equal" counts of eight, so that the sense of an agitated or impatient movement in Section I derives not only from the modification in the length and succession of the alternating blocks but equally from the repeated denial of a true sense of rhythmic and metric resolution.

"Procession of the Sage"

Stretching from no. 64 in the "Rival Tribes" to the end of the "Procession," a condensed version of the climactic Section III is shown in Example 39. There are three principal fragments: a G–F–E–D motive in the strings at nos. 64–66, the G♯–G(F♯)–G♯–A♯–C♯ theme of the Sage in the tubas at nos. 64–71, and a D or A–D–C–D reiteration in the horns which enters at no. 65 + 2 and, along with the tuba fragment, continues to the close of the "Procession." And as noted, the G–F–E–D string motive stems from Block D, while the tuba fragment's G♯–F♯ whole-step reiteration derives from Block C. Indeed, to return briefly to the chronology of the sketchbook, the superimposition at no. 64 actually preceded the composition of Block C in Sections II and III. The material at no. 64 appears already on page 12 of the sketchbook, the first page devoted exclusively to the "Rival Tribes" and the "Procession." Similarly, the three-against-four motive of the bass drum was an early conception, appearing already on page 12 in two separate entries. (Some of these initial sketches were discussed in Chapter 2 in conjunction with Table 1 and

EXAMPLE 39

"Ritual of the Rival Tribes"

(continued)

EXAMPLE 39 *(continued)*

"Procession of the Sage"

Examples 5 and 6.) In addition, there is an important G♯/D basso ostinato which enters in the bassoons and contrabassoons at no. 66. This is subsequently complemented by a host of ostinatos, a thick, instrumental "fill" largely ignored in Example 39.

The construction of Section III conforms to Type II; the three fragments in the strings, tubas, and horns repeat according to periods, cycles, or spans that vary independently of, or separately from, one another. And of special note is the extreme mobility of the periods defined by each of these fragments. For not only do the periods vary independently of one another, they are in themselves unstable, being of unequal duration. (Compare, in Example 39, this instability with the spans of the bass drum motive, spans which, although varying separately from those of the three principal fragments, define a stable duration of three quarter-note beats.) Thus the duration of the horn's D or A–D–C–D reiteration, detached by rests until no. 70, is constantly altered. Bracketed in Example 39, the first appearance, at no. 65 + 2, spans six quarter-note beats; the second, at no. 65 + 3, eight beats; the third, at no. 66, thirteen beats (this is repeated twice); and the sixth, at no. 68 + 2, a full seventeen beats in a final stretching in this gradual expansion. And while, beginning at no. 64, the conflicting periods of the tuba fragment divide into "equal" or "rational" groupings of four and eight quarter-note beats in support of the steady $\frac{4}{4}$ meter, they, too, are mobile. Until no. 67, the number of G♯–G(F♯) reiterations that precede each G♯–A♯–C♯ repeat is sometimes one, sometimes two, but most often three.

All the same, as this massive block draws to a close at no. 70, the mobility is eventually curbed. The periods of the horn's A–D–C–D reiteration reach a stable duration of eight quarter-note beats, while, at no. 67, those of the tuba fragment attain a sequence of three G♯–G(F♯) reiterations to one G♯–A♯–C♯ repeat, a total of sixteen beats. Hence the conflict is resolved as the periods of these fragments, mobile or irregularly spaced at nos. 64–70, unite and stabilize in accord with the assigned $\frac{4}{4}$ meter.

But beyond these statistics, the conflict at nos. 64–71 stems far more readily from the play of fixed metric identity and displacement. As with most passages adhering to Type II, a steady meter is imposed: a $\frac{4}{4}$ meter at nos. 64–70, and a $\frac{6}{4}$ meter at no. 70. And apart from the network of pulsating ostinatos, this $\frac{4}{4}$ framework is by and large a reflection of the tuba fragment, whose periods, although mobile or irregularly spaced at nos. 64–67, divide into "rational" groupings of four and eight quarter-note beats. Then, set against this steady $\frac{4}{4}$ periodicity, the "irrational" counts of thirteen and seventeen beats prompt weak-strong or upbeat-downbeat contradictions on the part of the horn's A–D–C–D fragment. Entering on the fourth beat of the $\frac{4}{4}$ bar at no. 67, A–D–C–D is introduced as an upbeating succession. This is then contradicted at nos. 68 and 69 by strong-beat placements, A–D–C–D entering on the first and the third beat, respectively. Finally, at no. 70, and in keeping here with the resolution of the conflict, the initial upbeat identity is restored.

Nonetheless, in direct opposition to these displacements, the articulation of the A–D–C–D fragment remains unchanged. Irrespective of A–D–C–D's placement relative to the $\frac{4}{4}$ meter, fixed stress and slur markings intone a stubborn, counteracting sameness in identity; the A and D are always stressed, while the D–C–D unit is always slurred. Indeed, as in previous illustrations, these twin edges of fixed identity and displacement do eventually challenge the $\frac{4}{4}$ meter in a brief moment of disorientation. For after A–D–C–D's initial appearance at no. 67, the listener is apt to identify its stress and slur articulation with an upbeating identity. And while the first displacement, at no. 68, might be heard and understood as such, the second, at no. 69, is likely to provoke real uncertainty as to the "true" metric identity of A–D–C–D. And with the momentary loss of such identity (the loss of an orientation, really) comes the simultaneous loss of felt periodicity; listeners seeking to hold on to the initial identification might here begin to doubt the stability of the $\frac{4}{4}$ framework. Hence the forces of fixed identity and displacement reach an impasse; for a brief moment listeners might find themselves unable to place their trust in either one. Hence too, the resolution of the conflict at no. 70 comes more immediately, in the form of a restoration of fixed metric identity in relation to the $\frac{4}{4}$ mold. And while the meter shifts at this point to $\frac{6}{4}$, all the principal fragments adhere to a continuing $\frac{4}{4}$ division. The $\frac{6}{4}$ meter merely accommodates the conflicting accentuation of the percussion parts, accents which result in a further thickening of the texture at this point.

"Ritual of Abduction"

As with the "Rival Tribes" and the "Procession," the block structure of the "Ritual of Abduction" can be divided into three principal sections as shown below in Chart 4. Here, however, the construction of each section conforms in one way or another to Type I.

Focusing for the most part on Block A, Example 40 is taken from Sections I and II. Notice that while the "Abduction" has a $\frac{9}{8}$ meter as its point of departure, a $\frac{6}{8}$ scheme would have been at least equally plausible in this respect. The accompaniment figures of Block B at nos. 38 and 40+6 and those of Block A at nos. 40 and 44 fully underscore the $\frac{6}{8}$ division. (The assigned meter does in fact shift to $\frac{6}{8}$ at no. 42.) And as bracketed in Example 40, the $\frac{6}{8}$ meter invariably arrives on target as successive block statements are concluded. Indeed, with relatively crucial passages like those at no. 37+2 and nos. 44–47, the $\frac{6}{8}$ scheme yields considerable regularity at higher levels of structure. And this is true even with the wildly irregular climactic stretch at no. 46, labeled Section II in Chart 4.

Earlier, in connection with Example 14 in Chapter 3, attention was drawn to the principal fragment of Block A at nos. 37 and 40 and to its subsequent dissection at no. 46. Introduced within a $\frac{9}{8}$ framework (or, as bracketed in Example 40, within a $\frac{6}{8}$ framework), the fragment is carved up into irregular units of eighth-note beats; the new formation at no. 46 yields two alternating blocks, a punctuation of F which paces or marks off successive entrances of the irregularly sliced units. The impact of the passage is disruptive; both the meter and the pulse (here the dotted quarter-note

CHART 4: "Ritual of Abduction"

Section I:	nos. 37–46	II: no. 46	III: no. 47
	A B C A B C D A	A plus F-punctuation	Fragment derived from A plus chordal punctuation

EXAMPLE 40: "Ritual of Abduction"

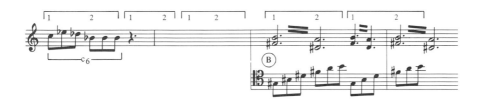

(continued)

EXAMPLE 40 *(continued)*

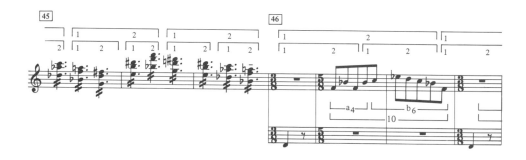

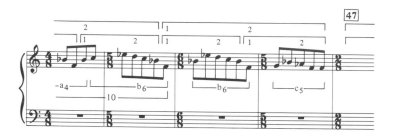

with a tempo marking of 132) are disturbed. And while the listener's attention might at first be directed toward some form of accommodation with the preestablished dotted quarter-note pulse, the persistence of the irregularity will more than likely force an abandonment of this effort—and of the established pulse in favor of the almost impossibly rapid eighth-note beat. This, in brief, is the nature of the disturbance.

Of course, as this disruptive stretch draws to a close at no. 47, the $\frac{6}{8}$ meter arrives on target with the foreground irregularity. And as is shown by the brackets in Example 41, regularity at higher levels of structure may readily be inferred. (The steady $\frac{9}{8}$ meter would also have emerged on target at no. 47, although with different hypermeasure implications.) Yet, as re-barred in Example 41, this climactic section seems curiously improbable. As the realization of a possible $\frac{6}{8}$ backdrop against which the disruptive effect is measured, it is singularly unconvincing.

EXAMPLE 41: "Ritual of Abduction" (re-barred)

There are several reasons for this. First, the punctuation of F on any beat other than a metrically accented one is bound to seem strange. Listeners bent on accommodation are apt to spot the punctuating F as an anchor, as a downbeat or metrically accented pitch, and to regulate the surrounding material accordingly. Second, and perhaps more especially, the metric identity of the reiterating fragment as re-barred in Example 41 fails to correspond to the initial identities as introduced at nos. 37 and 40. In other words, while the metric identity of the motive b6 (which is isolated as a separate entity at no. 40 + 3) remains constant, this fixed identity fails to conform to the earlier announced identities in relation to the steady $\frac{9}{8}$ or $\frac{6}{8}$ meter. Hence, if no. 46 does subtly admit to a steady background reference which the dissection seeks momentarily to challenge and overturn (and according to which the conservative listener might be expected to stake a claim), then it cannot persuasively rest with the re-barring as outlined in Example 41. Hence, too, in marked contrast to virtually all previous illustrations, the conveniently targeted sample proves unsatisfactory in the present case.

As is shown above in Example 40, Block A's reiterating fragment encompasses two separate identities. And in each of the block statements at nos. 37 and 40 these are presented successively; the motivic unit labeled b6 is repeated and shifted forward by an eighth-note beat. Thus, too, transposed to the level designated by no. 46, these two identities (or *placements* in relation to the $\frac{9}{8}$ or $\frac{6}{8}$ meter) are isolated and aligned vertically in Examples 42a and 42b. In Example 42a, the placement of motive a4 is such that the uppermost pitch E♭ falls on the accented dotted quarter-note beat, while in Example 42b, a4's placement shifts, allowing E♭ to fall forward by an eighth-note beat.

More simply, of course, these separate identities are part of a pattern of cyclical displacement. Taking as model the initial a4–b6 motivic order, the sum of ten eighth-note beats misses nine by one. Hence, as outlined in Examples 42a–42c, the overlapping tens are part of a sequential displacement on the part of the reiterating fragment. Example 43 offers a somewhat different view of these implications, where the sum of seven beats misses six by one. Following the third placement in the third and fourth measures of this example, a fourth shift forward would merely

EXAMPLE 42: "Ritual of Abduction"

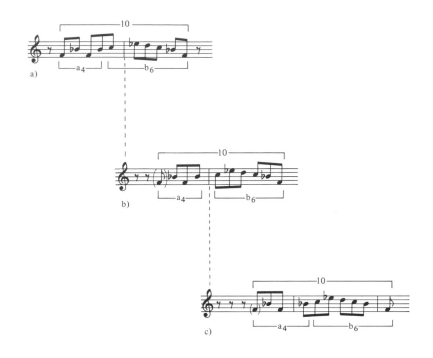

EXAMPLE 43: "Ritual of Abduction"

return the cycle to its point of departure. (Note that the third and final placement in Examples 42c and 43, ignored at nos. 37 and 40, corresponds to that proposed and rejected in connection with the targeted re-barring of no. 46 in Example 41.) The point of these illustrations is that in approaching the climactic passage at no. 46, the disruption will entail not merely the prior metric identity of a reiterating fragment but a patterned cycle of displacement in relation to the steady $\frac{9}{8}$ or $\frac{6}{8}$ meter.

Of course, the fact that the a4–b6 motivic order misses the sum of nine by one beat does eventually become the bone of contention, at no. 46. Severed from its initial $\frac{9}{8}$ or $\frac{6}{8}$ metrical bearings and hence from its sequential pattern of displacement, a4–b6 becomes isolated as a fixed component. Framed by the punctuation of F, which retains the dotted quarter-note beat as a stable duration, the sum of ten becomes "irrational" and hence disruptive in character. Further along, in the fourth, fifth, and sixth bars at no. 46, an elided a4–b6 order is followed by repeats of b6, a succession deceptively mirroring that at nos. 37 and 40.

Indeed, efforts at accommodation are likely to be subject to the following conditions: (1) that the punctuations of F fall on metrically accented dotted quarter-note beats, and (2) that subsequent repeats of motive b6 conform to one of the two identities exposed earlier at nos. 37 and 40 and outlined in Examples 42a and 42b. Both conditions are met by the re-barring proposed in Example 44. Thus, if the initial F of the a4–b6 motivic order is heard and understood as falling not on the dotted quarter-note beat but, as shown, on the eighth-note immediately preceding the beat (with a slight pause allotted to the initial F-punctuation), then the entire stretch until the final $\frac{5}{8}$ bar falls neatly into the framework as introduced at nos. 37 and 40. Following the initial bar, the metric identity of a4–b6 is repeated in slightly elided form, while all subsequent repeats of b6 are fixed in accord with the identity as defined in Example 42b.

But as an ironic twist to this conservative reading, the re-barred version of Example 44 is without the convenience of a target. Having shifted the climactic stretch backwards by an eighth-note beat, the proposed $\frac{6}{8}$ periodicity cannot emerge on target with the foreground irregularity at no. 47. Thus, in the final $\frac{5}{8}$ bar, the terminating motive c is stubbornly c5 (as earlier, at no. 37+4), not c6 (as later, at no. 40+4). And so there is in the final analysis no way of averting or "beating" the disruption; sooner or later its effect is felt, and an adjustment will have to be made to the difficult eighth-note beat. Still, the exercise of seeking out a logical, periodic alternative is far from futile. For as was indicated in Chapter 3, it is only by pursuing a path of accommodation that insight can be gained into the nature of the disruption, an effect that is in turn dependent on preestablished or readily inferrable implications of pulse, periodicity, and fixed metric identity.

As a final item here, the somewhat curious nature of the composer's initial notations for the music of the "Abduction" should be noted. For, as is shown in Example 3b in Chapter 1, the first entry for this movement appears already on page 7

EXAMPLE 44: "Ritual of Abduction" (re-barred)

of the sketchbook, a page that is ostensibly devoted to the "Spring Rounds." And this entry shows the sum of ten divided into two "irrational" bars of $\frac{5}{8}$, which are in turn followed by two bars of $\frac{6}{8}$ and $\frac{5}{8}$, respectively; in other words, a version of the principal fragment that very closely approximates that of the climactic section at no. 46 in the printed score. Indeed, transposed to the level of no. 46, virtually the same sketch appears on page 30—and here, too, before any sketches have appeared for the initial statement of the fragment at nos. 37 and 40. Under these circumstances it is difficult to imagine how the irregular barring of no. 46 could in fact have been conceived without reference to the steady periodicity of nos. 37 and 40; that is to say, without reference to the disruptive effect of this barring in relation to the earlier $\frac{9}{8}$ or $\frac{6}{8}$ periodic conceptions. On the other hand, the "Abduction" fragment had as its source melody no. 142 in the Juszkiewicz anthology of Lithuanian folk songs. And although, as was shown in Example 3a, this melody has a $\frac{2}{4}$ meter and is without any implications of cyclical displacement, a repeat structure is evident. Having jotted down the irregular conception as a reminder, the composer may have decided to trust his memory with the $\frac{9}{8}$ point of departure, but this, too, is conjecture. As a reflection of the compositional process, the sketchbook's first, occasional entries for the "Abduction" remain problematical.

5
Pitch Structure: A Russian Heritage

I was guided by no system whatever in *Le Sacre du printemps*. When I think of the other composers of that time who interest me—Berg, who is synthetic (in the best sense), Webern, who is analytic, and Schoenberg, who is both—how much more *theoretical* their music seems than *Le Sacre*; and these composers were supported by a great tradition, whereas very little immediate tradition lies behind *Le Sacre du printemps*. I had only my ear to help me. I heard and I wrote what I heard. I am the vessel through which *Le Sacre* passed.

Stravinsky and Craft, *Expositions and Developments,* pp. 147–48

To judge from the *Autobiography* and the later books of "conversation" with Robert Craft, Stravinsky harbored mixed feelings about his early years of apprenticeship with Rimsky-Korsakov.[1] At twenty-three years of age in 1905, he seems greatly to have liked and admired the patient, methodical ways of his teacher. Conducted twice a week and lasting for about three years, his lessons consisted in the main of assignments in orchestration. At the outset, piano reductions of Rimsky's operas were orchestrated and compared with the master's originals, and the young student must by these means have familiarized himself with nearly all of Rimsky's

[1]Igor Stravinsky, *An Autobiography* (New York: Norton, 1962), pp. 20–25; Igor Stravinsky and Robert Craft, *Memories and Commentaries* (Berkeley: University of California Press, 1981), pp. 54–60; Igor Stravinsky and Robert Craft, *Expositions and Developments* (Berkeley: University of California Press, 1981), pp. 41, 43–45.

scores. More significantly, his apprenticeship brought with it a recognition of both talent and serious intent, encouragement which seems to have been lacking within the confines of his immediate family circle. Rimsky had other composition students at the time, among whom Maximilian Steinberg, soon to become Rimsky's son-in-law, seems to have been regarded as the most promising. Yet there can be no overstating the spiritual and musical significance of this early bond. Stravinsky became a regular member of the Rimsky-Korsakov household, and for a time enjoyed the close friendship of Rimsky's two sons, Vladimir and Andrei. (*The Firebird* is dedicated to Andrei Rimsky-Korsakov.) Something like a father-son relationship must also gradually have transcended the teacher-pupil formality, and Rimsky was at this time, as Stravinsky later confessed, quite simply "*sans reproche.*"[2]

As these years drew to a close, however (Rimsky died in June, 1908), Stravinsky may well have become increasingly conscious of his teacher's limitations as a composer and instructor of composition. Although Rimsky was well versed in harmony and practical orchestral writing, his knowledge of composition itself "was not at all what it should have been."[3] Rimsky had in fact become something of a reactionary in his later years. He disliked the music of Debussy, and his retort following a performance of the latter's music has become legend: "Better not to listen to him; one runs the risk of getting accustomed to him, and one would end up by liking him."[4] Stravinsky, on the other hand, had become increasingly sympathetic to Debussy's music, as the opening pages of *The Nightingale*, composed in 1908–09 and in obvious imitation of "Nuages" in *Nocturnes*, clearly demonstrate. The influence can likewise be felt in the early cantata *Faun and Shepherdess* (1906), whose whole-tone passages affronted Rimsky's conservative bent.[5] Stravinsky would later quip that Rimsky's own "modernism" had at this time consisted of little more than "a few flimsy enharmonic devices."[6]

In both his operas and his symphonic poems Rimsky had drawn a distinction between the magical scenes or characters and the real or natural ones by complementing the former with music that was chromatic and instrumentally decorative and the latter with diatonic folk material (borrowed or pseudo) that was set rather simply in comparison. The chromatic side of this approach was often non-tonal; that is, it consisted of harmonic and melodic patterns that implied referential collections with interval orderings (scales) other than that of the diatonic collection and its familiar major and minor modes. The resultant scales were often symmetrical, outlining an (0, 4, 8) major-third or (0, 3, 6, 9) minor-third partitioning of the octave.

The general approach can be traced back to Mikhail Glinka. In *Ruslan and Lud-*

[2]Stravinsky and Craft, *Memories and Commentaries*, p. 57.
[3]Ibid.
[4]Stravinsky, *An Autobiography*, p. 18.
[5]Stravinsky and Craft, *Memories and Commentaries*, p. 59.
[6]Ibid.

milla (1842), the material that accompanies the evil sorcery of Chernomor in Act IV is a descending whole-tone scale, which, unadorned, is subsequently transposed down a fourth. Shown in Example 45, these implications are situated within a securely fastened diatonic framework whose tonal, E-major focus is never seriously undermined. Even the whole-tone transposition is in imitation of the tonic-dominant relationship.

Somewhat more elaborate is the passage shown in Example 46c from the overture to the opera. Here, a whole-tone scale on D descends in the bass, while major triads on D, B♭, and F♯ are outlined in the treble parts. The latter triads, whose roots define an (0, 4, 8) major-third partitioning of the octave, yield, in pitch-class content, the symmetrical (D C♯ B♭ A F♯ F (D)) set. Yet both chromatic hexachords, the (D C B♭ A♭ F♯ E (D)) whole-tone set and the (D C♯ B♭ A F♯ F (D)) set, are framed by material that is solidly diatonic and tonal, here in the key of D-major. The stressed connecting links between these sets are (1) the D, which, as a point of departure and return, assumes overall priority and determines scalar order; (2) the (0 4 8) augmented triad in terms of (D B♭ F♯), which is shared by the two chromatic hexachords; and (3) the (D F♯ A) tonic triad itself, shared by the D-major scale and the (D C♯ B♭ A F♯ F (D)) set. (If B♭ is interpreted as the flatted submediant in D-major—it functions as such earlier, in Example 46b—then (D B♭ F♯) becomes a pivot between all three referential categories. Indeed, since the (0, 4, 8) major-third cycle *descends* from the tonic in both Examples 45 and 46c, its first downward notch serves as a conspicuous link between the tonal, flatted submediant interpretation—the (B♭ D F) triad in Example 46c—and the cycle's symmetrical, non-tonal implications.)

EXAMPLE 45: *Ruslan and Ludmilla*

EXAMPLE 46: *Ruslan and Ludmilla*, Overture

D-major scale   Whole-tone scale

Given the obvious classical credentials of Glinka's opera, some of these deductions may seem a bit fussy. The overture follows the Italian model of the period in both form and general character. And the points of intersection are, as noted already, highly conspicuous: in Example 46c, the descending whole-tone scale is a variant of the tonal, chromatic descent earlier in Example 46b, while, motivically speaking, the (D, B♭, F♯) symmetrically defined triads are derived from the principal D-major theme. Yet it is these details of intersection or linkage that would become critically a part of Rimsky's application and, later, of Stravinsky's. In Stravinsky's case, reiterating fragments are often conspicuously preserved as connecting links or pivots between blocks or sections of material that are otherwise referentially distinct.

Rimsky's symmetrical patterns, although occasionally derived from the whole-tone scale or the (0, 4, 8) relation, spring more persistently from what has become known as the *octatonic pitch collection*.[7] This is a set of eight distinct pitch classes which, confined to the octave and arranged in scale formation, yields the symmetrical interval ordering of alternating half and whole steps or whole and half steps. (In his autobiography, Rimsky identified the scale according to its half step–whole step ordering.)[8] And apart from the diminished-seventh chord, there are two principal schemes of partitioning, the first of these harmonic in conception, the second exclusively melodic: in harmony, a partitioning or slicing up of the collection (with overlapping pitch content) by major and minor triads and dominant-seventh chords, and, in melody, a partitioning by the so-called minor or Dorian tetrachord whose 2–1–2 or whole step–half step–whole step interval ordering yields a pitch numbering of (0 2 3 5), reading up or down. (Conventional terminology is employed for purposes of identification. The larger symmetrical sets preclude tonally functional relations, which are founded referentially on the major-scale ordering of the diatonic set.)

In the passage from *Sadko* (1896) in Example 47, the major triads and dominant sevenths partition the octatonic octave at C, E♭, F♯, and A, the latter pitches constituting the roots of the triadic succession. The pitch-class content, shown in Example 47, yields the (C D♭ E♭ E F♯ G A B♭ (C)) octatonic reference collection. On the other hand, in Example 48 from Scene I in *Kastchei the Immortal* (1902), the reiterating (C D E♭ F) melody at no. 33 is subsequently transposed to (F♯ G♯ A B); the two (0, 6) tritone-related (0 2 3 5) tetrachords jointly yield the (C D E♭ F F♯ G♯ A B (C)) collection and ordering. Later, at nos. 38 and 43 in Scene I, this material in Example 48 is restated as a cohesive octatonic block. Notice the 0–11 or major-seventh interval that spans the (C D E♭ F) (F♯ G♯ A B) tetrachords, C–B, and the (C E♭ F♯ A) diminished-seventh figuration in the accompaniment.

---

[7] The first to examine octatonic pitch relations systematically in Stravinsky's music was Arthur Berger in his "Problems of Pitch Organization in Stravinsky," in Benjamin Boretz and Edward T. Cone, eds., *Perspectives on Schoenberg and Stravinsky* (New York: Norton, 1972), pp. 123–54. Berger's conclusions are further developed in Pieter C. van den Toorn, *The Music of Igor Stravinsky* (New Haven: Yale University Press, 1983).

[8] *My Musical Life*, trans. Judah A. Joffee (New York: Tudor, 1935), p. 72.

EXAMPLE 47: *Sadko*

The octatonic passages in Stravinsky's early works do not differ significantly from those of Rimsky. In fact, *The Firebird* adheres closely to the dual approach outlined above. The music of King Kastchei and of the magical scenes generally is accompanied by symmetrical patterns (often octatonic, as in the Introduction and, later, at the beginning of the *Danse infernale*), while the natural or sentimental scenes are for the most part diatonic in character (as in the Khorovod and the Finale). Moreover, a pattern of alternating major and minor thirds in the Introduction is clearly derived from Rimsky's *Kastchei the Immortal*; compare, in Example 49, the two passages from Scene I in Rimsky's opera to the figuration at mm. 1–9 in *The Firebird*, Example 50.[9]

---

[9]For a more detailed analysis of *The Firebird* introduction see van den Toorn, *The Music of Igor Stravinsky*, pp. 1–17. The *Kastchei-Firebird* connection is pursued at greater length in Richard Taruskin, "Chernomor to Kastchei: Harmonic Sorcery; or, Stravinsky's 'Angle,' " *Journal of the American Musicological Society* 38, 1 (1985): 72–142.

EXAMPLE 48: *Kastchei the Immortal*

EXAMPLE 49: *Kastchei the Immortal*

EXAMPLE 50: *The Firebird*

More specifically, too, the octatonic vocabulary in these early Stravinsky works is in large part drawn from Rimsky. Completed just before Rimsky's death, the *Scherzo fantastique* (1908) contains passages that exemplify both the harmonic and melodic conceptions as detailed above. Three (0, 3, 6, 9) symmetrically defined successions of triads and dominant sevenths are shown in Example 51, while a succession of overlapping (0 2 3 5) tetrachords appears in Example 52. And these are only a few of the many octatonic sequences that may readily be inferred from the *Scherzo*. Like a whirlwind, the piece moves from one such sequence to the next, often on an explicit basis, wholly unimpaired by "outside" interference. Moreover, the emphasis on the (B C D D♯ F F♯ G♯ A (B)) set, to which all four sequences in Examples 51 and 52 adhere, is no accident. Tonally, the *Scherzo* begins and ends in B major, with the (B D♯ F♯) triad, common to the B-major scale and the (B C D D♯ F F♯ G♯ A (B)) set, serving as the principal point of intersection. And note, in Example 52, the (D♯ F♯ A C) diminished-seventh chord sustained as an accompaniment to the (0 2 3 5) tetrachordal fragments. This relates conspicuously to Rimsky's (0 2 3 5) tetrachordal application in Example 48 from *Kastchei the Immortal*.

More directly to the point here: all of these formulae are as pertinent to *The Rite* as they are to the early *Scherzo fantastique* and *The Firebird*. Indeed, *The Rite* is one of the most thoroughly octatonic of Stravinsky's works, rivaled in the explicit nature

EXAMPLE 51:   *Scherzo fantastique*

EXAMPLE 52: *Scherzo fantastique*

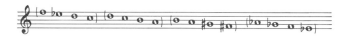

and persistence of this reference only by pieces such as the cited *Scherzo*, *Petrushka*, and, much later, the *Symphony of Psalms* (1930) and the *Symphony in Three Movements* (1945). And to an astonishing degree, the vocabulary that informs this referential commitment remains intact: triads, dominant sevenths, and (0 2 3 5) tetrachords. The distinction rests primarily with the technique of superimposition. In *The Rite*, the (0, 3, 6, 9) symmetrically defined units no longer succeed one another, harmlessly, as they do in the operas of Rimsky or in the early Stravinsky passages cited above. These units are now superimposed—played simultaneously. And this is an invention from which startling implications accrue not only in pitch organization but, as a consequence, in rhythm and instrumental design as well. It radically alters the conditions of octatonic confinement, opens up a new dimension in octatonic thought that Stravinsky, beginning with *Petrushka* and *The Rite*, was to render peculiarly his own.

Thus, in Example 53, from the "Ritual of Abduction" in *The Rite*, the (0, 3, 6, 9)–related dominant sevenths on C, E♭, F♯, and A are now superimposed. And in Example 54, from the "Ritual of the Rival Tribes," a reiterating (G F E D) tetrachord in the strings is superimposed over its lower (0, 6) tritone-related (C♯ (B) A♯ G♯) tetrachord in the tubas.

True enough, as illustrations of earlier formulae these two passages in Examples 53 and 54 are relatively straightforward. *The Rite* encompasses in addition a strong diatonic current, evident particularly in the dance movements of Part I,

EXAMPLE 53: "Ritual of Abduction"

along with significant chromatic vertical structures which, if not entirely unrelated to the octatonic framework, are at least locally non-octatonic in appearance. (See the ornamental F♯ in Example 54 which, substituting occasionally for the G, lies outside the octatonic reference collection indicated.) Moreover, the technique of superimposition, however closely identified with Stravinsky's music, is by no means without precedent. Although *Petrushka*'s tritone-related (A♯ C♯ F♯/C E G) chord is routinely cited as the first instance of superimposition, the first case of a "bitonal" clash, earlier examples are available. In his monumental study of the early Russian origins of Stravinsky's music, Richard Taruskin has unearthed similar

EXAMPLE 54: "Ritual of the Rival Tribes"

configurations in the music of Maximilian Steinberg.[10] Steinberg's *Prélude symphonique* (1908), composed, like Stravinsky's *Chant funèbre* (1908),[11] in memory of Rimsky-Korsakov, contains *Petrushka*-like chords that are undoubtedly among the very first of their kind. Midway into this piece the (B D♯ F♯) and (F A C) triads are *superimposed*, and even the tremolo, a specifically pianistic conception in *Petrushka*, is in evidence. Without question, the octatonic vocabulary of Rimsky and his school, however radically transformed by techniques of superimposition and by the rhythmic-metric innovations surveyed in earlier chapters, remains a fundamental part of the harmonic and melodic design of *The Rite*.

Indeed, the peculiar "dissonance" of *The Rite* can often be traced to the 0–11 or major-seventh span of the octatonic scale's 2–1 or whole step–half step ordering; see, in Example 54 from the "Ritual of the Rival Tribes," the metric accentuation of the G♯–G span which, reading down, encompasses the two reiterating (0 2 3 5) tetrachords, (G F E D) and (C♯ (B) A♯ G♯). Elsewhere in *The Rite* it is merely the upper of these two tritone-related tetrachords that stands in a kind of fixed, polarized opposition to a lower pitch number 11. Either way, the effect is insistent and

---

[10]An as yet untitled manuscript to be published by the University of California Press. The example from Steinberg's *Prélude symphonique* is also cited in Richard Taruskin, "*Chez Petrouchka*: Harmony and Tonality *Chez Stravinsky*," *19th Century Music*, forthcoming. A source of many of these tritone-related configurations was the Coronation scene in Mussorgsky's *Boris Goudunov*, where dominant sevenths alternate on D and A♭. These chords are not superimposed, however, but merely oscillate over a C–F♯ pedal.

[11]The score of this early *Chant funèbre* for wind instruments was unfortunately lost during the First World War. See Stravinsky and Craft, *Memories and Commentaries*, p. 59.

harsh, and it accounts in large measure for the consistency that may be inferred throughout on the part of the octatonic component.

Pierre Boulez once described *The Rite* as a piece in which a "vertical chromaticism" stood opposed to a "horizontal diatonicism."[12] By this he meant that while the vertical alignment is often chromatic, the individual parts are in themselves often simple and diatonic. Here, of course, the just-noted 0–11 interval span may define the "vertical chromaticism," while the (0 2 3 5) tetrachord often accounts for the simple "diatonicism" of the principal parts. And the "conflict" which has always seemed such an essential aspect of *The Rite* can no doubt revealingly be defined in terms of a vertical-horizontal, chromatic-diatonic opposition, as can, apropos of its "horizontal diatonicism," the fact that the term *dissonance* may yet seem appropriate even if conventional considerations of treatment no longer apply.[13]

Beyond this, however, Boulez's description quickly became deceptive. For as can be seen from the illustrations in this chapter, the (0 2 3 5) tetrachord is a subset of both the octatonic and the diatonic collections. In fact, by way of this neutrality, it often serves as an articulative connecting link between blocks or sections of material that are referentially distinct in this respect. Hence, too, the "conflict" or "opposition" in pitch structure has as much to do with the symmetrical conditions of octatonic confinement, and with the articulation of the octatonically conceived 0–11 vertical interval span, as with the vertical-horizontal or chromatic-diatonic oppositions noted by Boulez.

In a similar vein, Boulez drew attention to the techniques of superimposition, juxtaposition, and repetition; these, he averred, were the key to Stravinsky's art.[14] Curiously, however, these references were never amplified by a study of pitch structure that is in any way comparable to his analysis of rhythm, and many of his more concrete observations are seriously misleading. Although cognizant of the vocabulary of triads, dominant sevenths, and (0 2 3 5) tetrachords, and of the static implications that arise from the superimposition of this vocabulary, Boulez discussed these matters in a generally unsympathetic tone. Superimposition was viewed as an "irreducible aggregation," a "coagulation" that creates for the superimposed fragments and chords a "false counterpoint," all of this "eminently static in the sense that it coagulates the space-sound into a series of unvarying stages."[15] More significantly, "coagulation" was defined solely in terms of "complexities grafted onto the old organization,"[16] "complexities" that in turn constitute little more than a "surcharge of an existent [tonal] language."[17] In other words, it was the conventional diatonic (even tonal) identification of the triads, dominant sev-

---

[12]Pierre Boulez, *Notes of an Apprenticeship*, trans. Herbert Weinstock (New York: Knopf, 1968), p. 74.

[13]See Arnold Whittall, "Music Analysis as Human Science? *Le Sacre du Printemps* in Theory and Practice," *Music Analysis* 1, 1 (1982): 33–34. The idea of a "conflict" being tied to a dissonance-consonance distinction is central to Whittall's thesis, although he fails to define the specific terms of this relationship.

[14]Boulez, *Notes of an Apprenticeship*, pp. 61–62.

[15]Ibid., pp. 249–50.

[16]Ibid., p. 74.

[17]Ibid., p. 250.

enths, and (0 2 3 5) tetrachords that attracted his attention. He overlooked the new referential status, the octatonically conceived nature of the vocabulary, of the superimposition, "vertical chromaticism" or "coagulation." Similarly, the notion of "polarity," of an ambiguity in pitch-class priority, was interpreted not in terms of the (0, 3, 6, 9) symmetrically defined partitioning elements of the octatonic collections (as is often conspicuously the case in *The Rite* and indeed in much of Stravinsky's music), but, anachronistically again, in terms of a subdominant-tonic-dominant relation.[18]

Indeed, Boulez's critique revolved around an unsettling impasse. On the one hand, the vertical structures, being static, "easily manageable materials," allow for an "extreme boldness" in the rhythmic design (which for Boulez is the real treasure of *The Rite*).[19] On the other hand, these same vertical structures, which comprise the harmonic vocabulary and syntax of *The Rite*, are at the heart of the "Stravinsky Impossibility," of a "miserable insolvency" in compositional technique that rendered the neoclassical change of heart, the meek "nostalgia" of Stravinsky's neoclassical ways, all but inevitable.[20] Far from an aesthetic volte-face, for Boulez neoclassicism was an escape, a move of practical necessity triggered by the backwardness of the composer's harmonic and melodic materials. The idea of Stravinsky having lacked a "melodic gift" and of his consequent dependence on borrowed "stuff" also figures in Boulez's account, although this argument receives greater emphasis in the criticism of Cecil Gray, Constant Lambert, and Theodor Adorno, as surveyed earlier in Chapter 3.

Of course, triadic succession of the kind illustrated in the octatonic passages by Rimsky, Steinberg, and Stravinsky cited above *does* have a place in the tonal tradition. In Example 55 a passage from the second movement of Brahms's Third Symphony serves as illustration. Here, a transition leading back to the principal C-major theme is composed of a chromatic sequence that includes dominant-seventh chords on F and D; the second of these chords, serving as V–of–V, resolves to the tonic. The complete (0, 3, 6, 9) symmetrical sequence, with dominant sevenths on F, D, B, and A♭, sketched in Example 56, was a favorite of Brahms's. But seldom was the minor-third cycle allowed to run its course. In Example 55, from the Third Symphony, the sequence is transitory and incomplete; it stops at the second notch, the dominant seventh on D, and the symmetrical potential is in no way allowed to disrupt the tonal orientation. (A single instance in the whole of Brahms's *oeuvre* where this minor-third cycle is both complete and without the chromatic passing tones and chords of Examples 55 and 56 occurs in the closing measures of the song *Immer leiser wird mein Schlummer*, opus 105/2. Major triads on E, G, and B♭ appear in succession just before the final cadence on D♭.)[21]

---

[18]Ibid., p. 74.

[19]Ibid., p. 75.

[20]Ibid., pp. 14, 247.

[21]Much earlier examples of complete, locally realized major- and minor-third cycles are found in the opening measures of the Sanctus of Schubert's Mass in E♭ (1824), in the Coda of the first movement of

EXAMPLE 55: Third Symphony (Brahms)

EXAMPLE 56

On a more elementary level, the individual progressions in Examples 55 and 56 figure among the familiar "irregular resolutions" of the dominant-seventh chord. In Example 57, the dominant seventh on F is followed "irregularly" or "deceptively" by the dominant seventh of the submediant (in other words, down one notch in the (0, 3, 6, 9) minor-third cycle). And with proper voice-leading intact, this was of course standard fare from the Baroque era through the nineteenth century, available in the secondary-dominant realm and with all manner of variety in chordal disposition.

Schubert's C-Major Symphony, and in Liszt's first symphonic poem, *Ce qu'on entend sur la montagne* (1848). These and other examples of complete cycles are examined in detail in Taruskin, "Chernomor to Kastchei," pp. 79–92. Taruskin traces the origin of both the whole-tone and the octatonic scale to the imposition of passing tones between the three and four nodes of these two symmetrical scales (not, in other words, to the mere ornamentation of the augmented and diminished chords). More significantly, he shows that Rimsky's octatonicism derived specifically from these and similar passages in Schubert and Liszt. For a set-theoretic approach to Liszt's non-tonal music, see Allen Forte, "Liszt's Experimental Idiom and the Music of the Early Twentieth Century," *19th Century Music*, forthcoming.

EXAMPLE 57

Still, it is just this kind of associative factor, of a link between the tonal tradition of "enharmony" and the chromatic patterns of Rimsky-Korsakov and his school, that enables us to move quite smoothly from Boulez's comments on Stravinsky (Stravinsky's mere "surcharge of an existent [tonal] language") to Stravinsky's earlier-noted remarks on Rimsky-Korsakov. For it is altogether probable that when Stravinsky dismissed his teacher's "modernism" as having consisted of little more than "a few flimsy enharmonic devices," a variant of the tonal, enharmonic conception of the (0, 3, 6, 9) minor-third cycle, as demonstrted in Examples 55 and 56, lay somewhere in the back of his mind. True, according to his own testimony, Rimsky was conscious of the octatonic collection as a cohesive frame of reference, and hc followed through with its full (0, 3, 6, 9) symmetrical potential on an explicit and unimpaired basis. (See Example 47 from *Sadko*.) But Rimsky did not superimpose, nor did he juxtapose *à la* Stravinsky. Consequently, owing to triadic succession and conventional voice-leading, tonally conceived enharmony may have been—and may still be—as apparent as "octatonic accountability."

So, too, in his brief dismissal of Rimsky's "modernist" credentials, Stravinsky may well have forgotten both the nature and the scope of his debt.[22] Indeed, not once in his six books of "conversation" with Robert Craft did he mention the octatonic scale, or did he acknowledge, in his "composing with intervals," the frequent confinement of these intervals, in works of the early "Russian," neoclassical, and early serial periods, to the octatonic pitch collection. Given the evidence, however, there can be little question but that Stravinsky, like his predecessors, remained conscious of the octatonic collection as a constructive and referential factor. And it is toward a proper definition of these implications that the present analysis of pitch structure will largely be directed.

[22]Stravinsky and Craft, *Memories and Commentaries*, p. 59.

6

Part I: Pitch Structure

Sketches for the "Augurs of Spring"

Page 3 of the sketchbook of *The Rite*, reproduced in Figure 3 and transcribed in Example 58, consists of nine entries for the beginning of the "Augurs of Spring." At first glance it would appear that the fifth and sixth lines at the bottom of this page, each with four staves, were composed as a single entry. However, if these lines are read as a continuation of the fourth line directly above (where the "Augurs of Spring" or "motto" chord first appears), then the last three lines constitute, in proper succession, a remarkably accurate account of nos. 13–17 of the score. (Observe that the accentual pattern of the repeated chord, eight measures in length, is fully realized. The score itself extends, at the end of the fourth line, the Db–Bb–Eb–Bb ostinato from two to four measures. The syncopated offbeat figure of the first measure of the last line is eliminated, while the sustained octave C of this line, "2 ob.," becomes a syncopated, upbeat reiteration.) Moreover, inasmuch as pages 4–5 (not shown here) are a further continuation of this sketch extending all the way to the "break" at no. 22, these first three pages of musical notation in turn constitute an accurate account of nos. 13–22. The instrumental cues attached to the last three lines of page 3 are also of considerable interest. The mark "x" at the fifth measure of the last line refers back to the second line's third entry: the latter, inserted sideways and in red ink, was added as an instrumental footnote to the syncopated chord of fifths.

FIGURE 3: Early jottings and sketches for the "Augurs of Spring," page 3 of the sketchbook of *The Rite. The Rite of Spring (Le Sacre du Printemps) Sketches*, 1911–1913, © copyright 1969 Boosey & Hawkes Music Publishers Ltd. Reprinted by permission of Boosey & Hawkes, Inc.

EXAMPLE 58:   Sketchbook, p. 3 ("Augurs of Spring")

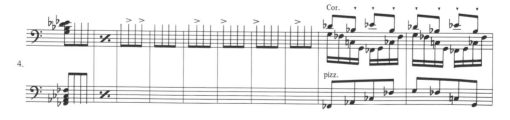

(continued)

EXAMPLE 58 *(continued)*

EXAMPLE 58 *(continued)*

In his commentary to the sketchbook, Robert Craft has remarked that such details were unusual at so early a stage in the conception of a Stravinsky work.[1]

Pages 5 and 6 are likewise ostensibly devoted to the "Augurs of Spring." They include a sketch for the "break" at no. 22, entries for the new horn melody at no. 25, and a brief jotting at the bottom of page 5 for the transition or "modulation" at no. 30. Most elaborate, however, is a six-stave sketch at the top of page 6 for the beginning of the first climactic block at nos. 28–30. The latter even includes the melody, introduced by the trumpets at no. 28 + 4 of the score, that would subsequently serve as the principal motive of the "Spring Rounds." Following its appearance at the top of page 6, the succeeding material of pages 7–9 is in fact given almost entirely to the "Spring Rounds." (Recall that this was the original order of the dances: "Spring Rounds" followed the "Augurs of Spring," while the "Ritual of Abduction" came after the "Rival Tribes" and its succeeding "Procession." According to Craft, the "Spring Rounds" melody was one of Stravinsky's earliest ideas.)[2] The sketches for the "Augurs of Spring" on pages 3–6 underscore the prin-

[1]Robert Craft, "Commentary to the Sketches," Appendix I in the accompanying booklet to Igor Stravinsky, *The Rite of Spring: Sketches 1911–1913* (London: Boosey and Hawkes, 1969), p. 4.
[2]Ibid., p. 6.

cipal divisions of this movement as a whole. At the end of the Introduction there is a brief preparation or transition at no. 12. This is followed at nos. 13–22 by Section I, where the motto chord is first introduced, and then at nos. 22–30 by Section II, where two new melodies appear and the motto chord is dropped. Finally, the transition or "modulation" at no. 30 leads to Section III at nos. 31–37, the final climactic block of the "Augurs of Spring."

Somewhat puzzling in relation to the extended sketch are the initial jottings at the top of page 3. Not that the relationship of these entries to the "Augurs of Spring" at nos. 13–22 is in any way obscured. Except for the second line's second entry, where the chords are part of the Introduction's preparatory block at no. 12, all entries refer unambiguously to the extended sketch on pages 3–5. Puzzling, rather, is the immediacy of some of these jottings compared to the surprising gaps evidenced by others. The third notation of the first line is an accurate spelling of m. 3 of the last line. On the other hand, the first entry's syncopated offbeat figure is inaccurate, down a whole step from its pitch at m. 5 in the fifth line.[3] And the (B♭ A♭ G F) melody of the third line, while prefacing (C B♭ A G) at m. 6 in the last line and (B♭ A♭ G F) in the bassoons on page 4 (no. 19 in the score), is, in relation to the latter, two octaves too high and in sixteenth-notes.

All these jottings were undoubtedly composed in preparation for what follows below. Yet the extended sketch, in its overall comprehension and detail, exhibits such a stunning command of the "Augurs of Spring" at nos. 13–22 that the discrepancies revealed by some of these entries are not easily reconciled. Irrespective of whether pages 3–5 do comprise Stravinsky's first notations for the "Augurs of Spring," it is tempting to suppose that the extended sketch had been with the composer for some time prior to actual notation and that the prefatory jottings on page 3 were entered as "soundings" with a preexistent view toward the more precise plan of action detailed below.

Noteworthy in this respect are the sketchbook's initial entries for the "Glorification of the Chosen One" on pages 52, 59, 61, and 66–67 and those for the "Sacrificial Dance" on pages 84–85. These, as noted in Chapter 2, reveal a similarly developed character. And the role of the piano in Stravinsky's inventive processes, early on as an aid in improvisation and then in a constant "testing" of the ear, cannot sufficiently be stressed. Notice, for example, the easy right-hand–left-hand "lie" of the motto chord itself, which underscores the chord's compound nature, its triadically sealed top and bottom "halves." Here, too, then, the pianistic element is most conspicuous in those entries which are at the outset highly developed, suggesting the early, improvisational origin of this material. In contrast, the sketches for the Introduction to Part II and the "Mystic Circles of the Young Girls," material that lacks such a pianistic orientation, are among the most extensive and seemingly arduous in the sketchbook.

---

[3] Recall from Chapter 1 that this upbeat figure accompanied one of the composer's earliest ideas for the stage action, namely, that of "the old woman in a squirrel coat."

Indeed, when Stravinsky first examined the sketchbook after a period of some fifty years, he cited as his first notation on page 3 not the initial jottings but the motto chord at the fourth line (along, presumably, with its rhythmic pattern, eight measures in length).[4] And the foundational status of this chord has long been taken for granted. Earlier in the century, in his revisionist interview with *Comoedia*, Stravinsky claimed that the "embryo" of *The Rite*, "strong and brutal" in character, had been conceived while completing *The Firebird* in the spring of 1910.[5] André Schaeffner's biography, where much of the information is known to have come from the composer himself, acknowledged the chord as "the first musical idea," composed, however, during the summer of 1911.[6] Craft gave a similar account: the composer continued to single out the "focal chord" of *The Rite*, the E♭ dominant seventh superimposed over (E G♯ B), as his initial idea.[7] (Craft in turn analyzed the top half of the chord, the dominant seventh itself, as "a root idea of the entire piece.") Indeed, in an added reflection that points to both its keyboard, improvisational origin and its apparent isolation from whatever else might at the time have been engaging the composer musically, Stravinsky recalled that he had initially been unable to explain or justify the chord's construction, but that his ear had nonetheless "accepted it with joy."[8] (The chord's immediate "justification" is readily apparent on page 3, in its relationship to the D♭–B♭–E♭–B♭ ostinato and the (E G♯ B) arpeggio of the second line, a relationship which is in turn stressed registrally at the end of the fourth line.) But Craft later reversed himself. Citing his intimate acquaintance with the composer's working habits, he concluded in his commentary to the sketchbook that there was no reason to doubt the left-to-right and top-to-bottom "chronological order" of page 3: the melodic conception of the chord, the D♭–B♭–E♭–B♭ ostinato and its (E G♯ B) accompaniment in the initial jottings, had come first, while the chord at the fourth line had come as a subsequent verticalization of this conception. He discussed the matter with the composer, who later agreed that this was "probable."[9]

At issue, of course, is not the authenticity of a left-to-right and top-to-bottom reading of page 3 (with the jottings preceding the fourth line), but whether this "chronological order" can be taken as representing the very earliest invention.

To recapitulate here for a moment: it is almost universally agreed that, following performances of *Petrushka* in Paris, Stravinsky began to compose his sketches for the "Augurs of Spring," "Spring Rounds," and possibly even the "Ritual of the Rival Tribes" during the summer of 1911 at Ustilug, Russia. He may have begun

[4]Craft, "Commentary to the Sketches," p. 4.

[5]"Les Deux *Sacres du printemps,*" *Comoedia*, December 11, 1920. Reprinted in François Lesure, *Le Sacre du Printemps: Dossier de presse* (Geneva: Editions Minkoff, 1980), p. 53. For an English translation of the interview, see Igor Stravinsky, "Interpretation by Massine," in Minna Lederman, ed., *Stravinsky in the Theatre* (New York: Pellegrini and Cudahy, 1949), p. 24.

[6]*Strawinsky* (Paris: Rieder, 1931), p. 39.

[7]Robert Craft, "*The Rite of Spring*: Genesis of a Masterpiece," *Perspectives of New Music* 5, 1 (1966): 23.

[8]Ibid., p. 24.

[9]Craft, "Commentary to the Sketches," p. 4.

EXAMPLE 59

in July, either before or after his visit with Nicolas Roerich, at which time the scenario and the titles of the dances were decided upon. Little could have been accomplished in August. The composer made trips to Karlsbad to settle the commission with Diaghilev, to Warsaw and Lugano to meet with Alexandre Benois, and finally to Berlin to visit his publisher, Russischer Musik Verlag, on matters pertaining to *Petrushka*. In fact, Craft estimates that the initial notations for the "Augurs of Spring" were entered after the composer's return from Berlin, on or around September 2.[10]

In a letter to Roerich dated September 26, 1911, Stravinsky informed his collaborator of his new address in Clarens, Switzerland, explaining that he had already begun to compose a dance, his description of which fits the "Augurs" movement.[11] Yet it is entirely possible—indeed probable, as suggested—that these sketches were preceded not only by considerable improvisation (both at and away from the piano), but by additional sketch material as well. The existence of sketches as much as a year earlier is confirmed by two letters from Stravinsky to Roerich dated July 2, 1910, and August 9, 1910.[12] And Craft has published what he believes to be the earliest extant sketch for *The Rite*: pre-dating the sketchbook, and given here as Example 59, it shows an E♭ dominant seventh superimposed over an A (rather than an E), and with general contours and rhythms that anticipate sections from both the "Ritual of the Rival Tribes" and the "Sacrificial Dance."[13] In

---

[10]Vera Stravinsky and Robert Craft, *Stravinsky in Pictures and Documents* (New York: Simon and Schuster, 1978), p. 596.

[11]"Letters to Nicholas Roerich and N. F. Findeizen," Appendix II in the accompanying booklet to Stravinsky, *The Rite of Spring: Sketches 1911–1913*.

[12]Ibid., pp. 27–29.

[13]V. Stravinsky and Craft, *Stravinsky in Pictures and Documents*, p. 597.

other words, the order of the entries on page 3, even if authentic, in no way discounts the possibility that the motto chord of the fourth line might indeed have been the composer's first idea.

But how significant is the which-came-first argument? Can it matter all that much whether, as Craft now claims, the motto chord of the fourth line was derived from the D♭–B♭–E♭–B♭ ostinato and its (E G♯ B) chordal affiliation in the initial jottings, or whether, as has generally been assumed, the chord came first and spawned its melodic conception? In the extended sketch for nos. 13–22, as in the score itself at no. 13, the chord appears first, while the ostinato and its (E G♯ B) accompaniment detach themselves from this construction eight measures later. On the other hand, if the preparation at no. 12 is taken into account, then the ostinato is first heard, pizzicato in the second violins, as a melodic component in anticipation of the chord at no. 13. The real miracle, however, is that the impact of the chord, the shock of its hammer-like, percussive action, is so entirely dependent on the "loose," contrapuntal network of the "awakening of nature" in the Introduction and that this latter should not have been composed until after the first three dances, and possibly even after the whole of Part I, as Stravinsky later maintained.[14]

Clearly the essentials here are: (1) that the notations for the "Augurs of Spring" on pages 3 and 4 of the sketchbook, whether in their most original form or not, probably represent the composer's earliest ideas for *The Rite*; and (2) that these ideas, forming the very cornerstone of *The Rite*, introduce vertical and linear arrangements that are of paramount concern not only to a consideration of the "Augurs of Spring" but of succeeding movements as well. Regardless of which came first, the chord or its melodic conception, these arrangements are central to our analytic-theoretical perspective.

1. The three pitches of the D♭–B♭–E♭–B♭ ostinato constitute, respectively, the dominant seventh, fifth, and root of the E♭ dominant-seventh chord, the top half of the motto chord. This relationship is sustained registrally in the concluding two measures of the fourth line.

2. The disengagement from the motto chord of E♭, D♭, and B♭ as an ostinato and of (E G♯ B) as its accompaniment underscores the compound nature of the chord; that is, the *superimposition* of the E♭ dominant seventh and of the D♭–B♭–E♭–B♭ ostinato over (E G♯ B).

3. Vertical or linear in conception, the superimposed quality of the configuration points in turn to the essential triadic makeup of the harmony in these initial pages.

4. Apart from arpeggios, melody is represented most prominently by the (B♭ A♭ G F) tetrachord of the third line and by (C B♭ A G) at m.5 in the last line. Encountered in Chapter 5, this is the minor or Dorian tetrachord with in-

[14]Igor Stravinsky and Robert Craft, *Expositions and Developments* (Berkeley: University of California Press, 1981), p. 141.

terval order 2–1–2 (whole step–half step–whole step) and with a pitch numbering of (0 2 3 5). The D♭–B♭–E♭–B♭ ostinato may in this connection be regarded as an incomplete (E♭ D♭ (C) B♭) tetrachord.

5. The (C E G) triad, substituting occasionally for (E G♯ B) in the accompaniment, forms, in combination with the E♭ dominant seventh or the D♭–B♭–E♭–B♭ ostinato above, another prominent configuration in *The Rite*, especially in the "Ritual of Abduction" and later in the Introduction to Part II at nos. 86–89.

6. The outer pitches of the motto chord, E♭ and E reading down (the roots of the two triadic subcomplexes), define a 0–11 or major-seventh vertical span that is sustained statically and very nearly continuously throughout *The Rite*.

And so pages 3 and 4 of the sketchbook introduce groupings or arrangements central to the "Augurs" movement and to the work as a whole: the vocabulary of *The Rite* consists in large part of 0–2 whole-step reiterations, (0 2 3 5) tetrachords, major and minor triads, dominant-seventh chords, and 0–11 or major-seventh vertical interval spans. (Again, as in earlier chapters, conventional terminology is employed for purposes of identification, with no intention of invoking tonally functional relations.) And although, given the reputation of this piece as one of considerable complexity, this reduction might seem a bit fanciful, we can narrow the scheme somewhat. The (0 2 3 5) tetrachord, as the principal melodic fragment not only of *The Rite* but of Stravinsky's "Russian" period generally, surfaces by way of all manner of reiterating, folkish tunes. As such, it is invariably articulated in the tightest or closest arrangement, confined to the interval of 5, the fourth (without interval complementation, in other words). It may nonetheless be either (0 2 5) or (0 3 5), incomplete, as noted already, with the D♭–B♭–E♭–B♭ ostinato or (E♭ D♭ (C) B♭) unit, which lacks the C, pitch number 3 reading down.

The triads and dominant sevenths also assume a characteristic disposition: as with the (0 2 3 5) tetrachord, the tight or close arrangement. This is not always the case but is customary, especially in the treble registers. The typical dominant-seventh placement is exemplified by the top half of the motto chord: closed position, "first inversion." Starting with the chord's E♭ dominant seventh at no. 13, Example 60 traces continued reference to this disposition throughout *The Rite*. All these fixed arrangements are bound to be of consequence to a local or global reading of *The Rite*, a matter to which we shall therefore be returning for further comment. But note, for the moment, how closely this tight articulation is linked to the melodic repetition and then to the rhythmic-metric implications of this repetition. In other words, given the superimposed, layered structure of *The Rite*, a construction in which fragments, fixed registrally and instrumentally, repeat according to the two rhythmic types outlined in preceding chapters, the tight or limited fragmental compass becomes inevitable.

By contrast, the 0–11 vertical span is rarely melodic in character (fragmental or linear), but defines, harmonically or vertically, the span between pitches of unmistakable priority among superimposed, reiterating fragments or chords. Thus, as noted above, the Eb–E span of the motto chord and its subsequent melodic formulation; or, in Example 60, the subsequent pitch realizations of this span further along in Parts I and II. In Example 61 from the "Ritual Action of the Ancestors" in Part II, the (0 2 3 5) tetrachord, (C♯ B A♯ G♯) here in the trumpets, is superimposed over a D–Bb ostinato in the bassoon. Reading down, the 0–11 span is therefore C♯–D as defined between the C♯ of the upper (C♯ B A♯ G♯) tetrachord and the low D of the D–Bb unit. Similarly, in Example 54 in Chapter 5, from the "Ritual of the Rival Tribes," a reiterating (G F E D) tetrachordal fragment is superimposed over a lower G♯; the 0–11 span is G–G♯, reading down again. And starting with the

EXAMPLE 60

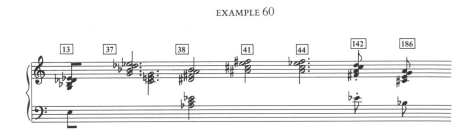

EXAMPLE 61: "Ritual Action of the Ancestors"

motto chord at no. 13, note the metric accentuation of the 0–11 span in these illustrations, an accentuation that typifies its articulation throughout *The Rite*, rendering it highly conspicuous from one block or movement to the next.

The Octatonic Pitch Collection

Listed above are thus the principal articulative units, the common denominators, so to speak, often with dispositions of marked character. What may in turn be judged the referential glue of this vocabulary, what binds within and between blocks and sections, is very often the octatonic pitch collection. More precisely, the referential character of this vocabulary is very often determined by its confinement, for periods of significant duration, to one of the three octatonic collections of distinguishable content.

As was defined in Chapter 5, the octatonic collection is a set of eight distinct pitch classes that, arranged in scale formation, yields the interval ordering of alternating 1s and 2s (half and whole steps). Such an arrangement obviously yields only two possible interval orderings or scales, the first of these with its second scale degree at the interval of 1 from its first (a 1–2, half step–whole step ordering), the second with its second scale degree at the interval of 2 from its first (a 2–1, whole step–half step ordering). These are shown in Example 62, with the 1–2 ordering and consequent (0 1 3 4 6 7 9 10 (0)) pitch numbering on the left side, the reverse 2–1 ordering and (0 2 3 5 6 8 9 11 (0)) numbering on the right. And the issue as to which of these orderings might pertain to a given context naturally hinges on questions of priority, vocabulary, and articulation. Thus the (0 2 3 5) tetrachord with its 2–1–2 ordering suggests the 2–1 ordering as cited on the right side in Example 62. And octatonic contexts which are (0 2 3 5) tetrachordally oriented will tend therefore to

EXAMPLE 62

suggest this 2–1 ordering as the most favorable approach in scale formation. Similarly, when octatonically conceived, the 0–11 vertical interval span invariably suggests the 2–1 ordering and its consequent (0 2 3 5 6 8 9 11 (0)) numbering on the right side in Example 62; the latter is in fact closely linked to *The Rite*'s (0 2 3 5) tetrachordal articulation. (Note, in other words, the 0–11 span of this numbering.) On the other hand, the (0 1 3 4) tetrachord, of only slight consequence in *The Rite*, and the root-positioned (0 4 7/0 3 7) major and minor triads tend more readily to suggest the 1–2 ordering on the left side of Example 62.

The collection is limited to three transpositions; there are only three octatonic collections of distinguishable pitch content. These are also shown in Example 62, labeled I, II, and III. Thus, respecting Collection I with the 1–2 ordering on the left side in Example 62: had we, following the initial C♯, transposed beyond D (Collection II) and E♭ (Collection III) to E, this final transposition would merely have yielded the initial collection (Collection I), starting only with the E rather than the C♯. Moreover, since this transposition to E defines the interval of 3 (the minor third) with the initial C♯ (as pitch number 0), transpositions at 6 and 9 will entail similar duplications. And it follows that this minor-third (0, 3, 6, 9) symmetrically defined partitioning is fundamental to the integrity of the single octatonic collection: given an octatonic fragment, transpositions at 3, 6, and 9 will remain confined to that collection.

Finally, note that the 1–2 ordering on the left side in Example 62 ascends, while the reverse 2–1 ordering on the right descends. This is in principle in order to allow representation of longer spans of material, spans that, confined to a single collection, may nonetheless in vocabulary and articulation implicate both orderings. In other words, respecting Collection I again, with the ascending 1–2 ordering at C♯ on the left side: were we to switch to the 2–1 ordering and yet remain committed to the customary ascending approach in scale representation, the resultant scale would no longer represent Collection I but, rather, Collection III. However, by *descending* with the 2–1 ordering from C♯, not only do we remain confined to Collection I but the (0, 3, 6, 9) symmetrically defined partitioning elements in terms of (C♯, E, G, B♭) remain the same.

Still, the descending formula, the reading-down situation on the right side of Example 62, is not wholly a question of analytical convenience. In many "Russian" pieces it is often an "upper" (0 2 3 5) tetrachord, along with an "upper" pitch number 0, that assumes priority by means of doubling, metric accentuation, and persistence in moving from one block or section to the next. And if the scalar ordering and pitch numbering are to reflect these conditions, the descending formula is the logical course. Throughout large sections of the "Augurs of Spring," the "Ritual of Abduction" and "Spring Rounds" in Part I, a punctuating E♭, along with an (E♭ D♭ C B♭) tetrachord with which this E♭ identifies articulatively, assume priority. And it is by descending from the E♭, with the (0 2 3 5) tetrachordal numbering synchronized with the principal (E♭ D♭ C B♭) unit, that the priority of these units is properly represented: (0 2 3 5 6 8 9 11) in terms of (E♭ D♭ C B♭ A G F♯ E), Collection III. (Again, to *ascend* from the E♭ with the 2–1 ordering would have yielded a different octatonic collection, in this case Collection II.) Moreover, the symmetrical discipline conveniently allows for options of this kind. The 2–1–2 ordering and consequent (0 2 3 5) pitch numbering of this present tetrachord remain the same whether ascending or descending.

In general summation, Examples 63 and 64 partition the octatonic collection by means of the various articulative groupings cited above.[15] In Example 63 the 2–1 ordering is shown on the left side, where brackets outline the four overlapping (0 2 3 5) tetrachords at 0, 3, 6, and 9. Notice the two non-overlapping (0, 6) tritone-related tetrachords, which together yield the all-important 0–11 vertical span. Separate realizations are given below for each of the three content-distinguishable collections.

On the right side in Example 63 the familiar disposition of the dominant-seventh chord is applied in similar fashion. Here, too, superimposed over its (0, 3) minor-third-related major triad, the compound configuration, encountered already in terms of (E♭ D♭ B♭ G) (C E G) in the "Augurs of Spring," likewise encompasses the 0–11 span. More essential, however, is the exposed, upper interval of 5, or the fourth of the dominant seventh's closed, first-inversion articulation. Thus the E♭–B♭ fourth or incomplete (E♭ D♭ (C) B♭) tetrachord of Collection III's (E♭ D♭ B♭ G) dominant seventh connects with the (E♭ D♭ C B♭) tetrachord on the left side of Example 63. Associations of this type are crucial to the special registral and articulative layout of *The Rite*. Indeed, as will be noted, the descending scale is applied to both the triadic and the tetrachordal side of Example 63, and in recognition not only of the "upper" conditions of priority noted already but of this essential link between the typically closed, first-inversion articulation of the dominant seventh and the (0 2 3 5) tetrachord.

Example 64 offers a different view of these formulae. The three collections are partitioned at four successive levels, by their (0, 3, 6, 9) partitioning elements at the first level and by their (0 2 3 5) tetrachords at the second. At the third level the 0–11 vertical span encompasses the upper 0–5 fourth of the (0 2 3 5) tetrachord, while brackets encircle the lower of the two tritone-related fourths to cover those fewer instances where the lower or both of the collection's (0 2 3 5) (6 8 9 11) tetrachords prevail. Hence the 0–11 designation becomes 0–5, 11, or, more comprehensively still, 0–5/6, 11.[16] Indeed, in light of its comprehensive application, 0–5/6, 11 may

---

[15]See Pieter C. van den Toorn, *The Music of Igor Stravinsky* (New Haven: Yale University Press, 1983), pp. 48–60. In this earlier volume, the triadic and (0 2 3 5) tetrachordal groupings, yielding the ascending and the descending forms of the scale, respectively, are represented by two separate schemes labeled Model A and Model B. This strict separation was maintained in order to pinpoint critical distinctions involving the whole of Stravinsky's music, from the early "Russian" period to neoclassicism and early serialism. Here, however, with the analysis confined to the articulative routine of *The Rite*, these models are easily condensed to a single descending mode of representation.

[16]In connection with Béla Bartók's music, this 0–5/6, 11 vertical span was identified as "cell z" by Leo Treitler in his "Harmonic Procedure in the Fourth Quartet of Béla Bartók," *Journal of Music Theory* 3, 2 (1959): 292–98. Treitler's designation came in partial response to an earlier study by George Perle, where two other "cells" were labeled "x" and "y"; see George Perle, "Symmetrical Formations in the String

EXAMPLE 63

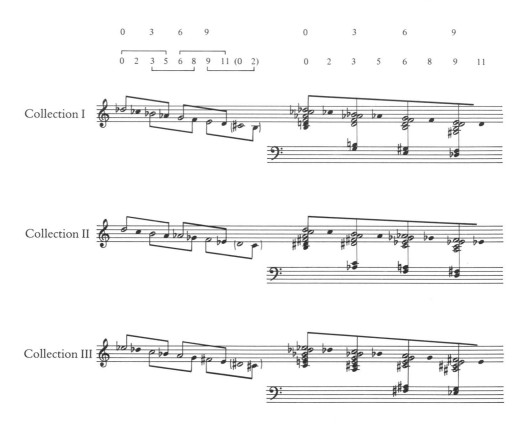

be envisioned as a kind of basic sonority in *The Rite*, the shell of its octatonic content. As was noted in Chapter 5, it accounts in large measure for the static "vertical chromaticism" that may be inferred: the upper (0 2 3 5) tetrachord or 0–5 fourth is made to stand in a fixed, polarized opposition to the lower pitch number 11.[17] At the final level in Example 64 the (0, 3, 6, 9) partitioning elements of each of the three scales are represented by round notes.

Quartets of Béla Bartók," *Music Review* 16 (1955): 300–312. The role of "cell z" in Bartók's music generally—its relationship to other symmetrical cells, interval cycles, and various octatonic and diatonic orderings—is discussed at length in Elliott Antokoletz, *The Music of Béla Bartók* (Berkeley: University of California Press, 1984), pp. 67–137.

[17]The kind of upper-lower or treble-bass opposition or polarity implied by the 0–5/6, 11 vertical stance could be dealt with by using a descending pitch numbering and lettering for the upper contingent and an ascending numbering and lettering for the lower contingent. This method could eventually lead to confusion, however, and in view of the greater emphasis placed on the upper of these contingents, the descending formula is here applied throughout. Note, however, that the (E♭ D♭ B♭ G) (C E G) label in these pages encompasses a pitch-lettering that does in fact reflect this upper-lower polarity.

EXAMPLE 64

Collection I

Collection II

EXAMPLE 64 *(continued)*

Collection III

Preliminary Survey

In its coverage of both Parts I and II, the analytical portion of Example 65 en-compasses four successive stages.[18] Moving from a least to a most determinate stage, the first of these levels recognizes the (0 2 3 5) tetrachord as that unit which, complete or (0 2 5/0 3 5) incomplete, is shared by blocks and sections of varied articulative and referential implications, and hence as that unit which is more or less globally determinate or continuously operative with respect to the whole of *The Rite*. At the second stage the (0 2 3 5) tetrachord attaches itself to the octatonically conceived 0–5/6, 11 vertical span or shell, a formula that applies to passages of octatonic or octatonic-diatonic content, not to the few scattered patches of unimpaired diatonicism in Part I. The local articulation of these global units, acknowledged at the third level, yields the reference collection at the fourth level, where beams, parentheses, and the like confirm earlier-noted pri-orities and partitionings.

[18]The format of Example 65 corresponds somewhat to that of Example 27 in van den Toorn, *The Music of Igor Stravinsky*, pp. 102–22. Here, however, the process has been streamlined. With a view toward *The Rite* as a whole, the dance movements of both Part I and Part II are taken into account, while the blocks selected for detailed treatment are often different. The accompanying graph, compressed in Example 66, also reflects a concern for *The Rite* in its entirety.

EXAMPLE 65

(continued)

EXAMPLE 65 *(continued)*

Collection II   Collection I   D-scales on F and B♭

(continued)

EXAMPLE 65 *(continued)*

"Augurs of Spring"

Collection III

EXAMPLE 65 *(continued)*

Collection III   Collection I

(continued)

EXAMPLE 65 *(continued)*

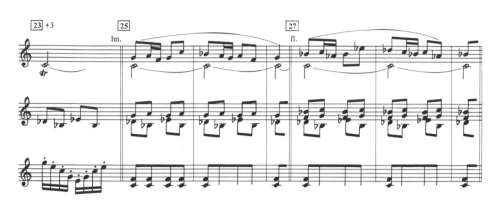

Collection III

D-scales

(continued)

EXAMPLE 65 *(continued)*

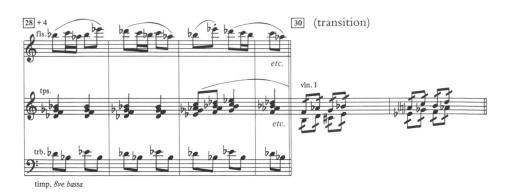

D-scale on E♭   Collection I   Collection II

(continued)

EXAMPLE 65 (continued)

"Ritual of Abduction"

Collection II   Collection III   D-scale on A

(continued)

EXAMPLE 65 *(continued)*

(continued)

EXAMPLE 65 *(continued)*

Collection III   Collection III

(continued)

EXAMPLE 65 *(continued)*

Collection II

(continued)

EXAMPLE 65 *(continued)*

Collection II   D-scale on F

5-cycle

(continued)

EXAMPLE 65 *(continued)*

(continued)

EXAMPLE 65 *(continued)*

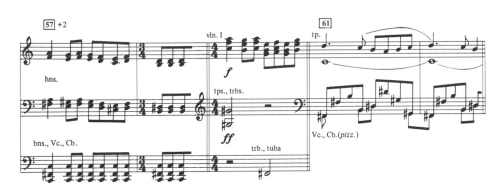

Collection II Collection II Collection II

(continued)

EXAMPLE 65 *(continued)*

Collection I　　　　Collection III　　　　Collection II

(continued)

EXAMPLE 65 *(continued)*

(continued)

EXAMPLE 65 *(continued)*

"Dance of the Earth"

(continued)

EXAMPLE 65 *(continued)*

Introduction

Strings

cls.

hns.

b. cls.

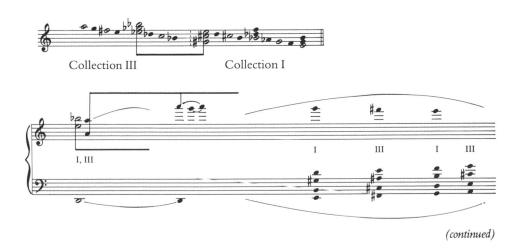

Collection III   Collection I

(continued)

EXAMPLE 65 *(continued)*

Collection I   Collection III

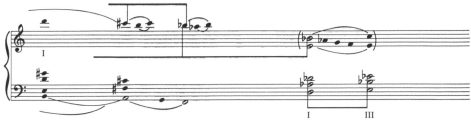

(continued)

EXAMPLE 65 *(continued)*

(continued)

EXAMPLE 65 *(continued)*

Collection I   Collection III

(continued)

EXAMPLE 65 *(continued)*

Collection I

(continued)

EXAMPLE 65 *(continued)*

"Sacrificial Dance"

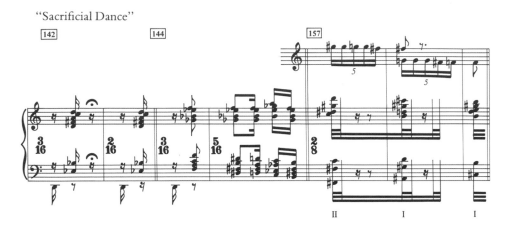

Collection II

(continued)

EXAMPLE 65 *(continued)*

(continued)

EXAMPLE 65 *(continued)*

Collection I

(continued)

EXAMPLE 65 *(continued)*

Collection III

The graph that runs at the foot of Example 65, pages 149–73, shows the general direction of the block and sectional transpositions, a sketch that is further compressed in Example 66. For the moment it will be useful to survey some of the initial realizations.

At no. 6 in the Introduction, the (0 2 3 5) tetrachord in the English horn—(0 (2) 3 5), incomplete in terms of (Bb (Ab) G F)—is the principal melodic fragment. Traced to the climactic block at no. 10, (Bb (Ab) G F) is confined to a Bb–B vertical span, defined at no. 6 between the tetrachord's Bb and the low B sustained in the bassoon. At no. 10 the dominant seventh on E is significantly second inversion, allowing B to remain stationed in the bass. Note the (G F E D) tetrachord in the alto flute at no. 6, which relates to (Bb (Ab) G F) by the interval of 3. This (0, 3) relationship between superimposed fragments is one that persists in the movements directly ahead.

These relations are sustained in terms of (Eb Db (C) Bb) and Eb–Bb, E at nos. 13 and 14 in the "Augurs of Spring." The principal fragment is the Db–Bb–Eb–Bb ostinato in the English horn, an (0 2 (3) 5) incomplete tetrachord in terms of (Eb Db (C) Bb). The contour of the ostinato is foreshadowed by the Introduction's opening bassoon melody, whose C–A–D–A phrase identifies with Db–Bb–Eb–Bb.[19] Hence the vertical arrangement at nos. 13–14 is Eb–Bb, E, with the (Eb Db (C) Bb) incomplete tetrachord of the (Eb Db Bb G) dominant seventh and ostinato superimposed over a lower E in the bass.

Critical at nos. 13–19 is the mixed (0 2 3 5) tetrachordal, triadic, and dominant-seventh articulation. As noted already, (Eb Db Bb G) preserves, in simultaneity, the ostinato's incomplete (Eb Db (C) Bb) tetrachord; Eb, Db, and Bb of the ostinato merely become the root, seventh, and fifth, respectively, of (Eb Db Bb G). And so the rationale of the tight, first-inversion articulation of the dominant seventh is as follows: registrally fixed at nos. 13–15, this disposition exposes the persistence of Eb, Db, and Bb as a tightly articulated (Eb Db (C) Bb) tetrachord. Hence, too, the frequent (0 2 5) incomplete articulation of the (0 2 3 5) tetrachord in *The Rite*; (0 2 5) becomes the connecting link between these tetrachordal and dominant-seventh partitionings of the octatonic collection. In addition, the (0, 3) relationship persists in terms of (Eb, C). This is realized tetrachordally in terms of the Db–Bb–Eb–Bb ostinato and the (C Bb A G) fragment in the flutes at no. 16, and then triadically in terms of (Eb Db Bb G) and the (C E G) triad. At nos. 14 and 16 (Eb Db Bb G) (C E G) preserves the Eb–E vertical span, with E as the major third of (C E G). Hence the 0–5, 11 octatonic presence is realized articulatively by means of an upper (0 2 3 5) tetrachord sustained over a lower pitch number 11 or by means of a dominant seventh, closed position, first inversion, superimposed over a (0, 3)–related major triad, also closed position. Note the (E G C) first-inversion articulation of the (C E G) triad at no. 14, with E as pitch number 11 in the bass.

---

[19] A more detailed account of Part I's Introduction is given in van den Toorn, *The Music of Igor Stravinsky*, pp. 102–6, 124–26.

EXAMPLE 66

(continued)

EXAMPLE 66 *(continued)*

"Rival Tribes"

"Procession"   "Dance of the Earth"

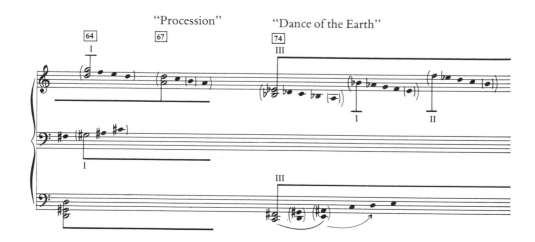

Introduction

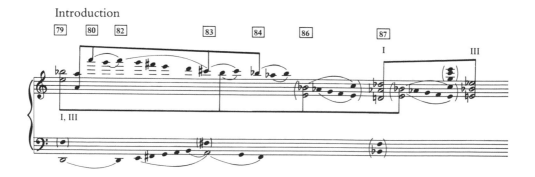

(continued)

EXAMPLE 66 *(continued)*

(continued)

EXAMPLE 66 *(continued)*

The transposition of the (C B♭ A G) flute melody at no. 16 to (B♭ A♭ G F) in the bassoons at no. 19 introduces an added complexity: (B♭ A♭ G F) refers not to Collection III but, rather, to Collection I. Indeed, the transposition points to the hybrid character of the celebrated motto chord itself, which is not an octatonic entity; its (E♭ D♭ B♭ G) top half refers to Collection III, while its (E G♯ B) bottom half refers to Collection I. True, the prominence of the (E♭ D♭ B♭ G) dominant seventh and its superimposition over E guarantee Collection III's hegemony throughout most of the "Augurs of Spring" and the succeeding "Ritual of Abduction" as well; see, especially, Collection III's triadic and tetrachordal articulation at nos. 13–19, 22–25, 37, and 42. Yet both G♯ (A♭) and B of the motto chord are foreign to Collection III, while, excluding the important E♭, the pitch content of the chord refers equally to Collection I. Hence, as shown in Example 65, the chord may smoothly accommodate blocks referring to either Collection III or Collection I. And in addition to the transposition to (B♭ A♭ G F) at no. 19, note the B/E–G♯/C♯–B♭ syncopated, upbeat figure at no. 15, where the material, once again excluding E♭ as root of the (E♭ D♭ B♭ G♭) dominant seventh, refers wholly to Collection I.

Indeed, the embedded fourths in this Collection III–Collection I exchange at no. 19 (E♭–B♭ over B♭–F, for example) point to yet another referential factor in *The Rite*, that of the interval–5 cycle or cycle of fourths.[20] There is much explicit evidence to support its role, and with particular reference to the many diatonic fragments in Part I, a topic to be discussed just below. Consider,

---

[20]The role of the interval-5/7 cycle in *The Rite* is briefly discussed in George Perle, "Berg's Master Array of the Interval Cycles," *Musical Quarterly* 63, 1 (1977): 10–12, and in Elliott Antokoletz, *The Music of Béla Bartók*, pp. 313–18. Pursuant to *The Rite*'s (0 2 3 5) tetrachords and the present descending approach in scale formation, emphasis is here placed on the *descending* 5-cycle rather than on the complementary 7-cycle (although, of course, explicit 7-cycle segments do occasionally arise in the "Augurs of Spring"). Chart 5, Example 68, and Charts 7–11 just ahead are plotted accordingly.

however, the broader implications of the cycle's intersecting role as suggested by the transposition to (B♭ A♭ G F) at no. 19 and its superimposition over the motto chord. Reading from left to right in Chart 5, four different rotations of the interval–5 cycle are aligned vertically in accord with the 0–5/6, 11 span. This arrangement yields twelve 0–5/6, 11 verticals, which are numbered accordingly. In addition, the collectional affiliations of these verticals are shown, while lines and beams trace the degree of emphasis exercised by each in Parts I and II. Verticals 3 and 4 are of obvious concern in the first part of the "Augurs of Spring," while vertical 5 is crucial to the "Rival Tribes" until the climactic section at no. 64, at which point vertical 7 surfaces. The "Dance of the Earth" at nos. 75–79 consists almost entirely of transpositions involving verticals 3, 4, and 5 or, alternatively, the E♭–B♭–F–C segment of the 5-cycle. Part II exhibits a different set of priorities. The blocks at nos. 132, 134, and 138 in the "Ritual Action of the Ancestors" expose vertical 1, while transpositions of the opening section of the "Sacrificial Dance" entail verticals 8, 1, and 9, respectively. The four rotations in Chart 5 could have been cut off at the tritone, since the upper and lower tritone-related fourths merely begin a series of duplications at this point. In view of the significance attached to upper and lower placement, however, it seemed advantageous to include all the relevant formations. Whether the actual block-by-block progressions defined by these verticals exhibit, with respect to the interval–5 cycle and/or collectional affiliation, a meaningful hierarchical scheme for *The Rite* as a whole is a matter to be considered presently.

Returning to the purely local conditions of the "Augurs of Spring," the introduction of the new (C B♭ A G F) fragment in the horn at no. 25, transposed to (E♭ D♭ C B♭ A♭) at no. 27, undermines the octatonic advantage. The fragment anticipates the climactic stretch at nos. 28–30, a diatonic block im-

CHART 5

Vertical:	1	2	3	4	5	6	7	8	9	10	11	12
Collection:	I	II	III	I	II	III	I	II	III	I	II	III

Part I

0	D♭	A♭	E♭	B♭	F	C	G	D	A	E	B	F♯
5	A♭	E♭	B♭	F	C	G	D	A	E	B	F♯	C♯
(6)	(G)	(D)	(A)	(E)	(B)	(F♯)	(C♯)	(A♭)	(E♭)	(B♭)	(F)	(C)
11	D	A	E	B	F♯	C♯	G♯	E♭	B♭	F	C	G

Part II

EXAMPLE 67: Sketchbook

plicating the D-scale (or Dorian scale) on E♭. Here, E♭ and the upper (E♭ D♭ C B♭) tetrachord prevail as connecting links, while the remaining non–Collection III elements are eliminated; A, G, and E are gradually replaced at nos. 25 and 27 by A♭, G♭, and F.

Interestingly, the new (C B♭ A G F) fragment at no. 25 was initially conceived as part of a more fully committed Collection III framework. Reproduced in Examples 67a and 67b are two entries from pages 5 and 6 of the sketchbook, where the fragment's (C B♭ A G) tetrachord is superimposed over its lower tritone-related (G♭ (F♭) E♭ D♭) unit.[21] In the second of these sketches, Example 67b, this explicit 0–5/6, 11 configuration, C–G/G♭, D♭, is superimposed over the D♭–B♭–E♭–B♭ ostinato. Yet, at the bottom of page 6 these overt octatonic overtones are purged in favor of the more ambiguous octatonic-diatonic setting as it presently stands. Only the F of the (C B♭ A G F) fragment remains foreign to Collection III at no. 25, however. The D♭–B♭–E♭–B♭ ostinato and its tritone-related A–G whole-step reiteration in the second violins continue to mark Collection III's presence.

Coming by way of the transition at no. 30, the (E♭ D♭ C B♭) tetrachordal emphasis at nos. 13–30 is transposed to (D C B A) at nos. 31–37. The 0–5, 11 vertical span perseveres in terms of D–A, E♭, with E♭ positioned in the bass.

The Diatonic Component

As can readily be seen in Example 65, the transposition to (D C B A) in the final climactic block of the "Augurs" movement is foreshadowed by the C–

---

[21]The first of these sketches on page 5 of the sketchbook, Example 67a, is crossed out.

A–D–A phrase of the opening bassoon melody and by the (D C B A) fragment at no. 6 + 4. Of concern at no. 37 in the "Ritual of Abduction," however, is the abrupt return to Collection III's (E♭ D♭ B♭ G) dominant seventh and its superimposition over (D C B A), which is now articulated as part of a new (A G F♯ E) (D C B A) D-scale fragment. In addition, the (E G♯ B) bottom half of the motto chord is dropped altogether in favor of the (C E G) triad, the compound octatonic configuration now (E♭ D♭ B♭ G) (C E G). Transposed to Collection II in terms of (B A F♯ D♯) (A♭ C E♭) at nos. 38 and 40 + 6, this configuration persists with remarkable consistency throughout the "Abduction," rendering this movement one of the most thoroughly octatonic in *The Rite*. A punctuating F♯ in the percussion solidifies Collection III's initial presence at no. 37, while, in the climactic block at no. 42, (E♭ D♭ B♭ G) is complemented by dominant sevenths on F♯ and A. At no. 44 the configuration is transposed to Collection II, where (F E♭ C A) is superimposed over D–A. Here, the D–A horn call or (D C B A) tetrachord, foreign to Collection III at nos. 37 and 40, is fully octatonic, accountable to Collection II. Note that in all these block transpositions entailing Collections III and II, the dominant seventh stubbornly preserves its closed, first-inversion articulation.

Still, patches of unimpaired diatonicism occasionally arise. The D-scale (or Dorian) fragment introduced at no. 37 returns in transposed form at no. 46. And in moving from the octatonic block at no. 44 to the unimpaired D-scale on F at no. 46, the connecting link or pivot, that which is in turn shared by these two blocks of distinct referential character, is the (0 2 3 5) tetrachord.

Thus the presiding (F E♭ C A) dominant seventh at no. 44 preserves, in tight formation, the incomplete (F E♭ (D) C) tetrachord. And as indicated by the brackets in Example 65, (F E♭ (D) C) is retained by the succeeding diatonic block at no. 46, where the (F E♭ D C) (B♭ A♭ G F) tetrachordal articulation implicates the D-scale on F. A condensed layout of the scheme appears in Chart 6.

Indeed, similar equations pertain to those blocks and passages of Part I where the octatonic and diatonic collections may be said to *interpenetrate*. At no. 10 in the Introduction two diatonic fragments in the clarinet piccolo and oboe are superimposed over Collection I's B♭–F, B framework. In this octatonic-diatonic interaction, (B♭ A♭ G F) is shared by Collection I and the D-scales on F and B♭. Similarly, at no. 37 in the "Abduction," Collection III's (E♭ D♭ B♭ G) (C E G) configuration is introduced along with the (A G F♯ E) (D C B A) D-scale fragment. Shared by these two interpenetrating references is the (A G F♯ E) unit, the lower of Collection III's (E♭ D♭ C B♭) (A G F♯ E) tritone-related tetrachords.[22]

---

[22]The dotted lines in the analytical portions of Example 65 signify octatonic-diatonic interpenetration, with the octatonic component on the left side, the diatonic on the right. At the collectional level, brackets mark off the (0 2 3 5) units held in common.

CHART 6: "Ritual of Abduction," nos. 44–47

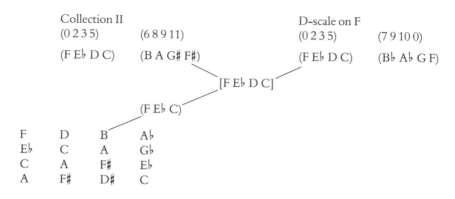

Collection II				D-scale on F		
(0 2 3 5)	(6 8 9 11)			(0 2 3 5)	(7 9 10 0)	
(F Eb D C)	(B A G# F#)			(F Eb D C)	(Bb Ab G F)	

[F Eb D C]

(F Eb C)

F	D	B	Ab
Eb	C	A	Gb
C	A	F#	Eb
A	F#	D#	C

In sum, the two adjoining (0 2 3 5) tetrachords of the octatonic scale are (0, 6) tritone-related while those of the diatonic D-scale are (0, 7) fifth-related. (The octatonic scale contains four overlapping (0 2 3 5) tetrachords, which, in passages of octatonic-diatonic interaction, could imply eight possible D-scales. Here we consider only the two adjoining ones.) And as shown in Chart 6, the critical point of distinction is likely to arise at the pitch-number 6/7 juncture of the two tetrachords. In moving from an octatonic to a diatonic or octatonic-diatonic framework, pitch number 7, replacing number 6, does in fact often intrude to signal this shift. At no. 25 in the "Augurs of Spring," only F of the (C Bb A G F) diatonic fragment is foreign to Collection III. Here, Gb (F#) in place of F, as indeed originally contemplated by the composer, would have tipped the balance more favorably toward Collection III and a possible (0 2 3 5) (6 8 9 11) formation in terms of (C Bb A G) (Gb (Fb) Eb Db), reading down. (Actually, the original conception, shown in Examples 67a and 67b, includes both the F and the Gb. Collection III at this point might well have seemed a bit cluttered and over-committed to the composer, in view of the upcoming D-scale on Eb at nos. 28–30, for which the blocks at nos. 25 and 27 serve as a preparation. The score defines a very gradual shift toward the unimpaired D-scale on Eb reference at nos. 28–30.)

Hence, as a subset of both the octatonic and diatonic collections, the (0 2 3 5) tetrachord serves as the principal connecting link between blocks of octatonic, diatonic, and octatonic-diatonic content. And when (0 2 (3) 5) is incomplete, it may in addition connect an (0 2 3 5) partitioning of the octatonic collection with a dominant-seventh partitioning, closed-position, first inversion. Hence, too, as a surface-articulative unit, it embodies matters of deep structural concern to the harmonic, contrapuntal, and referential character of *The Rite.*

The Interval–5 Cycle

Explicit delineations of the interval–5 cycle are found in the "Augurs of Spring," the "Ritual of Abduction," and the "Dance of the Earth." Most telling in the "Augurs" movement is the E♭–B♭–F–C ostinato in the lower strings at nos. 15–18 and 28–30, the vertical piling-up of fourths just prior to no. 18, and the transposition of the (0 2 3 5) tetrachord along the cycle's E♭–B♭–F–C segment, to which reference has already been made. At no. 45 in the "Abduction," the bass descends from A to F by way of the cycle, while at nos. 74–79 in the "Dance of the Earth" the initial (E♭ D♭ C B♭) tetrachordal fragment is transposed to (B♭ A♭ G F) and (F E♭ D C). The cycle is of particular assistance whenever the question of pitch-class or tetrachordal priority, and hence of scalar ordering, is in doubt. And here, as with the D-scale ordering of the diatonic collection, intersection with the octatonic scale by way of the (0 2 3 5) tetrachord or its encompassing fourth can handily be taken into account.

Indeed, even with the diatonic fragments of Part I, fragments whose framing octaves and (0 2 3 5) tetrachordal formations readily suggest the D-scale ordering, openly articulated fourths can point to the 5-cycle as a constructive and referential factor. Shown in Examples 68a–68c are five diatonic fragments taken from the Introduction and the "Abduction." Separate columns in this example reveal the (0,2,5,7) pitch-class set, the D-scales, and the compression of these latter scales as segments of the 5-cycle. The two diatonic fragments at no. 10 in the Introduction are framed by octaves and exhibit an explicit (0 2 3 5) tetrachordal articulation, circumstances that readily imply the two D-scales on F and B♭ as shown in the third column of Example 68b. Yet the embedded fourths of these fragments, together with the transposition of the scale up one notch along the 5-cycle, suggests the condensation as shown in the fourth column. The five-note segment here covers the pitch-class content of the two fragments while the box encircles the centric-like E♭–B♭–F–C series with its three fourths. (Given the scale's transposition at the fourth, the two D-scales in Example 68b could have been represented as a series of three adjoining (0 2 3 5) tetrachords, (F E♭ D C) (B♭ A♭ G F) (E♭ D♭ C B♭), in descending order; in other words, as two overlapping D-scales with the (B♭ A♭ G F) unit shared, and hence ultimately as a segment of the non-univallic cycle with interval order 5–2–5–2–5.) Similar observations pertain to the two fragments at nos. 46 and 47 in the "Abduction." The sharply articulated fourths along with the transposition at the fourth suggest a six-note segment with the B♭–F–C–G series as centric.

In Chart 7 the content of the Introduction's climactic block at no. 10 is displayed as a nearly complete 5-cycle.[23] The pitch-class content of the diatonic fragments in the flutes, clarinet piccolo, and oboe (see Example 68b)

---

[23]Charts 7–10 are modeled after a design used in Elliott Antokoletz, *The Music of Béla Bartók.*

EXAMPLE 68

(a) Introduction   (0, 2, 5, 7)   D-scales   5-cycle

(b) Introduction

(c) "Ritual of Abduction"

CHART 7: Introduction

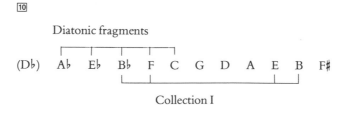

yields the Ab–Eb–Bb–F–C segment, while the Bb–F/E, B vertical span of Collection I's framework is indicated directly below. Here, the point of intersection or connecting link is the Bb–F fourth or (Bb Ab G F) tetrachord, as was discussed in connection with Example 65 and octatonic-diatonic interpenetration.

CHART 8: "Augurs of Spring"

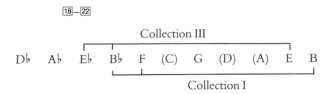

CHART 9: "Augurs of Spring"

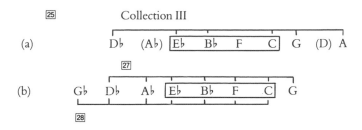

Similarly, the embedded fourths in the superimposition of (B♭ A♭ G F) over the motto chord at nos. 18–22 suggest the gapped segment shown in Chart 8. The 0–5, 11 spans for Collections III and I are shown, and the embedded fourths in this compound configuration yield the E♭–B♭–F segment. The gradual erosion of Collection III's content is in turn traced in Chart 9. Notice, once again, that notwithstanding the prominent fourths at no. 25 (the F/C accompaniment figure in the lower strings along with E♭ and B♭ of the ostinato), only F in this gapped segment remains foreign to Collection III. At no. 27 the seven-note diatonic segment still contains the G that is subsequently replaced by G♭ at no. 28. In Chart 10, derived from the "Dance of the Earth," the boxed-off area containing the E♭–B♭–F–C segment points to the transposition of the (E♭ D♭ C B♭) fragment to (B♭ A♭ G F) and (F E♭ D C). The octatonic implications of these levels are outlined above while the intersecting whole-tone scale or interval 2-cycle of the basso ostinato is shown below. Finally, intersection of the 5-cycle with the three octatonic collections is summarized in Chart 11. Since the fourths or (0 2 3 5) tetrachords of these collections are (0, 3, 6, 9)–related, each collection is represented as a gapped 5-cycle.

There are important connections among several of the 5-cycle segments traced in Example 68 and Charts 7–10. The E♭–B♭–F–C segment of the diatonic fragments in the Introduction persists in the "Augurs of Spring," where, as was indicated already, it becomes linked to the Collection III–Collection I hybrid character of the motto chord. In addition, E♭–B♭–F–C

CHART 10: "Dance of the Earth"

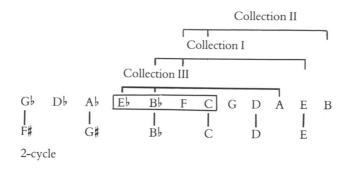

CHART 11

reappears in the "Dance of the Earth." Yet the limitations of the 5–cycle as an explanatory tool, even when it is applied in conjunction with other interval cycles, are at least equally apparent in these illustrations. The cycle tends to skirt essentials of vocabulary and disposition, especially the triads and dominant sevenths, groupings with special articulative and registral implications. And while its circumvention of priority and octave considerations is at times both convenient and appropriate, the (0 2 3 5) tetrachords and octatonically conceived 0–5/6, 11 spans can more often than not ensure the more determined conditions of a scalar ordering. (As should be evident, the analysis of Examples 65 and 66 provides a far more detailed and explicit picture of pitch organization on both a local and global scale.) Nor, as we shall see, is the cycle of much use when confronting *The Rite* as a whole. In order for it to be effective, inferred segments must exhibit pitch-adjacency or, if severely gapped, a pattern of some sort. Apart from some of the above-noted passages, this is seldom the case in *The Rite*.

Summations

The prevalence of E♭ and the (E♭ D♭ C B♭) tetrachord seems to invest these units with a certain priority in Part I. This priority extends to Collection III and its E♭–B♭, E vertical span, and, on the diatonic side of the coin, possibly to the D-scale on E♭ as well. A number of details have already been mentioned in this connection: respecting Collection III and the D-scale on E♭, the persistence of E♭ and (E♭ D♭ C B♭) at nos. 13–30 in the "Augurs of Spring," and the return to—and further enhancement of—Collection III at nos. 37, 40, and 42 in the "Abduction." To this might be added the explicit D-scale on E♭ reference at no. 50 in the "Spring Rounds," where the principal (E♭ D♭ C B♭) fragment is superimposed over an E♭–F–G♭ motion in the bass.

More critical still is the final return to E♭ and (E♭ D♭ C B♭) at nos. 74–79 in the "Dance of the Earth." In this concluding movement to Part I, a reiterating (E♭ D♭ C B♭) fragment perseveres for some thirteen measures at no. 74 as an unmistakable point of departure and return. Subsequent transpositions along the interval–5 cycle to (B♭ A♭ G F) and (F E♭ D C) at nos. 75 + 4 and 76 + 4 may suggest a recapitulation of earlier shifts in the "Augurs of Spring" and "Rival Tribes." (These shifts entail verticals 3, 4, and 5 in Chart 5.) In this sense, proximity along the cycle of fourths measures function or "closeness" in relation to E♭ and (E♭ D♭ C B♭), irrespective of collectional affiliation: (B♭ A♭ G F) refers to Collection I while (F E♭ D C) refers to Collection II. In Example 66 the "progressions" defined by these shifts are plotted by the upper beam on the top stave.

A second area of contention in Part I entails D and the (D C B A) tetrachord. Here, too, details have been noted: the (D C B A) fragment in the Introduction at m. 2 and no. 6 + 4, the transposition to (D C B A) at nos. 31–37 in the "Augurs of Spring," and the appearance of (D C B A) as part of a new D-scale fragment at no. 37 in the "Abduction." The affiliation of (D C B A) with Collection II materializes slowly and is first established at no. 44. In the "Procession of the Sage," the reiterating A–D–C–D fragment in the horns (an incomplete (D C (B) A) tetrachord) along with the G♯–F♯ reiteration in the tubas implicate Collection II.[24] This (D C (B) A) (G♯ F♯) delineation is anticipated earlier at no. 61 in the "Rival Tribes," where (D C B A) is superimposed over G♯–F♯ in the bass, and then at no. 63, where Collection II's (D F A) (A♭ C E♭) triads yield (D C A) in the upper parts, superimposed over an F♯. An important link connecting Collections II and III is the C–F♯ tritone, punctuated by the percussion at no. 37 and sustained in the bass at no. 57 + 2 in the "Rival Tribes." (In addition to the articulative units shown in Examples 63 and 64, an octatonic collection may be partitioned by two diminished-seventh chords; each of these chords will overlap one of those of the remaining two collections. Collections II and III share (C E♭ F♯ A), although the encompassed pitches do not represent, for Collection II, the (0, 3, 6, 9) partitioning elements they do for Collection III.)[25]

---

[24]As shown in Example 65, Collection I is also present at nos. 64–71, most forcefully in terms of the initial (G F E D) (C♯ (B) A♯ G♯) superimposition at no. 64. The G♯–D tritone is punctuated as the shared connecting link between these two octatonic collections.

[25]Throughout *The Rite*, tritone or diminished-seventh elements are frequently exposed in the bass as connecting links between octatonic collections on a block-by-block basis. Thus, the C–F♯ tritone, intro-

Note, finally, the persistence of Collection II's D–A, E♭ vertical in Part II, at no. 106 + 1 in the "Glorification" and again at nos. 142–49 in the opening section of the "Sacrificial Dance." In Example 66 successive block appearances of D, (D C B A), and D–A, E♭ are connected by the lower beam on the top stave. As a rule, the connecting beams on the top stave of this example are drawn with a view toward the collectional identity of the globally defined units from one block to the next. As shown by the roman numerals, connections are thus made on the basis of collectional affiliation.

Beyond these tetrachordal or collectional priorities, associations, and links, however, *The Rite* does not readily submit to the imposition of an all-embracing plot, one of intrinsic interest (exhibiting a form of symmetry, for example) or tied in some fashion to local details of significance. The interval-5 cycle is not a convincing model in this respect. Apart from its E♭–B♭–F–C segment at nos. 13–30 in the "Augurs" movement (verticals 3 and 4 in Chart 5), which derives from the Collection III—Collection I hybrid character of the motto chord, the cycle leaves too much unaccounted for. As plotted in Chart 5, specific areas of concentration, whether surveyed from the standpoint of actual succession or mere statistical prevalence, fail to convey a meaningful or coherent pattern.

Nor, for that matter, can the reduction of Example 66 be equated with a "Schenker graph." As a series of "progressions," the beams connect the various realizations or transpositions of important globally defined units from one block or movement to the next. And while these shifts inevitably yield a voice-leading path, the meaning or significance of this path is far from apparent.

The question, in other words, is why one particular octatonic or diatonic collection (or transposition) should necessarily succeed another. What, in the final analysis, accounts for "progress" in this piece? At nos. 38 and 40 + 6 in the "Abduction," for example, why should Collection III's (E♭ D♭ B♭ G) (C E G) triadic configuration alternate with Collection II's (B A F♯ D♯) (A♭ C E♭) formation, and then yield, with the Collection II block at no. 44, a condensed E♭–B–E♭–F♯–F trail in the upper parts?

No doubt Collection II's presence at nos. 38 and 40 + 6 is foreshadowed by the transposition to (D C B A) at nos. 31–37 in the "Augurs of Spring" and anticipates the Collection II block at no. 44. The original chronology of these dance movements, according to which the "Abduction" at no. 37 followed

---

duced at nos. 12, 37, and 57 + 2, returns in the timpani in the "Dance of the Earth," where, at no. 74, it accompanies the (E♭ D♭ C B♭) tetrachordal fragment and its affiliation with Collection III. Shared by Collections I and II, the D/G♯ tritone punctuated in the bassoons at nos. 64–71 in the "Rival Tribes" and "Procession" fulfills a similar role. In the "Ritual Action of the Ancestors" and "Sacrificial Dance" in Part II, the D, shared by Collections I and II, persists in the bass at nos. 129, 132, 134, and 142. Most of these long-range associations are acknowledged in Examples 65 and 66.

the "Rival Tribes," allows a more compelling explanation: the C–B fragment in the percussion and lower strings at nos. 38 and 40 + 6 served as an immediate link to the tuba's C–B fragment in the opening measures of the (then preceding) "Rival Tribes." And since, in relation to the opening (E♭ D♭ B♭ G) (C E G) configuration of the "Abduction," the B–F♯, C span (reading down) of this C–B fragment suggests (B A F♯ D♯) (A♭ C E♭), Collection II would have been the logical choice. Moreover, there are no entries among the initial sketches for the "Augurs of Spring" on pages 3–6 of the sketchbook for the transposition to (D C B A) at nos. 31–37; the latter might well have been conceived after the rearrangement of the movements. Hence, with the "Abduction" following the "Augurs of Spring," the transposition to (D C B A) at no. 31 could have come in anticipation of the new (A G F♯ E) (D C B A) fragment at no. 37 and of Collection II's pending role. Yet, however interesting and illuminating, these conjectures do not get much beyond the kinds of associations and links surveyed already in this chapter.

It should also be noted that conventional notions of harmonic progress, voice leading, and "directed motion" are qualified not only by the symmetrical implications of octatonic construction but also by the two types of rhythmic structure. In blocks and movements adhering to Type II, which include the "Procession of the Sage" and the "Dance of the Earth," pitch organization is necessarily static. Essentials here include the registrally fixed layers of reiterating fragments, the referential implications of these layers, points of intersection, and the varying periods defined by the repetition in relation to an assigned or readily inferable metric periodicity. Conventional voice-leading graphs applied to settings of this type would be essentially meaningless. Similar reservations pertain to the large block structures of Type I. The point of this invention rests with the modification and reshuffling of the juxtaposed blocks upon successive restatements, a juxtaposition in which the blocks often retain separate collectional identities. And since with larger block settings—as at nos. 57–62 in the "Rival Tribes" (Example 38 in Chapter 4)—the same blocks are always preceding or succeeding one another, a true sense of progress can come only with an abrupt cutting off of the entire section and with its further juxtaposition with something quite new in formal, rhythmic, registral and/or pitch-relational design. It is with these considerations in mind that the analysis of Example 65 and its accompanying graph in Example 66 are best understood.

7

Part II: Pitch Structure

Introduction

Greater complexity is generally ascribed to the six movements constituting Part II of *The Rite*. In the current view, this has principally to do with a more intimately paced relationship among the three transpositions of the octatonic collection. Contexts of transpositional purity (confined, that is, to a single collection) are of course still to be found. Shown in Example 61 in Chapter 6, the blocks at nos. 132 and 134 in the "Ritual Action of the Ancestors," where Collection I's (C♯ B A♯ G♯) (G F E D) tritone-related tetrachords are superimposed within a C♯–D vertical span, are as explicitly octatonic as any in this music. And the Collection II bar at no. 106 + 1 in the "Glorification of the Chosen One," shown here in Example 69, exposes the partitioning units of *The Rite* in a blunt, primitive fashion. Indeed, as was discussed in connection with Examples 65 and 66 in Chapter 6, there is little difficulty in tracing these units to the end of the "Sacrificial Dance" at nos. 186–201. Nonetheless, following subsequent repeats of the $\frac{7}{4}$ bar in the "Glorification," there occurs a sequence of 0–5/6, 11 verticals. And since these verticals relate to one another not by the intervals of 3, 6, or 9 (as would be necessary if the succession were confined to a single octatonic collection, one transpositional level), but delineate a 2–2–2–1 succession (with set affiliations shown below in Example 69), referentially, the formulae pursued thus far clearly carry a flexibility beyond that encountered in Part I.[1]

---

[1]This flexibility extends to the "Sacrificial Dance" as well, of course. In Examples 65 and 66 in Chapter 6, see the set affiliations as shown by the roman numerals for the succession of chords at nos. 157 and 160–

EXAMPLE 69: "Glorification of the Chosen One"

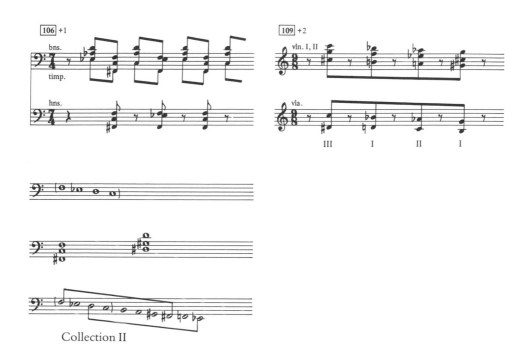

Collection II

It is as though the composer, having exposed an explicit octatonic hand in Part I, felt the necessity of venturing a bit further in Part II, upping the octatonic coherence stakes, as it were.

These implications are apparent in the very first measures of Part II's Introduction. Reproduced in Example 70, two minor triads, (E♭ G♭ B♭) and (C♯ E G♯) in the clarinets and flutes, move back and forth over a sustained (D F A) triad in the horns.[2] And like the verticals in Example 69, the relationship defined fails to con-

---

66(+4). Thus, too, while the 0–5, 11 or 0–5/6, 11 vertical span usually encompasses pitches of priority among superimposed, reiterating fragments and chords, in Part II it surfaces just as readily as a basic articulative unit of vocabulary, along with the (0 2 3 5) tetrachords, triads, and dominant sevenths. Apart from nos. 157 and 160–66(+4) in the "Sacrificial Dance," see the chromatic scale passages in the flutes and strings that directly precede the Collection II bar shown in Example 69 (with repeats at nos. 107, 108, and 117), passages which are all composed of 0–5, 11 verticals. Indeed, the consistency of this 0–5, 11 ornamentation in the "Glorification" may be compared to nos. 39 and 41 in the "Ritual of Abduction," where the initial triadic configuration at no. 37 persists in passages of "chromatic fill" between the principal (E♭ D♭ B♭ G) (C E G) and (B A F♯ D♯) (A♭ C E♭) units.

[2]Stravinsky's notation for (E♭ G♭ B♭) at no. 79 is (D♯ F♯ A♯). But since (E♭ G♭ B♭) conforms to Collection III's format in Example 62, and since the composer himself switches to (E♭ G♭ B♭) later, at no. 80, it seemed convenient to employ (E♭ G♭ B♭) from the start.

EXAMPLE 70: Introduction

form to the octatonically conceived (0, 3, 6, 9) arrangement. It is, rather, a 1–1–1 relationship, which means that each triad will refer to a different octatonic collection. These, too, are circumstances that do not readily lend themselves to an octatonic interpretation.

Yet when the configuration at no. 79 is heard and understood in relation to what follows, there is no mistaking its octatonic purpose. The oscillating (E♭ G♭ B♭) (C♯ E G♯) triads in the upper parts define an alternation between Collections III and I, the (E♭ G♭ B♭) triad referring to Collection III, (C♯ E G♯) to Collection I. And it is to this Collection III–Collection I alternation that succeeding measures and blocks in this introductory section conspicuously refer.

In the ⁴₄ measure directly following no. 79, shown in Example 71, Collection III's (E♭ G♭ B♭) triad remains fixed on the beat, while Collection I's contribution expands beyond (C♯ E G♯) to include (B♭ D♭ F) and (E G B)—triads that are (0, 3, 6, 9)–related to (C♯ E G♯), and so remain confined to Collection I. This Collection I expansion is underscored by the progression from the octave A to (B♭ D♭ F) in the strings, and then by the (E G♯ B D) dominant seventh in the bass. Moreover, these collectional shifts are patterned metrically. Collection III's (E♭ G♭ B♭) triad assumes a strong or downbeat identity, while Collection I's expansion unfolds either off the beat or on the upbeat.

The scheme perseveres at no. 79 + 5 (again, see Example 71). The (E♭ G♭ B♭) triad remains fixed on the first and third quarter-note beats of the ⁴₄ measure, while Collection I's minor triads at C♯, B♭, and E are sandwiched in between. Then, in the lengthy progression beginning at no. 82 + 1, Example 72, the bass rises from the D to an A. And the shifts are here stretched to ³₄ measures for each collection. The Collection I (B♭ D♭ F) (E G B) minor triads at no. 82 + 2 are followed in the succeeding measure by Collection III's (C E♭ G) (A C E) (F♯ A C♯) triads, which

EXAMPLE 71: Introduction

are in turn followed by the Collection I triads at no. 82+4. And, as earlier at no. 79+5, the bass line reinforces these Collection III–Collection I shifts with dominant sevenths on E and G (for Collection I) and on F♯ (for Collection III). From an initial triadic configuration seemingly without octatonic qualifications, an octatonic cohesion is thus brought to bear on the passage as a whole, and in the form here of a carefully patterned alternation between the minor triads and dominant sevenths of Collection III and those of Collection I.

A different version of the chordal progression at no. 82 appears later, at no. 161 in the "Sacrificial Dance." From what may be gathered from two separate entries on pages 85 and 104 of the sketchbook,[3] the progression was originally intended for the concluding "sacrifice" alone. Indeed, as with the "Augurs of Spring" chord (see Example 59 in Chapter 6), this idea may have been conceived in advance of the

---

[3]Being virtually identical, these two sketches fail to reflect the differences between the two final versions of the Introduction and the "Sacrificial Dance."

EXAMPLE 72: Introduction

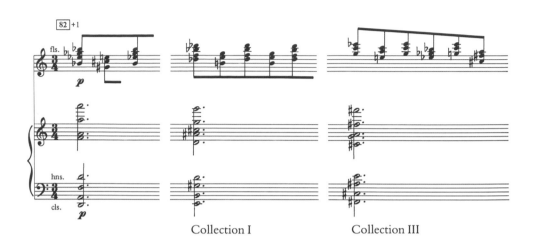

Collection I   Collection III

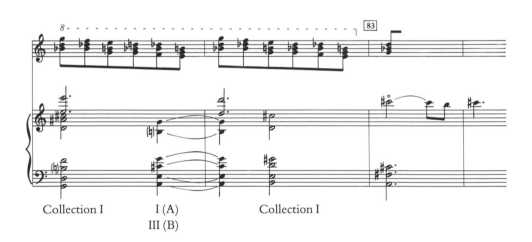

Collection I   I (A)   Collection I
                      III (B)

sketchbook. Transcribed in Examples 73a and 73b are two early sketches from a separate notebook,[4] which may be compared to the sketchbook's version of the progression on page 104 (Example 73c), and then to the two final versions as found

---

[4]The two early sketches appear in Vera Stravinsky and Robert Craft, *Stravinsky in Pictures and Documents* (New York: Simon and Schuster, 1978), p. 599, and are derived from the small notebook mentioned in Chapter 2 as dating from 1912 to 1918. Craft refers to it as the "Klychkov notebook," since it contains an unfinished setting of a poem by the symbolist poet Sergei Klychkov. He also dates the sketches "July, 1911," but there is in fact no evidence to suggest that they were not composed much later, during the actual composition of the "Sacrificial Dance." What seems clear is that both were intended for *The Rite* and that they predate the two notations on pages 85 and 104 of the sketchbook. They are reproduced in Figure 4.

FIGURE 4: Early sketches of the chordal progression at nos. 82 and 161 in the Introduction and "Sacrificial Dance." These are taken from the separate notebook dating from 1912 to 1918. Courtesy of the Paul Sacher Foundation.

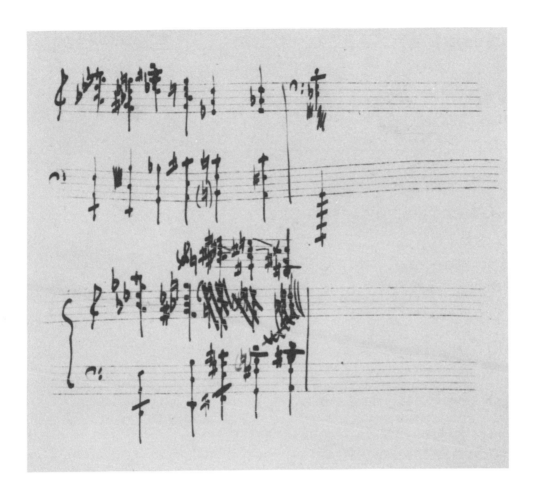

at no. 82 in the Introduction (Example 72) and at no. 161 in the "Sacrificial Dance" (Example 73d).[5] Notice that the contrary motion of the diatonic outer parts was not initially part of the conception, and that only three chords in the two early sketches in Examples 73a and 73b survive in the two final versions of the Introduction and the "Sacrificial Dance."

Most remarkable, however, is the manner in which the progression was re-

---

[5] The progression in the "Sacrificial Dance" is also given in Example 65. In the 1943 revision of the "Sacrificial Dance," the disposition of the chords was somewhat altered. In addition, the Db of the second chord (with E in the bass) was changed to a D, while the Eb of the third chord was changed to an E. These changes do not, however, affect the collectional identity of the chords.

EXAMPLE 73

(a)   (b)

II (B♭)   I   ?   ?   II (G)   II   ?   II (B♭)   I   III   ?   II

(c) Sketchbook, p. 104

II (B♭)   I   III   ?   II   III   I

(d)

II (B♭)   I   III   ?   II   III   I

composed with a view toward the referential conditions as surveyed already apropos of the opening measures of the Introduction. In his own brief survey of these early sketches, Robert Craft has called attention to the "evolution in harmonic content" and to the manner in which the composer "gravitated, instinctively and unconsciously, toward *The Rite*'s fundamental combinations."[6] This is clear from an

---

[6] V. Stravinsky and Craft, *Stravinsky in Pictures and Documents*, p. 599. In Allen Forte, *The Harmonic Organization of "The Rite of Spring"* (New Haven: Yale University Press, 1978), p. 199, the author points

octatonic standpoint. For although five of the seven chords of the sketchbook version are octatonic, these refer to Collections I, II, and III. Following the initial (D F
A) triad in the recomposed version for the Introduction, however (see Example
72), the succession is committed solely to Collections I and III, with each $\frac{3}{4}$ measure
implying one of these two collections. Moreover, the disposition of the rising
dominant sevenths in the bass remains fixed and derives from the (E G♯ B D) chord
at no. 79 + 1. The A of the dominant seventh at no. 82 + 4 refers to Collection III,
while the remaining pitches of this vertical, including the succession of minor triads
above, refer to Collection I. In other words, as a triadic unit, the dominant seventh
on A refers specifically to Collection III, but only its root is foreign to Collection I
and the broader implications of this latter commitment at no. 82 + 4. In Example
72 the brackets single out A as an "outside" element, a procedure applied in Examples 73a–73d, and earlier, in Example 65, as well.

Of course, the Khorovod tune of the Introduction, for which the sustained A
and the (D F A) triad at no. 79 are a preparation, has been overlooked. And the
Collection II implications of these components are occasionally evident. Example
74 shows one of the several variants of this tune. Introduced at no. 84, a Collection
II chord alternates with others implying Collections III and I. Most important,
however, is this tune's B♭–E tritone boundary, which refers back to the initial (E♭
G♭ B♭) (C♯ E G♯) triadic configuration at no. 79. Indeed, with the appearance of the
two trumpet fragments at no. 86 and then of the superimposition of these fragments over reiterating 0–5, 11 verticals in the strings at no. 86 + 3, the Collection
III–Collection I bond is further solidified—and here, as earlier in the Introduction,
with the specifics of the bond directly traceable to the triadic configuration at
no. 79.

Thus, as shown on the left side in Example 75, the upper part of the initial
configuration consists of a B♭–E tritone motion that refers to both Collection III
and Collection I (although B♭ and E are not among the (0, 3, 6, 9) symmetrically
defined partitioning elements for Collection III, as they are for Collection I). Beginning with the unison B♭ at no. 86 + 1, the second trumpet completes this B♭–E
interval by way of a (0 2 3 5) tetrachordal delineation in terms of (B♭ A♭ G F) and
then by a conclusion on E, the entire B♭–A♭–G–F–E succession accountable to
Collection I. Moreover, the accompanying B♭–C♭ reiteration of the first trumpet,
with C♭ (B) as pitch number 11 in relation to B♭, also refers to Collection I, the
complete succession now B–B♭–A♭–G–F–E. Nevertheless, as these two fragments draw to a close, the terminating C in the first trumpet together with the (C E
G) triadic outline refer not to Collection I but to Collection III. (In other words, the
C upsets the 1–2–1–2–1 ordering in terms of B–B♭–A♭–G–F–E. A C♯ (D♭), instead of the C, would have ensured this ordering's continuance, and hence continued confinement here to Collection I.) Hence the shift at this point from Collection

---

similarly to Stravinsky's "predilection" for this progression, noting that the two final versions in *The Rite*
"contain many, if not all, of the basic harmonies of the work."

EXAMPLE 74: Introduction

EXAMPLE 75: Introduction

I to Collection III, a shift duly confirmed by the entrance of the reiterating 0–5, 11 verticals at no. 86 + 3.

Shown in Example 76, these verticals also derive in straightforward fashion from the initial configuration at no. 79. Embedded in the configuration, below the B♭–E tritone motion in the upper parts, are the verticalized intervals of 5, two fourths (D♭/A♭ and E♭/B♭) that move back and forth. The D♭/A♭ fourth, being part of the initial (C♯ E G♯) triad, refers to Collection I; E♭/B♭, being part of (E♭ G♭ B♭), refers to Collection III. And the Collection I–Collection III implications of these fourths are neatly synchronized with those of the two trumpet fragments: D♭/A♭ relates to the B–B♭–A♭–G–F–E succession of Collection I, E♭/B♭ relates to the C and the (C E G) triad of Collection III. Furthermore, a pitch number 11 is added to both fourths, yielding the familiar 0–5, 11 vertical span in terms of D♭–A♭, D for Collection I, and E♭–B♭, E for Collection III. Finally, in the climactic block at no. 87, shown in Example 77, the (0, 3) relationship between superimposed fragments, so prominent a feature in Part I, also surfaces: a lower (B♭ D F) triad is added to Collection I's D♭–A♭, D span, while (C E G) accompanies E♭–B♭,

EXAMPLE 76: Introduction

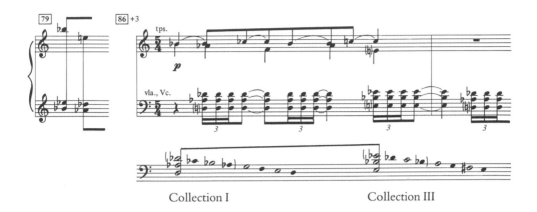

Collection I   Collection III

E. The second trumpet's (B♭ A♭ G F) tetrachord is of course (0, 3)–related to D♭–
A♭, D. Hence within this intimately paced alternation between Collections I and
III, stemming initially from the triadic configuration at no. 79, the principal articulative units and their characteristic dispositions, as examined in Part I, are conspicuously brought to the fore.

    Still, the harmonic distinction between Collections I and III, carefully paced
and patterned in the preparatory measures at no. 86, is eventually obscured at no.
87 + 1. And this is principally a rhythmic issue. For as is frequently the case with the
climactic settings of *The Rite*, the construction at nos. 87–89 conforms in general
outline to the second of the two rhythmic types as detailed in Chapter 4. The fragments, lines or parts, fixed registrally and instrumentally in repetition, are brought
together in a final, tutti summation; they repeat according to periods or cycles that
vary independently of one another, and hence effect a vertical or harmonic coincidence that is constantly changing. And given the inevitable overlapping in period-
duration, the initial harmonic synchronization as introduced at no. 86 + 3 will not
hold, and the fragments implicating Collection I will fuse with those implicating
Collection III. At no. 87 + 2, Collection III's E♭–B♭, E span enters prior to the clarinet's C, while Collection III's (C E G) triad in the flutes is a separate layer, superimposed over Collection I's contribution. Moreover, in place of the steady meter generally applied to constructions of this kind, the meter at nos. 87–89 shifts among $\frac{5}{4}$,
$\frac{4}{4}$, and $\frac{3}{4}$ in reflecting the varying periods defined by the reiterating fragments in the
clarinets and horn (fragments first introduced by the trumpets at no. 86). And al-
though a steady $\frac{3}{4}$ meter is imposed at no. 88 as these two fragments reach a stable
duration of three quarter-note beats, the conflict is never entirely resolved, as the
periods of the remaining fragments continue to overlap one another.

    A condensed layout of the scheme appears in Example 78. The first of the three

EXAMPLE 77

Collection I   Collection III

layers shows the successive repeats of the (C E G) triad in the flutes, the second layer those of the clarinet-horn fragments, and the third layer those of the reiterating 0–5, 11 verticals in the strings. In sum, the overlapping in period duration, together with the gradual harmonic fusion between Collections I and III, promote a truly remarkable richness in sound at nos. 87–89, in keeping with the climactic character of the passage and with the specifics of the collectional shifts as introduced earlier in this movement.

EXAMPLE 78: Introduction

"Sacrificial Dance"

In stunning contrast to the separate, climactic block of the Introduction at nos. 87–89, the opening section of the "Sacrificial Dance" conforms to the first of the two rhythmic types outlined in Chapter 4. Labeled A, B, and C in Example 79, three blocks are placed in rapid juxtaposition; within each of these blocks the lines or parts repeat according to the same rhythmic periods and are hence synchronized unvaryingly in vertical coincidence; and the invention has principally to do with the reordering, expansion, or contraction of these blocks and their motivic subdivisions upon successive restatements. Earlier, in Example 36 in Chapter 3, attention

EXAMPLE 79: "Sacrificial Dance"

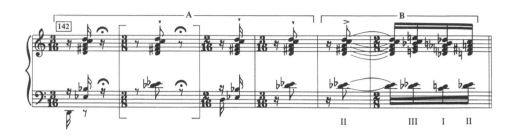

Collection II

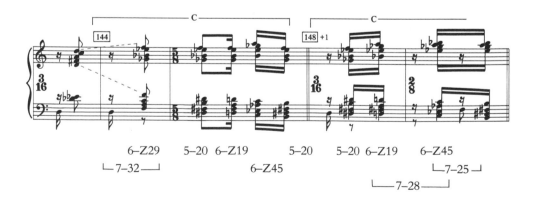

(continued)

EXAMPLE 79 *(continued)*

5–10

Collection II

was drawn to the two motives of Block B and to the upbeat–downbeat contradictions to which subsequent repeats of these motives were subjected in relation to a background $\frac{2}{8}$ periodicity.

No less apparent in Example 79, however, is the adherence at the outset of the "Sacrificial Dance" to *The Rite*'s by now standard pitch formulae. There is, first, the punctuating dominant seventh of Block A, here (D C A F♯), which refers to Collection II, and with the disposition of this unit exposing an upper, incomplete (D C (B) A) tetrachord. Typical, too, is the superimposition of this dominant seventh over a lower pitch number 11, which yields the 0–5, 11 vertical span, here in terms of D–A, E♭. Moreover, the rapid collectional shifts characteristic of Part II are apparent in Block B, where the dominant sevenths, enclosed within 0–11 spans, imply first Collection II, then Collections III and I, and finally Collection II again with (C A F♯ D), which thus frames the succession. Finally, in Block C the referential commitment to Collection II is restored and enhanced. With an F–G♭ span fixed in the upper parts, Collection II's major triads at F, B, D, and A♭ unfold underneath.

Indeed, Block C is in this respect favorably understood as a continuation of the collectional implications of Block A. Shown in Example 80, Blocks A and C are composed of four relatively static layers of material: (1) the (E♭ G♭ B♭) triad, where G♭, as the enharmonic equivalent of F♯, may be inferred from the punctuating (D C A F♯) dominant seventh; (2) the F–A figure later in Block C; (3) Collection II's descending triads, which begin with the (D C A F♯) dominant seventh of the opening bar; and (4) the D–F motion in the bass. Moreover, while the 1943 revision deleted the B♭ from the opening chord (as is shown by the bracketed measure in Example 79), its relationship to the (E♭ G♭ B♭) triad later on in Block C is clear. B♭

EXAMPLE 80: "Sacrificial Dance"

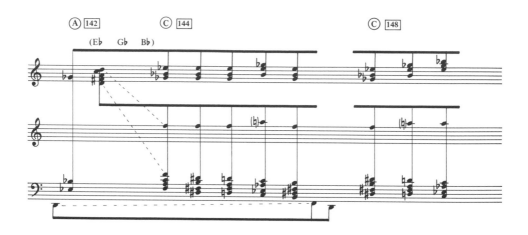

ensures (E♭ G♭ B♭)'s presence in the initial chord of Block A, which serves as the source of the upper parts further along in Block C. (As noted earlier, in Example 13 in Chapter 2, B♭ also enhances the long-range connection between the "Augurs of Spring" chord and the "Sacrificial Dance.") And while, as a triadic unit, (E♭ G♭ B♭) refers to Collection III rather than to Collection II, E♭ and G♭ are nonetheless a part of Collection II. Only B♭ is foreign to Collection II in Block C, a matter to which we shall presently be turning for further comment.

What thus emerges in Blocks A and C (Example 80) is the superimposition of the fixed (E♭ G♭ B♭) triad over Collection II's F–A figure, its descending triads at F, B, D, and A♭, and finally its D–F motion in the timpani and bass. More significantly, the D–F motion in the bass echoes the principal progression in the treble parts: the progression from D of the (D C A F♯) dominant seventh to F of the F–A figure, and, an octave lower, from D of the same dominant seventh to F of the (F A C) triad. The resultant "parallel octaves," as it were, are shown by the dotted lines in Example 80.

Subsequent transpositions of the opening section of the "Sacrificial Dance" are traced in Example 81. Earlier, in Example 65, the origin of the first of these transpositions at no. 167, down a half step from (D C A F♯) to (D♭ B A♭ F), was traced to the upper C♯–B and C♯–B–G♯ parts in the chords at nos. 157 and 166 + 2. (See the circled pitches in Examples 65 and 66.) Of special note here is the second and final version at no. 186, where the octatonic implications of Block C's descending triads are more explicitly brought into play. Transposed to Collection III, the material in the upper parts is omitted at nos. 193 and 194, with the triadic progression now harmonized with dominant sevenths rather than major triads. (Note that the familiar disposition of the dominant seventh can apply only at C, A, and F♯, at

EXAMPLE 81: "Sacrificial Dance"

Collection III

those pitches in the C–B♭–A–G–F♯ succession that are among the (C,A,F♯,E♭) symmetrically defined partitioning elements of Collection III, the roots of this collection's four triads and dominant-seventh chords.) Finally, the three transpositions are plotted in condensed form in Example 82. Here, the motion embedded in the upper parts of Block C, F–A–B♭ at no. 148, is mirrored (inverted) by these long-range transpositions, which in the upper parts read D–D♭–A. Thus, too, the transpositions implicate Collections II, I, and III, respectively.

But to return for a moment to the opening statement of Block A. Even the non-octatonic pitches in this initial stretch, the non–Collection II D♭, for example, derive from intercollectional relations of significance in Part II. Thus, as shown in Example 83, the two 0–11 verticals embedded in the initial "cluster" simultaneity, D–E♭ and C–D♭, are traceable to the oscillating E♭–E and D♭–D verticals at no. 87 + 1. The difference is that while these two (0, 2) whole step–related verticals define a collectional shift in the Introduction, they are wedded in the "Sacrificial Dance" as part of a single simultaneity. And in each case the verticals jointly yield the "chromatic" (0 1 2 3) tetrachord (shown in Example 83), with pitch number 2 lying outside the octatonic ordering, the D♭ lying outside Collection II in Block A.

EXAMPLE 82: "Sacrificial Dance" (transpositions)

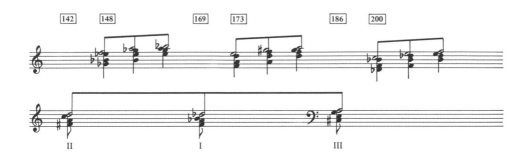

EXAMPLE 83: "Sacrificial Dance"

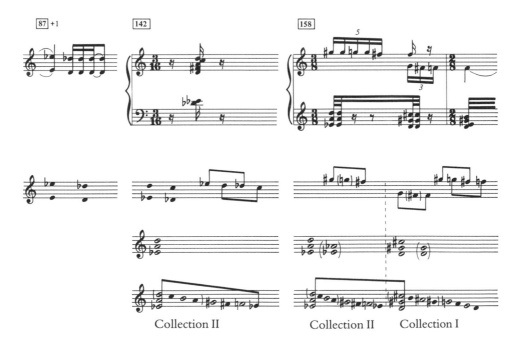

Ultimately of greater consequence, however, are the two upper and lower 2s or whole steps of this (0 1 2 3) tetrachord: that is, in Block A, D–C and E♭–D♭. (See, again, the brackets in Example 83.) For instead of the two 0–11 verticals, it is these two 2s or whole steps to which the collectional shifts in subsequent passages of the "Sacrificial Dance" make reference.[7] Thus, further along, at no. 158, shown in Example 83, the two oscillating 0–5, 11 verticals in the strings, D–A, E♭ and C♯–G♯, D, define a shift from Collection II to Collection I. This is neatly synchronized with the octatonic implications of the (G♯ G F♯ F) tetrachord's two 2s or whole steps, G♯–F♯ and G–F in the trumpets: for Collection II, G♯–(G)–F♯ is superimposed over D–A, E♭, while for Collection I, G–(F♯)–F is superimposed over C♯–G♯, D. By such means seemingly non-octatonic, "chromatic" elements in these passages derive from intercollectional shifts, and the octatonicism that may here be inferred acquires its special intricacy.

The Pitch-Class Set

Still, questions may linger about the completeness of the octatonic record in Part II, and in particular about the rapid collectional shifts and consequent "outside" pitch elements. Could the approach at this point benefit from, say, certain of Allen Forte's set-theoretic formulations? The answer here seems to be yes, but only up to a rather limited point. Readers familiar with Forte's analysis of Stravinsky's early works will have noted a number of correspondences. Forte frequently invokes the octatonic collection, the "superset" 8–28, and in connection with a passage from *Zvezdoliki* [*The King of the Stars*] (1911–12) cites it as "one of Stravinsky's hallmarks."[8] In Forte's *The Harmonic Organization of "The Rite of Spring,"* the (0 2 3 5) tetrachord, pitch-class set 4–10, is encountered throughout, while its (0 2 5/0 3 5) incomplete form, 3–7, is identified as "a kind of motto trichord."[9] In fact, most of the prominent sets in Forte's analysis are subsets of the octatonic collection. Of his two hundred and twenty pitch-class sets (sets of from three to nine elements, reduced to a "best normal order" by means of transposition or inversion followed by transposition), thirty-four are octatonic: seven from a possible twelve three-element sets, thirteen from the twenty-nine four-element sets, seven from thirty-eight five-element sets, six from fifty hexachords, and one from the thirty-eight seven-element sets, 7–31. These are easily spotted since the pitch numbering of these thirty-four "prime forms" will correspond to that either of the 1–2 half step–whole step ordering, (0 1 3 4 6 7 9 10 (0)), or the reverse 2–1 whole step–half step ordering, (0 2 3 5 6 8 9 11 (0)).

Beyond this point the two paths diverge as different objectives are brought into play. In particular, the segmentation, what Forte interprets as cohesive units in *The*

---

[7]The specific disposition of these two 2s or whole steps of the (0 1 2 3) tetrachord can be traced back to no. 64 in the "Ritual of the Rival Tribes," where (G F E D) in the strings is superimposed over (C♯ (B) A♯ G♯ G (F♯)) in the tubas. As was shown in Example 54, F♯ alternates with G as an inflection to the G♯, so that G–F of the upper (0 2 3 5) tetrachord is occasionally superimposed over G♯–F♯ in the lower unit.

[8]Allen Forte, *The Structure of Atonal Music* (New Haven: Yale University Press, 1973), p. 118.

[9]Forte, *The Harmonic Organization*, p. 36.

Rite, differs markedly from that proposed here. Reference is occasionally made to the dominant seventh, 4–27, but the triad, 3–11, is ignored altogether since, as Forte notes, trichords "are easily identifiable components of larger sets."[10] In the view expressed here, however, the triad—not just the three-element trichord, but the *triad*—assumes, even under conditions of superimposition, a registral, instrumental, and notational reality—and to an extent that, on a strictly observational basis, many sections of *The Rite* seem more overtly triadic than many pieces of the later nineteenth-century tonal tradition (pieces on behalf of which the triad is nonetheless routinely invoked as a fundamental unit of musical structure).

Moreover, an emphasis is here placed on disposition, on the fixed, registral identities of recurring tetrachords, 0–5/6, 11 vertical spans, triads, and dominant sevenths. These matters are often obscured when, for purposes of comparison, of gauging the relatedness of sets and complexes of sets, such groupings are regularly reduced to their "prime forms" (by means, as indicated, of transposition or inversion followed by transposition.) Thus, a prime determinacy in Part II's Introduction at nos. 79–84 is not the triad *tout court*, 3–11, nor the tight disposition of the triad, but its persistent (0 3 7) minor articulation. But since the major and minor triads are inversionally equivalent and reduce to the single pitch-class set 3–11, the distinction is likely to be obscured. A similar case can be made for the dominant-seventh chord, whose special content and disposition are of such marked consequence to an octatonic reading of Part I and of the "Sacrificial Dance" in Part II. This determinacy is also obscured when it is subsumed under the broader implications of the set 4–27 and its (0, 2, 5, 8) "prime-form" numbering. (The strict inversion of this form yields *The Rite*'s familiar disposition; the "prime form" itself is not a dominant-seventh chord.)

Similarly, the two interval orderings of the octatonic collection, along with the three transpositions of distinguishable content, reduce to the single set 8–28. But the question of an octatonic presence in *The Rite* has not to do merely with *the* octatonic collection (that is to say, 8–28 *tout court*) but equally with *an* octatonic collection. Contexts derive their octatonic character, their symmetrical cohesion, by virtue of their confinement to a single transpositional level for periods of significant duration. And this, too, points to a hearing and understanding of determinacy having as much to do with pitch and pitch-class identity as with interval-class identity.

This is not to suggest that these issues are ignored by Forte. Frequent reference is made to invariance in pitch-class content between transpositions or transformations of a given set, and then to the Rp relation, which has to do with pitch-class invariance among non-equivalent sets having the same number of elements. But here, too, Forte's conclusions are apt to vary from those reached from a predominantly octatonic or octatonic-diatonic perspective. Thus, Example 84 shows twelve single and "composite" sets invoked by Forte to identify the verticals and

---

[10]Ibid.

EXAMPLE 84

Collection II

linear successions of Block C at no. 144 in the "Sacrificial Dance" and its subsequent near-repeat at no. 148.[11] (Although in ascending "normal order," the pitch numbering of these sets has not been reduced to that of the "prime forms." Note that 0 = C.)[12] Only sets 5–10 and 6–Z23 are octatonic; the others are not subsets of the octatonic collection 8–28. But the fact that all ten non-octatonic sets miss the

---

[11]Forte, *The Structure of Atonal Music*, pp. 147–48. Forte uses the 1943 revision of the "Sacrificial Dance" for his analysis. The orchestration and barring of this passage are changed, but the chords themselves remain unaltered.

[12]With O = C (and with the sets not reduced to their "prime forms"), a (0 2 3 5 6 8 9 11) numbering will always—as is shown in Example 84—imply Collection II. A (0 1 3 4 6 7 9 10) numbering under these conditions will imply Collection III, while the numbering for Collection I (which lacks the C) will conform to neither of the two octatonic pitch-numberings.

octatonic order by a single step (at pitch number 10 here), or, more importantly, that all sets, excluding the B♭, refer to a single transpositional level, the octatonic Collection II, is of the highest importance for an octatonic hearing and understanding.[13] The articulative makeup of the block is thus conditioned referentially by its confinement to Collection II, a confinement that in turn refers back to the initial, punctuating (D C A F♯) dominant seventh of Block A. More specifically, too, the sets 6–Z19 and 6–Z45, which follow one another in Block C (see Example 79), are "maximally dissimilar" in interval content (the Ro relation: the interval vectors of the two sets have no common entries) and are said to be "completely detached."[14] Yet from an octatonic standpoint the sets are close, the distinction having to do with Collection II's succession of triads in the lower parts: Collection II's (D F♯ A) triad is part of 6–Z19, while (A♭ C E♭) is part of 6–Z45. Furthermore, in comparing versions of equivalent or Z-related sets, the invariants among the three occurrences of the complementary pair 6–Z23 and 6–Z45 are said to be "of little consequence," although all three refer, crucially, to Collection II.[15] Invariance among the four occurrences of 6–Z43 is likewise deemed "not significant," although this non-invariance has crucially to do with the collectional shifts respecting Collections II and I, as was indicated in Example 83.[16] In conclusion, Forte points to "the dearth of strongly represented Rp" in this music and to "the paucity of invariance among equivalent sets," noting that interval content, not pitch-class content, is of "prime importance."[17]

Incompatibility is not really the issue here. The notion of the pitch-class set and its attendant formulations ("similarity," "complementation," and so forth) can in no way be construed as "incompatible" with a more determined octatonic or octatonic-diatonic reading. At issue, rather, is the *referential* character of the octatonic and diatonic sets, the extent of their hegemony in *The Rite* and hence, ultimately, the degree of abstraction deemed necessary or desirable in formulating rules of equivalence and association that can account for the coherence or consistency of the harmonic and melodic materials.

Inevitably, a theorist's choices in this regard are to some extent guided by his preoccupations with other literatures and traditions. But this does not mean that the set-theoretic approach is awkwardly "neutral" or without an historical foundation. *The Rite* is unquestionably non-tonal, and frequently exhibits, as Forte has

---

[13]These observations apply equally to Forte's brief analysis of a passage from *Zvezdoliki* in his *The Structure of Atonal Music*, p. 114. In the first three measures eighteen sets are identified as cohesive groupings, ten of which are non-octatonic. While the significance of 8–28 is recognized, invariance, except insofar as it may be inferred from the pitch numbering, is ignored. As in Block C of the "Sacrificial Dance," all the sets refer to a single transpositional level, Collection II, while all non-octatonic sets are owing to the single non–Collection II A♯ (B♭). Moreover, in articulation, a triadic and dominant-seventh partitioning of Collection II at G♯ (A♭), F, D, and B is, in the view expressed here, unmistakable.

[14]Forte, *The Structure of Atonal Music*, p. 154.

[15]Ibid., p. 159.

[16]Ibid.

[17]Ibid., p. 166.

claimed, the kinds of harmonic structures prevalent in the "atonal" music of Schoenberg, Berg, and Webern.[18] Nonetheless, as an attempt to cope with a large number of seemingly intractable works, pitch-class set analysis represents a retreat to more lenient and broadly defined terms of relatedness and association. The question, then, is whether, for its proper definition, the logic of *The Rite* requires the greater generality afforded by this retreat or whether, by means of an octatonic-diatonic determination, the piece remains susceptible to the more determinate rulings of a more familiar mode of reckoning, one characterized by scales, scalar orderings and numberings, triads, pitch-class priorities, and the like. The present discourse has of course opted for the second of these alternatives. Yet the underlying assumptions of set theory have by no means been ignored. While frequently in disagreement with the meaning and significance of many of Forte's set-theoretic conclusions, the present perspective may nonetheless be placed in sharper focus by a careful consideration of those results.

Conclusions

As the last of the three big "Russian" ballets, *The Rite* exhibits features in rhythmic and pitch structure that were to remain characteristic of Stravinsky for the greater part of his composing career. The two types of rhythmic construction outlined in Chapters 3 and 4 are as conspicuously a part of pieces such as the *Symphony of Psalms* (1930) and the *Variations* (1964) as they are of *The Rite*. And while *Renard*, *Les Noces*, and *Histoire du soldat* mark a sudden preference for smaller, chamber-like ensembles, pitch relations in these works can be identified closely with those of *The Rite*. Even neoclassicism, for so long defined in terms of a sharp stylistic break with earlier trends, can often revealingly be heard and understood in relation to prior inclinations and concerns as detailed in these pages.

Of course, the octatonic articulation in neoclassical works often differs from that of *The Rite* and other works of the "Russian" category. Instead of the (0 2 3 5) tetrachord, an (0 1 3 4) tetrachord may frequently be inferred as a cohesive linear

---

[18] *Tonality* is here viewed in its restricted and historically oriented sense as a hierarchical system of pitch relations based referentially on the major-scale ordering of the diatonic set and encompassing an intricate yet fairly distinct set of harmonic and contrapuntal procedures commonly referred to as tonal functionality or "triadic tonality." The by now classic formulation of this view is given in Arthur Berger, "Problems of Pitch Organization in Stravinsky," in Benjamin Boretz and Edward T. Cone, eds., *Perspectives on Schoenberg and Stravinsky* (New York: Norton, 1972), p. 123. Berger writes: "Tonality . . . is defined by those functional relations postulated by the structure of the major scale. A consequence of the fulfillment of such functional relations is, directly or indirectly, the assertion of the priority of one pitch class over the others within a given context—it being understood that context may be interpreted either locally or with respect to the totality, so that a hierarchy is thus established, determined in each case by what is taken as the context in terms of which priority is assessed. It is important to bear in mind, however, that there are other means besides functional ones for asserting pitch-class priority; from which it follows that pitch-class priority per se: (1) is not a sufficient condition of that music which is tonal, and (2) is compatible with music that is not tonally functional."

EXAMPLE 85

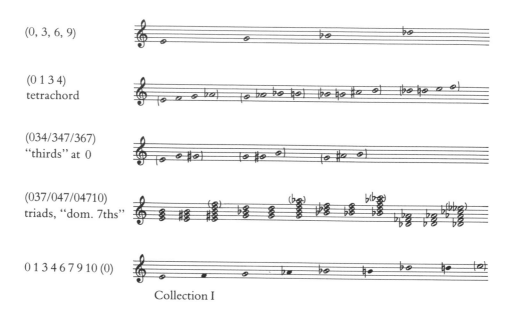

(0, 3, 6, 9)

(0 1 3 4)
tetrachord

(034/347/367)
"thirds" at 0

(037/047/04710)
triads, "dom. 7ths"

0 1 3 4 6 7 9 10 (0)

Collection I

grouping. Indeed, in the *Symphony of Psalms* it surfaces as a kind of "basic cell" in the first and second movements, as Stravinsky himself noted in one of his "conversations" with Robert Craft.[19] Complementing the (0 1 3 4) tetrachord are the (0 3 4/3 4 7/3 6 7) minor-major third units and, most conspicuously, the triads and dominant sevenths as cited in Chapters 5, 6, and 7 (but in neoclassical works with an overall approach in disposition more varied than that encountered in *The Rite* or in "Russian" pieces generally). The typical neoclassical format is summarized in Example 85: an (0, 3, 6, 9) symmetrically defined partitioning of Collection I in terms of this collection's (0 1 3 4) tetrachords, (0 3 4/3 4 7/3 6 7) minor-major thirds, triads, and dominant sevenths at E, G, B♭, and D♭. This partitioning implicates the 1–2, half step–whole step ordering, to which the customary ascending approach in scale formation is applied.

Such changes naturally coincide with changes in the diatonic articulation. In place of the D-scale ordering so prevalent in "Russian" contexts such as *The Rite*, the major scale is typical of neoclassicism, although both the E-scale and the A-scale may also at times be inferred. This major-scale reference is implied not only by the surface gesture and conventions of baroque and classical literature, but occasionally, and in however peripheral a manner, by certain tonally functional rela-

[19]Igor Stravinsky and Robert Craft, *Dialogues* (Berkeley: University of California Press, 1983), p. 77.

tions as well. What is often typical of the relations Stravinsky employed in these contexts can in turn be traced to an interacting partitioning of the octatonic collection as shown in Example 85; that is to say, to the manner in which this partitioning interacts with the gestures, conventions, and harmonic routines of the baroque and classical major-scale tradition.

These are obviously matters of considerable complexity, and have in fact been dealt with elsewhere in detail.[20] Consider, however, the tonic-dominant relationship insofar as this may here and there be felt as assuming a credible presence. The first movement of the *Symphony of Psalms* is a piece wherein octatonic blocks, accountable to Collection I with a background partitioning in terms of (E, G, Bb), interact with diatonic blocks implicating the E-scale on E. The (E G B) "*Psalms* chord," punctuated as a spacer, is articulatively shared between these two distinct collections and orderings of reference. Nonetheless, with (G B D F (Ab)) dominant-seventh and ninth supplementation, the equally shared G steadily gains the advantage and acquires, by virtue of the half-cadence on G that leads to the quasi–C-minor fugal exposition of the second movement, the characteristic "feel" of a dominant. Hence the peculiarity of Stravinsky's dominant. The G or (G B D) triad in *Psalms* identifies not only with the diatonic E-scale on E and the quasi–C-minor "resolution" of the second movement, but equally with the octatonic Collection I, in which connection it functions as an (E, G, Bb, Db) symmetrically defined partitioning element, placed in immediate juxtaposition with this collection's E and Bb and their (0 1 3 4) tetrachordal and triadic "support." Similar long-term tonic-dominant relationships, entailing both Collection I and a variety of (C Eb G/C E G) endings, govern a number of neoclassical ventures, among these the first and third movements of the Symphony in Three Movements (1945).

Hence the neoclassical perspective becomes conditioned by considerations of *The Rite* and other works of the "Russian" period. And the attraction of this approach is that a distinctive musical presence is in some measure brought to bear. For while individual pieces naturally yield their own rationales, these are most advantageously approached as parts of a greater whole, of a wider listening experience. And since, for most enthusiasts, the sense of a musical identity or distinctiveness on the part of this composer is unmistakable, speculation along these lines is likely to prove tempting for many years to come.

---

[20]See Pieter C. van den Toorn, *The Music of Igor Stravinsky* (New Haven: Yale University Press, 1983).

Bibliography

Adorno, Theodor W. *Philosophy of Modern Music*. Translated by Anne G. Mitchell and Wesley V. Bloomster. New York: Seabury Press, 1973.

Antokoletz, Elliott. *The Music of Béla Bartók*. Berkeley: University of California Press, 1984.

Asaf'yev, Boris. *A Book About Stravinsky*. Translated by Richard F. French. Ann Arbor: UMI Press, 1982.

Benjamin, William E. "A Theory of Musical Meter." *Music Perception* 1, 4 (1984): 355–413.

Berger, Arthur. "Problems of Pitch Organization in Stravinsky." Pp. 123–154 in *Perspectives on Schoenberg and Stravinsky*, edited by Benjamin Boretz and Edward T. Cone. New York: Norton, 1972.

Berry, Wallace. "Metric and Rhythmic Articulation in Music." *Music Theory Spectrum* 7 (1985): 7–33.

Boretz, Benjamin. "In Quest of the Rhythmic Genius." *Perspectives of New Music* 9, 2 (1972): 149.

Boulez, Pierre. *Notes of an Apprenticeship*. Translated by Herbert Weinstock. New York: Knopf, 1968.

Bullard, Truman C. "The First Performance of Igor Stravinsky's *Sacre du Printemps*." Ph.D dissertation, University of Rochester, 1971.

Cone, Edward T. "Stravinsky: The Progress of a Method." Pp. 155–164 in *Perspectives on Schoenberg and Stravinsky*, edited by Benjamin Boretz and Edward T. Cone. New York: Norton, 1972.

Cooper, Grosvenor, and Leonard B. Meyer. *The Rhythmic Structure of Music*. Chicago: University of Chicago Press, 1960.

Craft, Robert. "*The Rite of Spring*: Genesis of a Masterpiece." *Perspectives of New Music* 5, 1 (1966):20–36.

Craft, Robert, ed. *Stravinsky: Selected Correspondence*, vols. 1, 2, and 3. New York: Knopf, 1982, 1984, and 1986.

Cyr, Louis. "*Le Sacre du printemps*: Petite Histoire d'une grande partition." In *Stravinsky: Etudes et témoignages*, edited by François Lesure. Paris: Editions Jean-Claude Lattes, 1982.

———. "Writing *The Rite* Right." Pp. 157–73 in *Confronting Stravinsky: Man, Musician, and Modernist*, edited by Jann Pasler. Berkeley: University of California Press, 1986.

Druskin, Mikhail. *Igor Stravinsky: His Personality, Works, and Views*. Translated by Martin Cooper. Cambridge: Cambridge University Press, 1983.

Forte, Allen. *The Structure of Atonal Music*. New Haven: Yale University Press, 1973.

———. *The Harmonic Organization of "The Rite of Spring."* New Haven: Yale University Press, 1978.

Gray, Cecil. *A Survey of Contemporary Music*. London: Oxford University Press, 1924.

Grigoriev, S. L. *The Diaghilev Ballet, 1909–1929*. Translated by Vera Bowen. London: Constable, 1953.

Imbrie, Andrew. "'Extra' Measures and Metrical Ambiguity in Beethoven." Pp. 45–66 in *Beethoven Studies,* edited by Alan Tyson. New York: Norton, 1973.

Karlinsky, Simon. "The Composer's Workshop." *The Nation,* June 15, 1970, p. 732.

———. "Stravinsky and Russian Pre-Literate Theater." *19th Century Music* 6, 3 (1983): 232–240. Reprinted in *Confronting Stravinsky: Man, Musician, and Modernist,* edited by Jann Pasler, pp. 3–15. Berkeley: University of California Press, 1986.

Keller, Hans. "Rhythm: Gershwin and Stravinsky." *Score* 20 (1957): 19.

Kunstmuseum Basel and the Paul Sacher Foundation. *Strawinsky: Sein Nachlass, sein Bild.* Basel, 1984.

Lambert, Constant. *Music Ho! A Study of Music in Decline*, 3d ed. London: Faber and Faber, 1966.

Lederman, Minna, ed. *Stravinsky in the Theatre*. New York: Pellegrini and Cudahy, 1949.

Lerdahl, Fred, and Ray Jackendoff. *A Generative Theory of Tonal Music*. Cambridge, Mass.: MIT Press, 1983.

Lesure, François, ed. *Le Sacre du Printemps: Dossier de presse*. Geneva: Editions Minkoff, 1980.

Meyer, Leonard B. *Emotion and Meaning in Music*. Chicago: University of Chicago Press, 1956.

Morton, Lawrence. "Footnotes to Stravinsky Studies: *Le Sacre du Printemps*." *Tempo* 128 (1979): 9–16.

Pasler, Jann. "Music and Spectacle in *Petrushka* and *The Rite of Spring*." Pp. 53–81 in *Confronting Stravinsky: Man, Musician, and Modernist,* edited by Jann Pasler. Berkeley: University of California Press, 1986.

Perle, George. "Berg's Master Array of the Interval Cycles." *Musical Quarterly* 63, 1 (1977): 1–30.

Rahn, John. *Basic Atonal Theory*. New York: Longman, 1980.

Rimsky-Korsakov, Nicholas. *My Musical Life*. Translated by Judah A. Joffee. New York: Tudor, 1935.

Schaeffner, André. *Strawinsky*. Paris: Rieder, 1931.

Scherliess, Volker. "Bemerkungen zum Autograph des 'Sacre du Printemps.' " *Musikforschung* 35 (1982): 234–250.

Shepard, John. "The Stravinsky *Nachlass*: A Provisional Checklist of Music Manuscripts." *Music Library Association Notes* 40, 4 (1984): 719–750.

Smalley, Roger. "The Sketchbook of *The Rite of Spring*." *Tempo* 111 (1970): 2.

Spies, Claudio. "Editions of Stravinsky's Music." Pp. 250–67 in *Perspectives on Schoenberg and Stravinsky,* edited by Benjamin Boretz and Edward T. Cone. New York: Norton, 1972.

Stravinsky, Igor. *An Autobiography*. New York: Norton, 1962. (First published as *Chroniques de ma vie* [Paris: Denoël et Steele, 1935].)

———. *The Rite of Spring: Sketches 1911–1913*. London: Boosey and Hawkes, 1969.

———. *"Stravinsky Replies."* *The Nation*, August 3, 1970, p. 66.

Stravinsky, Igor, and Robert Craft. *Conversations with Stravinsky*. Berkeley: University of California Press, 1980.

———. *Memories and Commentaries*. Berkeley: University of California Press, 1981.

———. *Expositions and Developments*. Berkeley: University of California Press, 1981.

———. *Dialogues*. Berkeley: University of California Press, 1983.

Stravinsky, Vera, and Robert Craft. *Stravinsky in Pictures and Documents*. New York: Simon and Schuster, 1978.

Taruskin, Richard. "Russian Folk Melodies in *The Rite of Spring*." *Journal of the American Musicological Society* 33, 3 (1980): 501.

———. "*The Rite* Revisited: The Idea and the Sources of Its Scenario." Pp. 183–202 in *Music and Civilization: Essays in Honor of Paul Henry Lang*, edited by Edmond Strainchamps and Maria Rika Maniates. New York: Norton, 1984.

———. "Chernomor to Kastchei: Harmonic Sorcery; or, Stravinsky's 'Angle.' " *Journal of the American Musicological Society* 38, 1 (1985): 72.

———. "Stravinsky's 'Rejoicing Discovery' and What it Meant: Some Observations on His Russian Text-Setting." Pp. 162–99 in *Stravinsky Retrospectives,* edited by Ethan Haimo and Paul Johnson. Lincoln: University of Nebraska Press, 1987.

van den Toorn, Pieter C. "Some Characteristics of Stravinsky's Diatonic Music." *Perspectives of New Music* 14, 1 (1975): 104; 15, 2 (1977): 58.

———. *The Music of Igor Stravinsky*. New Haven: Yale University Press, 1983.

———. "Octatonic Pitch Structure in Stravinsky." Pp. 130–56 in *Confronting Stravinsky: Man, Musician, and Modernist,* edited by Jann Pasler. Berkeley: University of California Press, 1986.

Vershinina, Irina. *Stravinsky's Early Ballets*. Translated by L. G. Heien. Ann Arbor: UMI, 1986.

Walsh, Stephen. "Review Survey: Some Recent Stravinsky Literature." *Music Analysis* 3, 2 (1984): 201–208.

White, Eric Walter. *Stravinsky: The Composer and His Works*. Berkeley: University of California Press, 1966.

Whittall, Arnold. "Music Analysis as Human Science? *Le Sacre du Printemps* in Theory and Practice." *Music Analysis* 1, 1 (1982): 33–53.

Yaroustovsky, B. M., ed. *I. F. Stravinskii: Stat'i i materialy*. Moscow, 1973.

Yeston, Maury. *The Stratification of Musical Rhythm*. New Haven: Yale University Press, 1976.

Index